MATHEMATICS
for
AQA GCSE (Modular)
STUDENT SUPPORT BOOK
Intermediate Tier

Tony Banks and David Alcorn

Causeway Press Limited

Published by Causeway Press Ltd
P.O. Box 13, Ormskirk, Lancashire L39 5HP

First published 2002
Reprinted 2004

British Library Cataloguing-in-Publication Data.
A catalogue record for this book is available from the British Library.

ISBN 1-902796-57-8

Acknowledgements
Past exam questions, provided by the *Assessment and Qualifications Alliance*, are denoted by the letters AQA. The answers to all questions are entirely the responsibility of the authors/publisher and have neither been provided nor approved by AQA.

Every effort has been made to locate the copyright owners of material used in this book. Any omissions brought to the notice of the publisher are regretted and will be credited in subsequent printings.

Page design
Billy Johnson

Reader
Anne Alcock

Artwork
David Alcorn

Cover design
Waring-Collins Partnership

Typesetting by Billy Johnson, San Francisco, California, USA

Printed and bound by Scotprint, Haddington, Scotland

preface

This book provides detailed revision notes, worked examples and examination questions to support students in their preparation for AQA GCSE Mathematics (Modular) at the Intermediate Tier of Entry.

The book has been designed so that it can be used in conjunction with the companion book ***Mathematics for AQA GCSE (Modular) - Intermediate Tier*** or as a stand-alone revision book for self study and provides full coverage of AQA Specification B (Modular).

In preparing the text, full account has been made of the requirements for students to be able to use and apply mathematics in written examination papers and be able to solve problems in mathematics both with and without a calculator.

The detailed revision notes, worked examples and examination questions have been organised into 40 self-contained sections which meet the requirements of the National Curriculum and provide efficient coverage of the specifications for Modules 1, 3 and 5. Modules 2 and 4 are coursework tasks.

Module 1	Sections 1 - 7
Module 3	Sections 8 - 18
Module 5	Sections 19 - 40

At the end of Module 1 and Module 3 there is an examination questions section with a compilation of exam and exam-style questions, organised for non-calculator and calculator practice, in preparation for the exams.

In Module 5 a section review is provided at the end of Sections 19 - 26 (Algebra) and another at the end of Sections 27 - 40 (Shape, Space and Measures) to give further opportunities to consolidate skills. At the end of the module there is a further compilation of exam and exam-style questions, organised for non-calculator and calculator practice, in preparation for the exams.

Also available ***With Answers (ISBN 1-902796-56-X)***
The book has been designed so that it can be used in conjunction with the companion book ***Mathematics for AQA GCSE (Modular): Intermediate Tier (ISBN 1-902796-72-1)***

contents

Module 1

Sections 1 - 7

Module 3

Sections 8 - 18

Module 5

Sections 19 - 40

SECTION 1

Collection and Organisation of Data

What you need to know

- **Primary data** is data collected by an individual or organisation to use for a particular purpose. Primary data is obtained from experiments, investigations, surveys and by using questionnaires.
- **Secondary data** is data which is already available or has been collected by someone else for a different purpose. Sources of secondary data include the Annual Abstract of Statistics, Social Trends and the Internet.
- **Qualitative** data – Data which can only be described in words.
- **Quantitative** data – Data that has a numerical value. Quantitative data is either **discrete** or **continuous**. **Discrete** data can only take certain values. **Continuous** data has no exact value and is measurable.
- **Data Collection Sheets** – Used to record data during a survey.
- **Tally** – A way of recording each item of data on a data collection sheet.

  A group of five is recorded as ~~||||~~.
- **Frequency Table** – A way of collating the information recorded on a data collection sheet.
- **Grouped Frequency Table** – Used for continuous data or for discrete data when a lot of data has to be recorded.
- **Database** – A collection of data.
- **Class Interval** – The width of the groups used in a grouped frequency distribution.
- **Questionnaire** – A set of questions used to collect data for a survey. Questionnaires should:
  (1) use simple language,
  (2) ask short questions which can be answered precisely,
  (3) provide tick boxes,
  (4) avoid open-ended questions,
  (5) avoid leading questions,
  (6) ask questions in a logical order.
- **Hypothesis** – A hypothesis is a statement which may or may not be true.
- When information is required about a large group of people it is not always possible to survey everyone and only a **sample** may be asked.
  The sample chosen should be large enough to make the results meaningful and representative of the whole group (population) or the results may be **biased**.
- **Two-way Tables** – A way of illustrating two features of a survey.

Exercise 1

1 Pat is investigating how long students spend on homework each night.
The time, in minutes, taken by 30 students to do their homework on a Wednesday night is shown.

100	55	45	80	65	40	10	45	105	60	35	40	30	45	90
25	120	55	60	75	70	45	90	45	90	45	25	15	20	75

(a) Using equal class intervals, copy and complete the frequency table to show this data.

Time (t minutes)	Tally	Frequency
$0 \leqslant t < 30$		

(b) Which class interval has the highest frequency?
(c) Give two reasons why this data may not be typical for these students.

2 A newspaper headline states: More students eat less for breakfast.

You are asked to investigate this headline.
Design an observation sheet to collect the data you need.
Invent the first 10 entries on your data sheet.

3 Jamie is investigating the use made of his college library.
Here is part of his questionnaire:

Library Questionnaire

1. How old are you? ....

(a) (i) Give a reason why this question is unsuitable.
(ii) Rewrite the question so that it could be included.

(b) Jamie asks the librarian to give the questionnaires to students when they borrow books.
(i) Give reasons why this sample may be biased.
(ii) Suggest a better way of giving out the questionnaires.

4 The table shows the results of a survey of 500 people.

	Can drive	Cannot drive
Men	180	20
Women	240	60

A newspaper headline states: **Survey shows that more women can drive than men.**
Do the results of the survey support this headline?
Give a reason for your answer.

5 This sample was used to investigate the claim: **"Women do more exercise than men."**

	Age (years)			
	16 to 21	22 to 45	46 to 65	Over 65
Male	5	5	13	7
Female	25	35	0	0

Give three reasons why the sample is biased.

6 A mobile phone company wants to build a transmitter mast on land belonging to a school.
The company offers the school £50 000 for the land.
The local paper receives 20 letters objecting to the proposal and 5 letters in favour.
One of the paper's reporters writes an article in which he claims:

'Objectors outnumber those in favour by 4 to 1'

Give **two** reasons why the newspaper reporter's claim may **not** be correct. AQA

7 The two-way table shows the number of credit cards and the number of store cards owned by each of 50 shoppers.

Number of credit cards	Number of store cards: 0	1	2	3
0	3	2	1	0
1	5	4	3	1
2	8	6	4	3
3	4	3	2	1

(a) How many of the shoppers had two credit cards and one store card?
(b) How many of the shoppers had three credit cards?
(c) How many of the shoppers had exactly one card?
(d) How many of the shoppers had more credit cards than store cards? AQA

SECTION 2

Presentation of Data 1

What you need to know

- **Bar chart**. Used for data which can be counted.
Often used to compare quantities of data in a distribution.
The length of each bar represents frequency.
The longest bar represents the **mode**.
The difference between the largest and smallest variable is called the **range**.

> Bars can be drawn horizontally or vertically.
> Bars are the same width and there are gaps between bars.

- **Bar-line graph**. Instead of drawing bars, horizontal or vertical lines are drawn to show frequency.

Eg 1 The graph shows the number of goals scored by a football team in 10 matches.

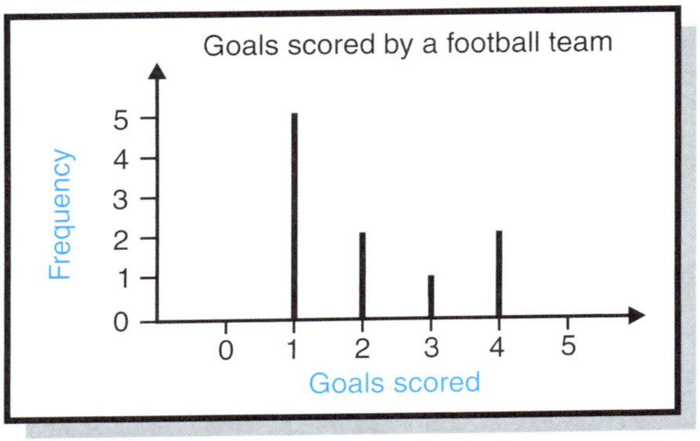

(a) Which number of goals scored is the mode?
(b) What is the range of the number of goals scored?

(a) The tallest bar represents the mode.
The mode is 1 goal.
(b) The range is the difference between the largest and smallest number of goals scored.
The range = 4 − 1 = 3

- **Pie chart**. Used for data which can be counted.
Often used to compare proportions of data, usually with the total.
The whole circle represents all the data.
The size of each sector represents the frequency of data in that sector.
The largest sector represents the **mode**.

Eg 2 The pie chart shows the makes of 120 cars.

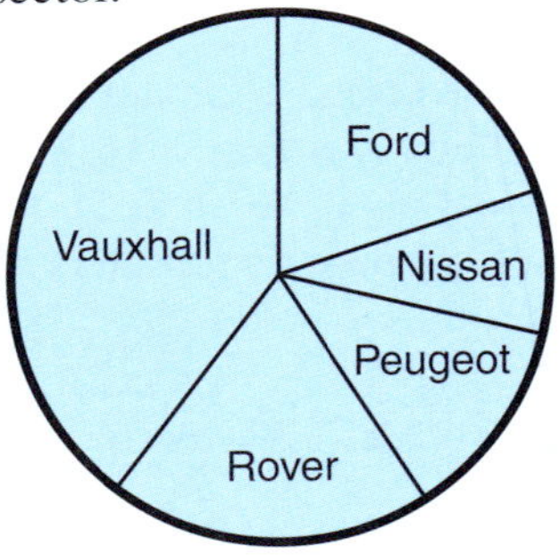

(a) Which make of car is the mode?
(b) How many of the cars are Ford?

(a) The sector representing Vauxhall is the largest.
Therefore, Vauxhall is the mode.
(b) The angle of the sector representing Ford is 72°.
The number of Ford cars $= \frac{72}{360} \times 120 = 24$

- **Stem and leaf diagrams**. Used to represent data in its original form. Data is split into two parts.
The part with the higher place value is the stem. e.g. 15 = stem 1, leaf 5.
A key is given to show the value of the data. e.g. 3 | 4 means 3.4 etc.
The data is shown in numerical order on the diagram. e.g. 2 | 3 5 9 represents 23, 25, 29.

Back to back stem and leaf diagrams can be used to compare two sets of data.

Eg 3 The times, in seconds, taken by 10 students to complete a puzzle are shown.

9	23	32	20	12
11	24	31	10	26

Construct a stem and leaf diagram to represent this information.

3 | 1 means 31 seconds

0	9			
1	0	1	2	
2	0	3	4	6
3	1	2		

Exercise 2

1 Causeway Hockey Club have a hockey team for men and a hockey team for women.
The bar chart shows the number of goals scored in matches played by these teams last season.

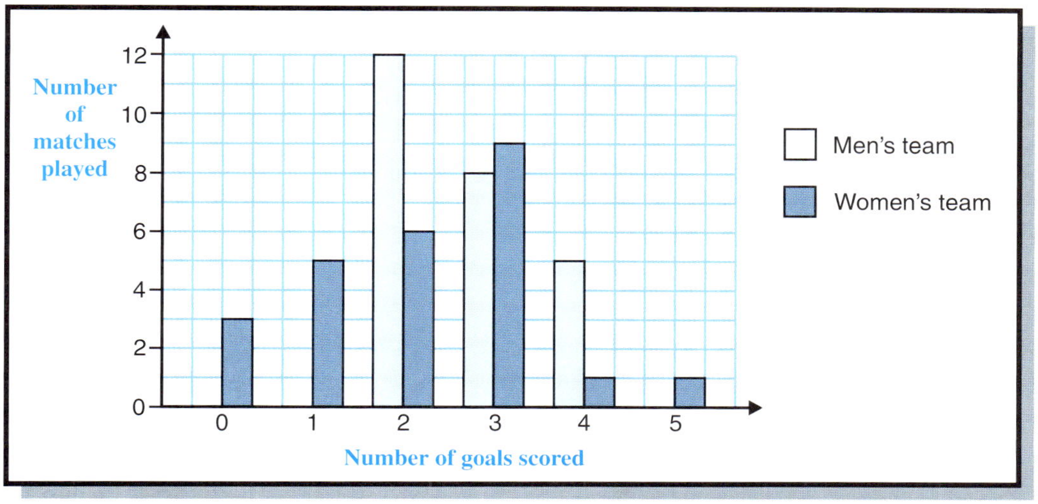

(a) How many matches did each team play?
(b) For the men's team, find the range and mode in the number of goals scored.
(c) Compare and comment on the goals scored by these teams last season.

2 The stem and leaf diagram shows the highest November temperature recorded in 12 European countries last year.

0 | 7 means 7°C

0	7 9
1	0 3 4 4 4 7 8
2	0 1 2

(a) How many countries are included?
(b) What is the maximum temperature recorded?
(c) Which temperature is the mode?
(d) What is the range of these temperatures?

3 The table shows the results of asking a group of children which pet they prefer.

Pet	Dog	Cat	Rabbit	Guinea pig
Number of children	8	5	7	4

Draw a clearly labelled pie chart to represent this information. AQA

4 The pie chart shows all the costs involved in making a dishwasher.

(a) Calculate what **fraction** of the total cost is for materials.
Give your answer in its lowest terms.

(b) Calculate what **percentage** of the total cost is for overheads.

(c) The total cost is £144.
Calculate the cost of the labour.

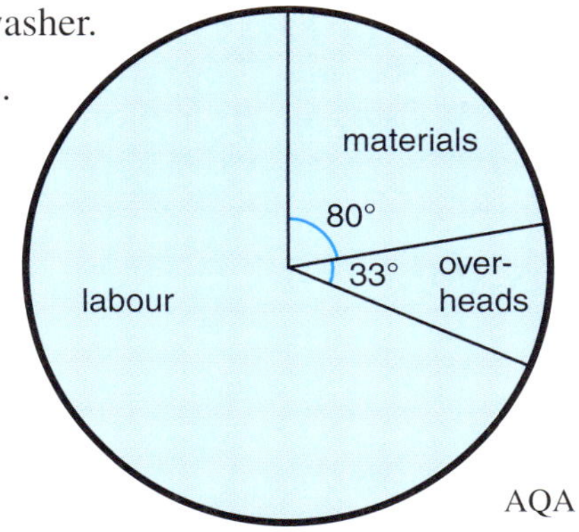

AQA

2

5 The bar chart shows information about the injuries of drivers involved in road accidents at a busy junction.

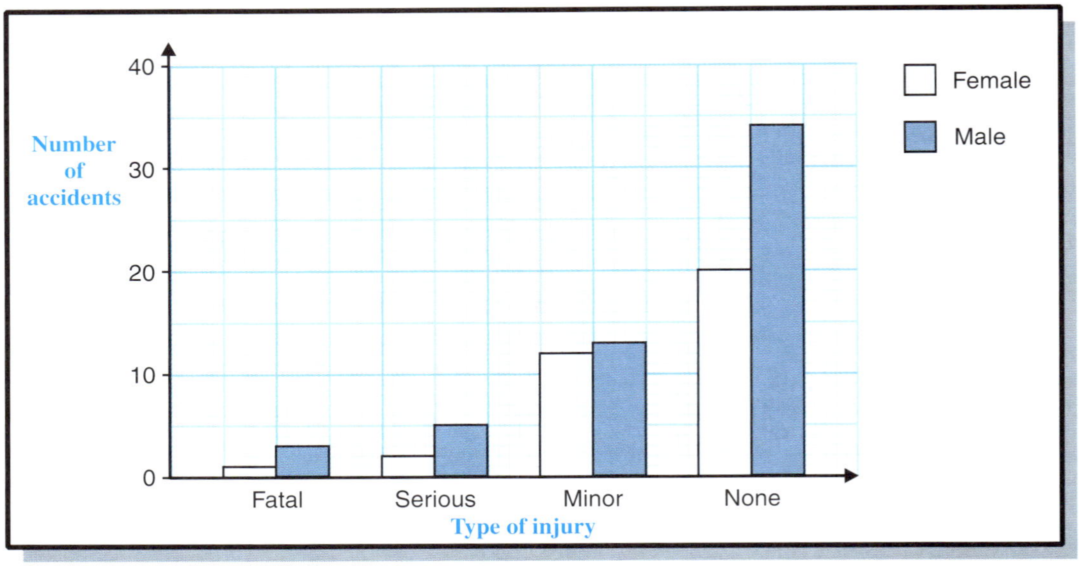

(a) What percentage of drivers had no injuries?
(b) What is the ratio of female to male drivers involved in these accidents? Give your answer in its simplest form.
(c) Draw a pie chart to illustrate the proportion of drivers with each type of injury.

6 Twenty children were asked to estimate the length of a leaf.
Their estimates, in centimetres, are:

Boys									
4.5	5.0	4.0	3.5	4.0	4.5	5.0	4.5	3.5	4.5

Girls									
4.5	5.0	3.5	4.0	5.5	3.5	4.5	3.5	3.0	2.5

(a) Construct a back to back stem and leaf diagram to represent this information.
(b) Compare and comment on the estimates of these boys and girls.

7 In a survey, parents were asked:

'Do you think the behaviour of children has improved in the last ten years?'

The results of the survey are shown in the pie chart.

(a) Estimate the fraction of parents who think that the behaviour of children has got worse.
(b) 75 parents in the survey said, 'Don't know'. This was 5% of all the parents. Calculate the number of parents that took part in the survey.

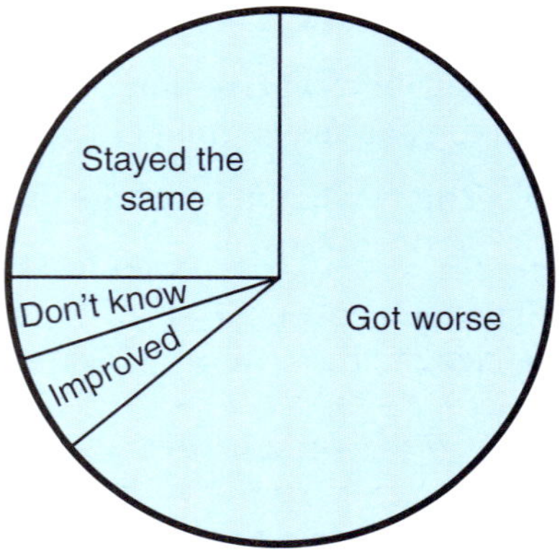

AQA

SECTION 3

Averages and Range

What you need to know

- There are three types of **average**: the **mode**, the **median** and the **mean**.

Eg 1 The number of text messages received by 7 students on Saturday is shown.

2 4 3 4 4 3 2

Find (a) the mode, (b) the median, (c) the mean, (d) the range.

> The **mode** is the most common amount.
>
> The **median** is found by arranging the data in order of size and taking the middle amount (or the mean of the two middle amounts).
>
> The **mean** is found by dividing the total of all the data by the number of data values.
>
> The **range** is a measure of **spread**.
> Range = highest amount − lowest amount

(a) The mode is 4.

(b) 2 2 3 (3) 4 4 4
The median is 3.

(c) The mean $= \frac{2+4+3+4+4+3+2}{7}$

$= \frac{22}{7} = 3.14\ldots$

$= 3.1$, correct to 1 d.p.

(d) The range $= 4 - 2 = 2$

- To find the mean of a **frequency distribution** use: $\text{Mean} = \frac{\text{Total of all amounts}}{\text{Number of amounts}} = \frac{\Sigma fx}{\Sigma f}$

Eg 2 The table shows the number of stamps on some parcels.

Number of stamps	1	2	3	4
Number of parcels	5	6	9	4

Find the mean number of stamps per parcel.

$\text{Mean} = \frac{\Sigma fx}{\Sigma f}$

$= \frac{1 \times 5 + 2 \times 6 + 3 \times 9 + 4 \times 4}{5 + 6 + 9 + 4}$

$= \frac{60}{24} = 2.5$

- To find the mean of a **grouped frequency distribution**, first find the value of the midpoint of each class.
Then use: $\text{Estimated mean} = \frac{\Sigma\,(\text{frequency} \times \text{midpoint})}{\text{Total frequency}} = \frac{\Sigma fx}{\Sigma f}$

Eg 3 The table shows the weights of some parcels.

Weight (w grams)	Frequency
$100 \leqslant w < 200$	7
$200 \leqslant w < 300$	11
$300 \leqslant w < 400$	19
$400 \leqslant w < 500$	3

Calculate an estimate of the mean weight of these parcels.

$\text{Mean} = \frac{\Sigma fx}{\Sigma f}$

$= \frac{150 \times 7 + 250 \times 11 + 350 \times 19 + 450 \times 3}{7 + 11 + 19 + 3}$

$= \frac{11\,800}{40} = 295$ grams

- Choosing the best average to use:
  When the most **popular** value is wanted use the **mode**.
  When **half** of the values have to be above the average use the **median**.
  When a **typical** value is wanted use either the **mode** or the **median**.
  When all the **actual** values have to be taken into account use the **mean**.
  When the average should not be distorted by a few very small or very large values do **not** use the mean.

Exercise 3

Do not use a calculator for questions 1 to 3.

1 The prices paid for eight different meals at a restaurant are:

£10 £9 £9.50 £12 £20 £11.50 £11 £9

(a) Which price is the mode? (b) Find the median price. (c) Calculate the mean price.
(d) Which of these averages best describes the average price paid for a meal? Give a reason for your answer.

2 (a) Calculate the mean of 13.9, 15.3, 11.7 and 16.2.
(b) Using your result from part (a), explain how to find quickly the mean of

14.9, 16.3, 12.7 and 17.2

(c) Calculate the median of the numbers in part (a).
(d) If the number 16.2 in part (a) was changed to 27.2, explain, without doing a calculation, whether the mean or the median would be more affected. AQA

3 The graph shows the distribution of goals scored by a football team in home and away matches.

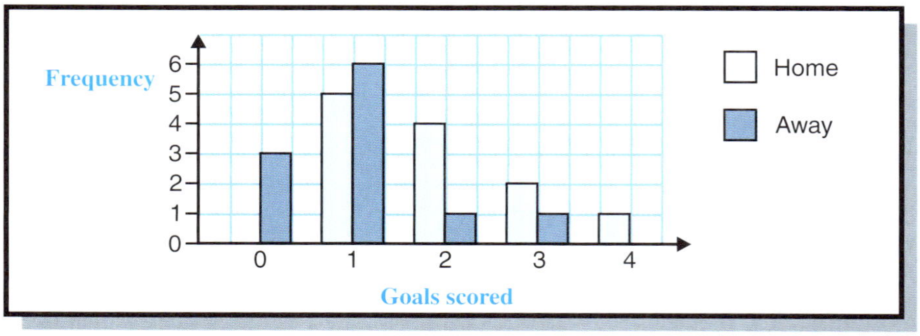

(a) What is the range of the number of goals scored at home matches?
(b) Calculate the mean number of goals per match for home matches.
(c) A supporter says, "The average number of goals per match is the same for both away matches and home matches." Which average is being used? AQA

4 Four taxi drivers recorded how many passengers they carried on each journey during one evening. The table shows the numbers of journeys they made with different numbers of passengers.

		Number of passengers carried			
		1	2	3	4
Taxi	A	6	6	4	0
	B	7	7	3	1
	C	5	7	2	0
	D	4	4	3	1

(a) Which taxi completed the most journeys that evening?
(b) Calculate the total number of journeys in which exactly 3 passengers were carried.
(c) There were 60 journeys made altogether.
Calculate the mean number of passengers per taxi journey. AQA

5 Fred records the time taken by 30 pupils to complete a cross-country run.

(a) Calculate an estimate of the mean time taken to complete the run.

(b) Which time interval contains the median time taken to complete the run? AQA

Time (t minutes)	Number of pupils
$20 \leqslant t < 25$	9
$25 \leqslant t < 30$	8
$30 \leqslant t < 35$	5
$35 \leqslant t < 40$	2
$40 \leqslant t < 45$	6

SECTION 4

Presentation of Data 2

What you need to know

- A **time series** is a set of readings taken at time intervals.
- A **line graph** is used to show a time series.

Only the plotted points represent actual values. Points are joined by lines to show the **trend**.

- Variations in a time series which recur with the seasons of the year are called **seasonal variations**.
- **Moving averages** are used to smooth out variations in a time series so that the trend can be seen.

Eg 1 The graph shows the amount of gas used by a householder each quarter over a period of 3 years.
The blue crosses show the 4-quarterly moving average values.
A line of best fit, drawn for the moving averages, shows the general **trend**.
The trend shows a slight increase in the amount of gas used.

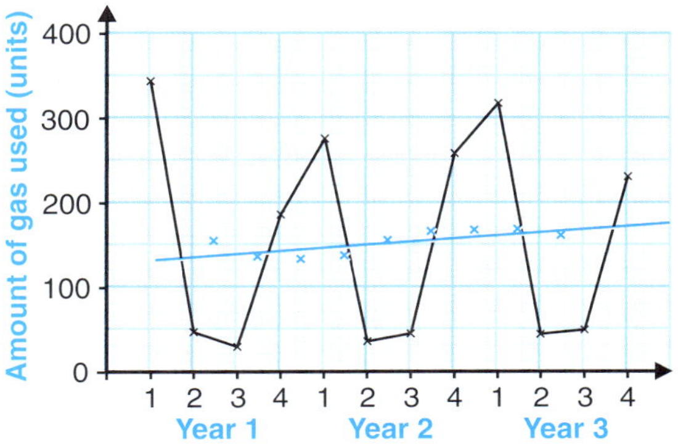

- **Histogram**. Used to illustrate **grouped frequency distributions.**
The horizontal axis is a continuous scale.
- **Frequency polygon**. Used to illustrate grouped frequency distributions.
Often used to compare two or more distributions on the same diagram.
Frequencies are plotted at the midpoints of the class intervals and joined with straight lines.
The horizontal axis is a continuous scale.

Eg 2 The frequency distribution of the heights of some boys is shown.

Draw a histogram and a frequency polygon to illustrate the data.

Height (h cm)	Frequency
$130 \leqslant h < 140$	1
$140 \leqslant h < 150$	7
$150 \leqslant h < 160$	12
$160 \leqslant h < 170$	9
$170 \leqslant h < 180$	3

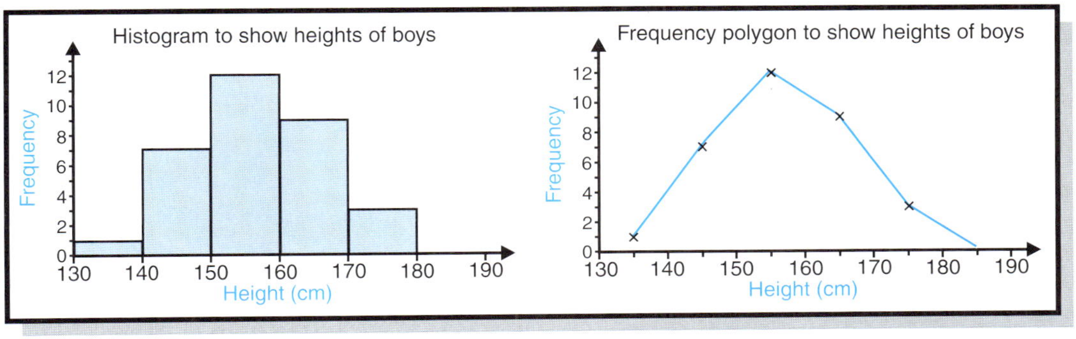

- **Misleading graphs**
Graphs may be misleading if:
the scales are not labelled, the scales are not uniform, the frequency does not begin at zero.

Exercise 4

1 On Sunday, Alfie records the outside temperature every two hours.
The temperatures he recorded are shown in the table.

Time of day	0800	1000	1200	1400	1600	1800
Outside temperature (°C)	9	12	15	17	16	14

(a) Draw a line graph to represent the data.
(b) What is the range in the temperatures recorded?
(c) (i) Use your graph to estimate the temperature at 1300.
(ii) Explain why your answer in (c)(i) is an estimate.

2 The amount of time spent by a group of pupils on their mobile phones in one week is recorded.
Here are the results.

Time (minutes)	**Number of pupils**
Less than 10 minutes	12
10 minutes or more but less than 20 minutes	9
20 minutes or more but less than 30 minutes	13
30 minutes or more but less than 40 minutes	6
40 minutes or more but less than 50 minutes	8
50 minutes or more but less than 60 minutes	2

(a) State the modal class.
(b) Draw a histogram to show this information. AQA

3 The number of words in the first 100 sentences of a book are shown in the table.

Number of words	1 to 10	11 to 20	21 to 30	31 to 40	41 to 50
Frequency	45	38	12	4	1

(a) Draw a frequency polygon for these data.
(b) Write down the class which contains the median. AQA

4 The graph shows the time taken to score the first goal in 20 football matches.

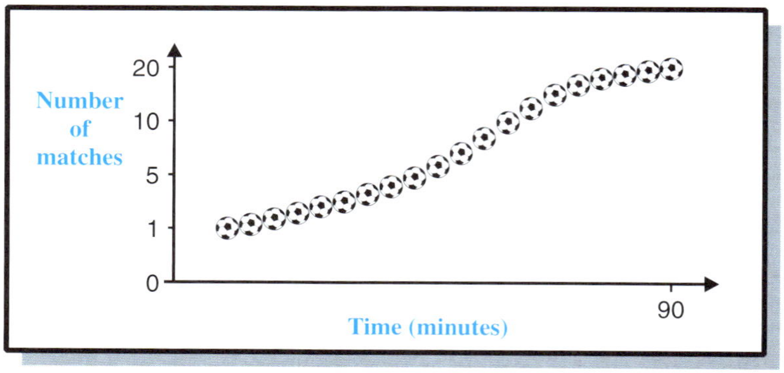

Explain why the graph is misleading.

5 The graph shows the age distribution of people in a nursing home.

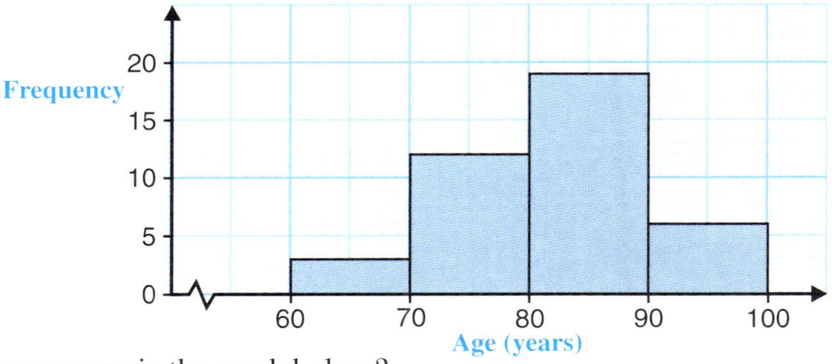

(a) Which age group is the modal class?
(b) How many people are in the nursing home?
(c) The table shows the age distribution of men in the home.

Age (a years)	$60 \leqslant a < 70$	$70 \leqslant a < 80$	$80 \leqslant a < 90$	$90 \leqslant a < 100$
Frequency	2	7	6	0

(i) Draw a frequency polygon to represent this information.
(ii) On the same diagram draw a frequency polygon to represent the age distribution of women in the home.
(iii) Compare and comment on the ages of men and women in the home.

6 The frequency polygon illustrates the age distribution of people taking part in a marathon.

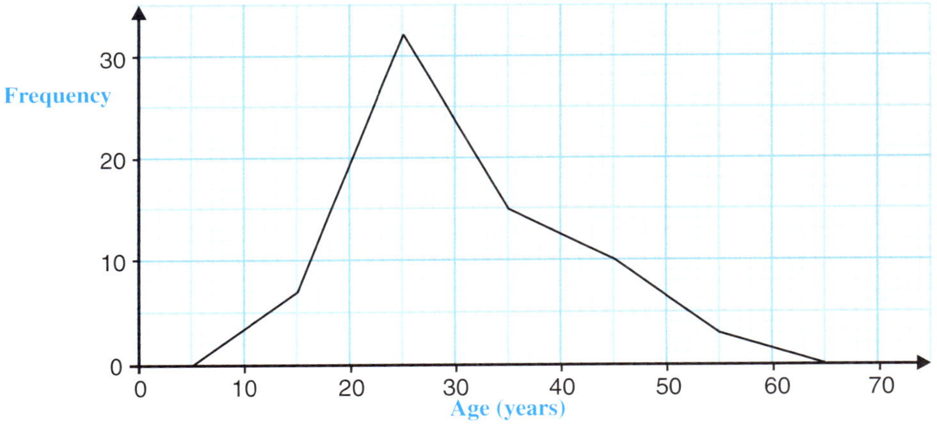

(a) How many people were under 20 years of age?
(b) How many people were over 50 years of age?
(c) How many people took part?

7 Calculate the second average in a 3-point moving average for these values.

15 23 19 12 17 22 28 20 16

8 The table shows the number of units of electricity used each quarter by a householder over a period of 3 years.

Year	1999				2000				2001			
Quarter	1	2	3	4	1	2	3	4	1	2	3	4
Units used	680	810	470	740	640	850	420	750	970	880	490	760

(a) Plot these values on graph paper.
(b) Calculate a 4-point moving average.
(c) Plot the moving average values on your graph.
(d) Comment on the trend in the units of electricity used.

SECTION 5

Scatter Graphs

What you need to know

- A **scatter graph** can be used to show the relationship between two sets of data.
- The relationship between two sets of data is referred to as **correlation**.
- You should be able to recognise **positive** and **negative** correlation.

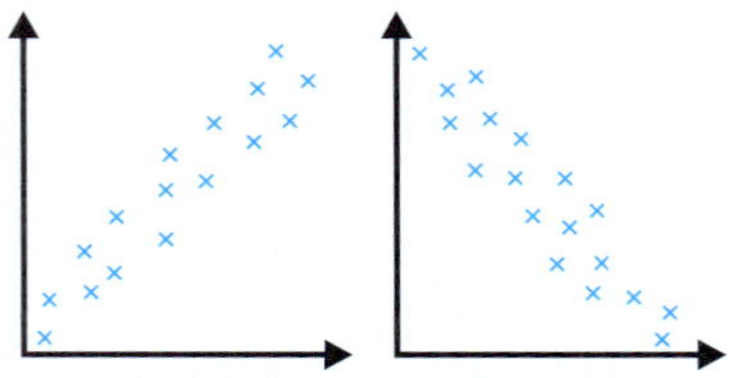

Positive correlation **Negative correlation**

- When there is a relationship between two sets of data a **line of best fit** can be drawn on the scatter graph.
  The correlation is stronger as points get closer to a straight line.
  Perfect correlation is when all the points lie on a straight line.

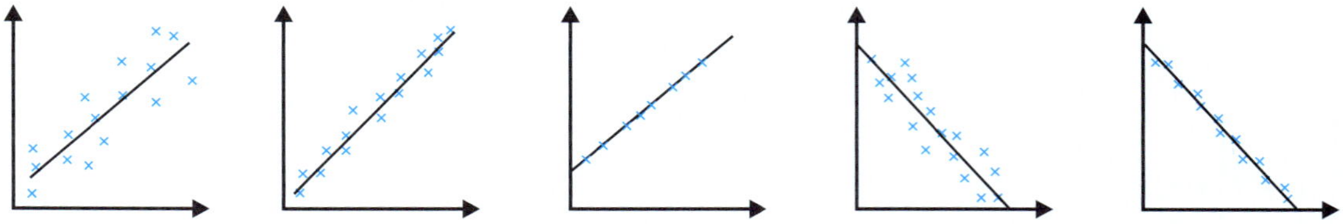

- The line of best fit can be used to **estimate** the value from one set of the data when the corresponding value of the other set is known.

Exercise 5

1 The scatter graphs below show the results of a questionnaire given to pupils who have jobs.

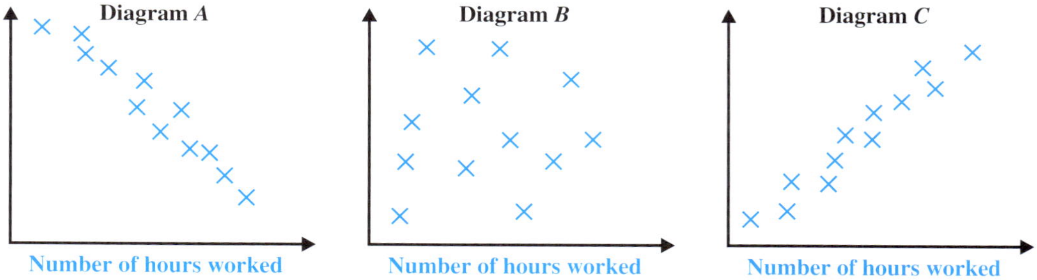

(a) Which scatter graph shows the number of hours worked plotted against:
   (i) the earnings of pupils,
   (ii) the time spent by pupils watching TV,
   (iii) the time taken by pupils to travel to work?

(b) State which one of the graphs shows a negative correlation. AQA

2 The table gives information about the engine size (in cc's) and the fuel economy (in kilometres per litre) of a number of cars.

Engine size (cc)	1800	1000	1200	1600	1400	800	2000	1500
Fuel economy (km/l)	6.5	11	10.5	8	9.5	12	6	8.5

(a) Draw a scatter graph to show this information.
(b) Describe the relationship between engine size and fuel economy.
(c) Draw a line of best fit.
(d) Explain how you can tell the relationship is quite strong.

3 The scatter graph shows the results of candidates in two examinations in the same subject.

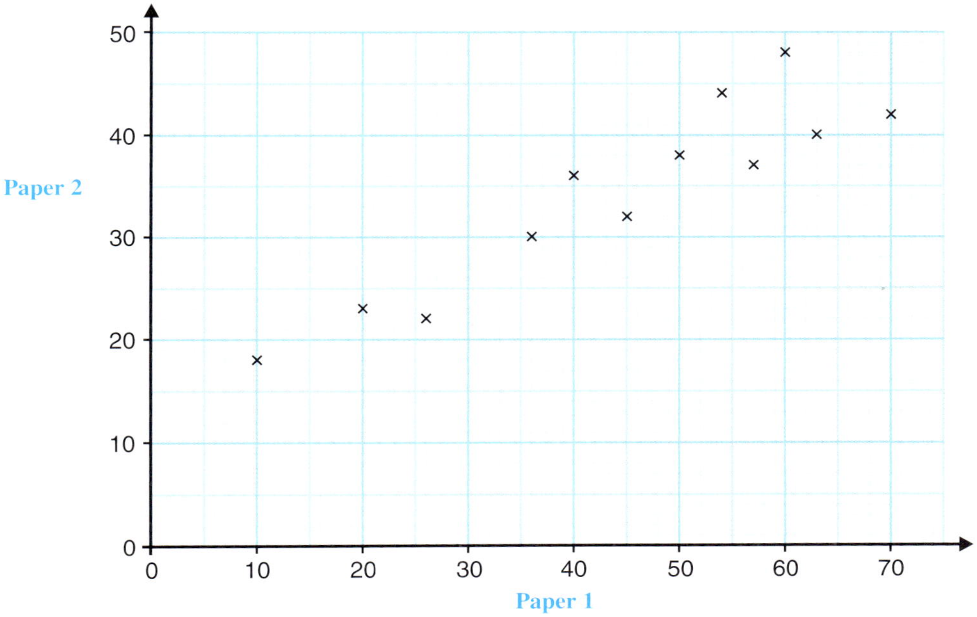

(a) One candidate scored 40 marks on Paper 1.
What mark did this candidate score on Paper 2?

(b) One candidate scored 48 marks on Paper 2.
What mark did this candidate score on Paper 1?

(c) Was the highest mark on both papers scored by the same candidate?

(d) Was the lowest mark on both papers scored by the same candidate?

(e) What type of correlation is there between the marks scored on the two exam papers?

4 The marks for 10 students in examinations in French and German are shown.

Mark in French	19	25	30	35	44	45	55	60	63	71
Mark in German	35	38	39	45	50	54	60	65	64	72

(a) Use this information to draw a scatter graph.
(b) What type of correlation is there between the marks in French and German?
(c) Draw a line of best fit.
(d) A student scored 50 marks in the French examination but was absent for the German examination.
Estimate the mark this student might have scored if he had taken the German examination.
AQA

5 The table shows the ages and heights of trees in a wood.

Age (years)	1	3	4	5	7	9	10
Height (m)	0.5	1.2	1.7	2.5	3.3	4.5	4.8

(a) Draw a scatter graph for the data.
(b) Draw a line of best fit.
(c) Use the graph to estimate the height of a tree which is
(i) 8 years old, (ii) 13 years old.
(d) Which of your answers in (c) is more likely to be reliable?
Give a reason for your answer.
AQA

SECTION 6 Cumulative Frequency

What you need to know

- The information given in a frequency table can be used to make a **cumulative frequency table**.
- You should be able to **draw cumulative frequency graphs**.

To draw a cumulative frequency graph:
1. Draw and label:
   the variable on the horizontal axis,
   cumulative frequency on the vertical axis.
2. Plot the cumulative frequency against the upper class boundary of each class.
3. Join the points with a smooth curve.

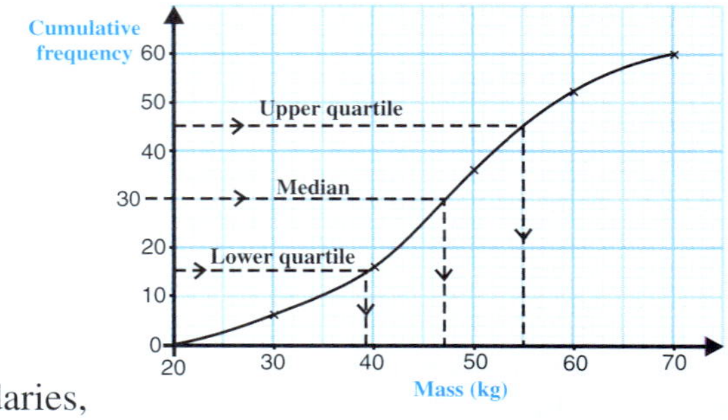

- If the question does not give the upper class boundaries, then the upper class boundary of each class is equal to the lower class boundary of the next class.
- When the classes have gaps between them then the upper class boundary is halfway between the end of one class and the beginning of the next.
- You should be able to **interpret cumulative frequency graphs**.

The **median** is the value of the middle number.
The **lower quartile** is the value located at $\frac{1}{4}$ of the total frequency.
The **upper quartile** is the value located at $\frac{3}{4}$ of the total frequency.
The **interquartile range** measures the spread of the middle 50% of the data.
Interquartile range = Upper Quartile − Lower Quartile

Eg 1 The times spent by students on the Internet one day are shown.

Time (t minutes)	$0 \leq t < 20$	$20 \leq t < 40$	$40 \leq t < 60$	$60 \leq t < 80$
Frequency	55	25	15	5

(a) Draw a cumulative frequency graph.
(b) Use your graph to find:
(i) the median, (ii) the interquartile range.

(a) Make a cumulative frequency table that can be used to draw the graph.

Time (mins) less than	0	20	40	60	80
Cumulative frequency	0	55	80	95	100

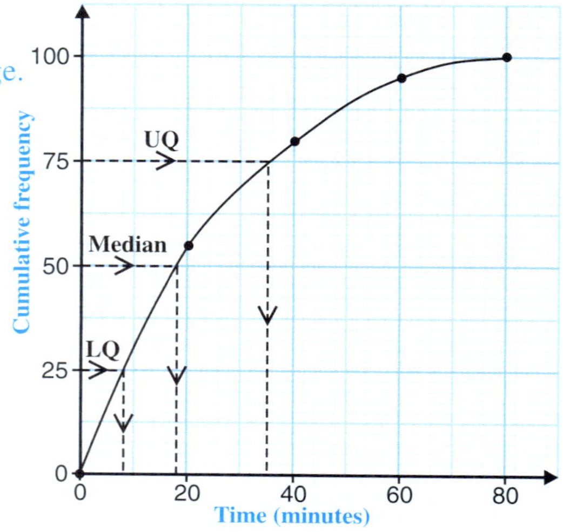

(b) Reading from the graph:
(i) Median = 18 minutes
(ii) Lower quartile (LQ) = 8 minutes
Upper quartile (UQ) = 35 minutes
Interquartile range = UQ − LQ = 35 − 8 = 27 minutes

- A **box plot** is used to represent the range, the median and the quartiles of a distribution.

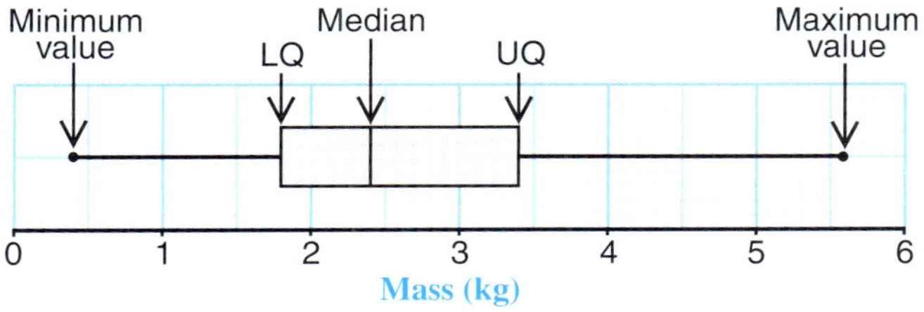

- The box plot shows how the data is spread out and how the middle 50% of data is clustered.
- Box plots can be used to compare two (or more) distributions.
- You should be able to draw and interpret box plots.

Eg 2 15 pupils were asked to estimate the size of an angle.
Their estimates, in degrees, are shown.
40 20 38 30 32 45 35 36 40 35 30 40 45 42 25
Draw a box plot to illustrate the data.

> Put the data in order and locate the median, lower quartile and upper quartile.
> Then use these values to draw the box plot.

20 25 30 (30) 32 35 35 (36) 38 40 40 (40) 42 45 45

LQ = 30, Median = 36, UQ = 40

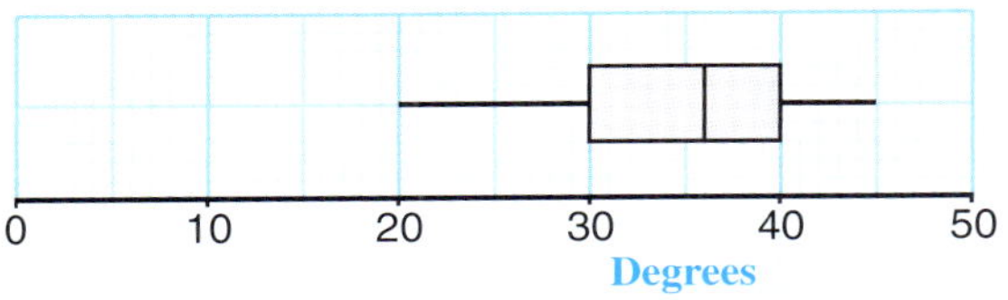

Exercise 6

1 As part of a lifesaving course a group of students were asked to swim as far as possible wearing shoes and clothes.
The cumulative frequency graph shows the distances swum.

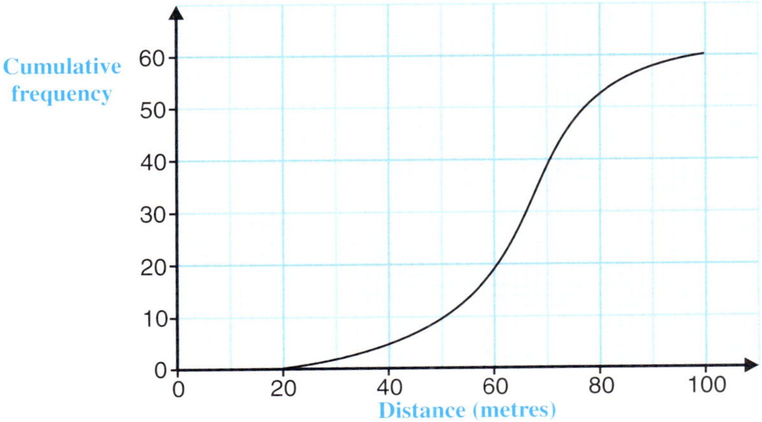

(a) Use the graph to find:
(i) the median distance, (ii) the interquartile range.
(b) Draw a box plot to illustrate the distances swum.

2 A group of children were asked to estimate the weight of a bucket of water.
Their estimates, in kilograms, are shown.

10	9	17.5	8	7.5	5	10	15	12.5	20	8	10	14	18	11

(a) Find (i) the median estimate, (ii) the interquartile range of these estimates.
(b) Draw a box plot to represent these estimates.

3 An English examination was taken by two groups of students.
The cumulative frequency graphs show information about the marks scored by each group.

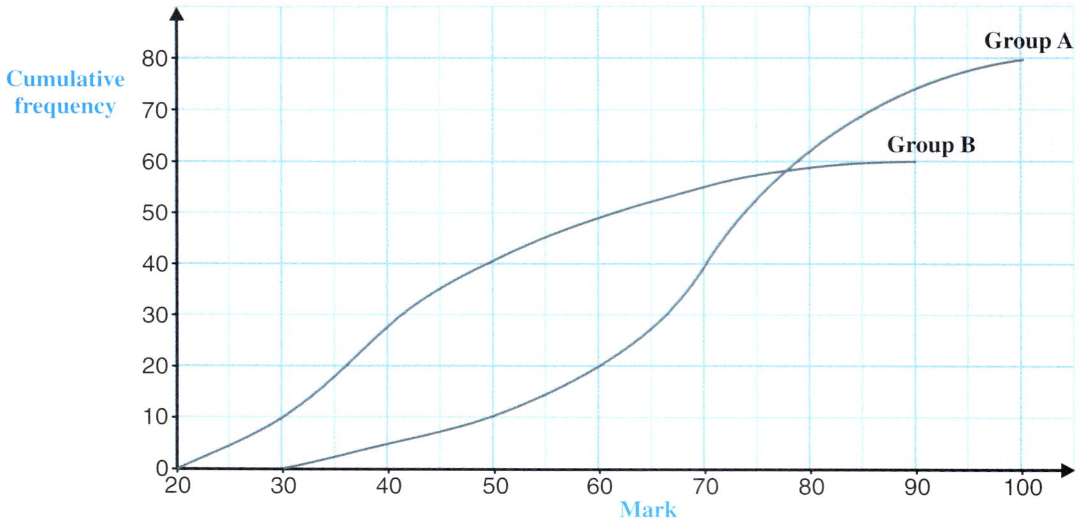

(a) Find the difference in the median marks of the two groups.
(b) (i) Which group had the larger interquartile range?
(ii) Find the interquartile range for this group.

AQA

4 The box plots illustrate the distribution of weights for a sample of eating apples and a sample of cooking apples.

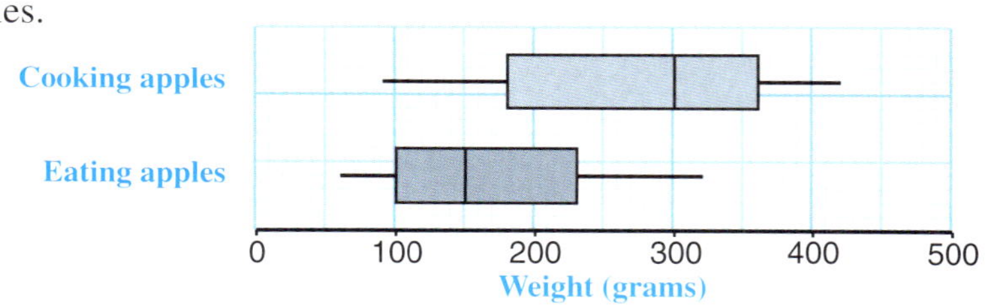

(a) What is the range in the weights of the eating apples?
(b) Which type of apple has the higher median weight?
(c) What is the interquartile range for cooking apples?
(d) Compare and comment on these distributions.

5 Laura and Joy played 80 games of golf together. The table below shows Laura's scores.

Scores x	$70 < x \leqslant 80$	$80 < x \leqslant 90$	$90 < x \leqslant 100$	$100 < x \leqslant 110$	$110 < x \leqslant 120$
Frequency	2	8	30	34	6

(a) Draw a cumulative frequency diagram to show Laura's scores.
(b) Use your graph to find: (i) Laura's median score,
(ii) the interquartile range of her scores.
(c) Joy's median score was 103. The interquartile range of her scores was 6.
(i) Who was the more consistent player? Give a reason for your choice.
(ii) The winner of a game of golf is the one with the lowest score.
Who won most of these 80 games? Give a reason for your choice.

AQA

Probability

What you need to know

- **Probability** describes how likely or unlikely it is that an event will occur.
  Probabilities can be shown on a probability scale.

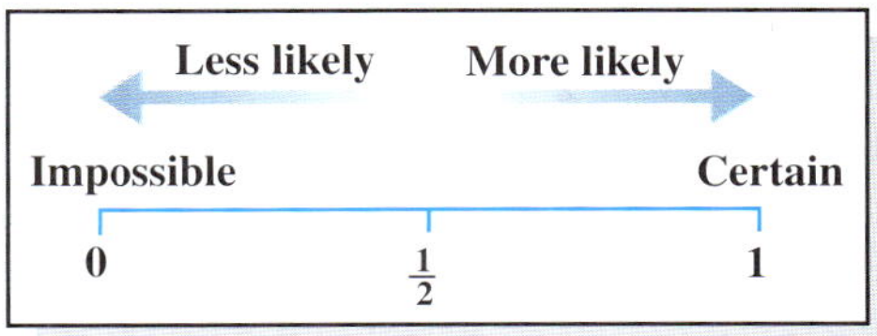

> Probability **must** be written as a **fraction**, a **decimal** or a **percentage**.

- How to work out probabilities using **equally likely outcomes**.

> The probability of an event $= \dfrac{\text{Number of outcomes in the event}}{\text{Total number of possible outcomes}}$

Eg 1 A box contains 7 red pens and 4 blue pens. A pen is taken from the box at random.
What is the probability that the pen is blue?

P(blue) $= \dfrac{\text{Number of blue pens}}{\text{Total number of pens}} = \dfrac{4}{11}$

> P(blue) stands for the probability that the pen is blue.

- How to estimate probabilities using **relative frequency**.

> Relative frequency $= \dfrac{\text{Number of times the event happens in an experiment (or in a survey)}}{\text{Total number of trials in the experiment (or observations in the survey)}}$

Eg 2 A spinner is spun 20 times. The results are shown.

4 1 3 1 4 2 2 4 3 3 4 1 4 4 3 2 2 1 3 2

What is the relative frequency of getting a 4?

Relative frequency $= \dfrac{\text{Number of 4's}}{\text{Number of spins}} = \dfrac{6}{20} = 0.3$

> Relative frequency gives a better estimate of probability the larger the number of trials.

- How to use probabilities to **estimate** the number of times an event occurs in an **experiment** or **observation**.

> Estimate = total number of trials (or observations) × probability of event

Eg 3 1000 raffle tickets are sold. Alan buys some tickets.
The probability that Alan wins first prize is $\frac{1}{50}$.
How many tickets did Alan buy? Number of tickets $= 1000 \times \frac{1}{50} = 20$

- **Mutually exclusive events** cannot occur at the same time.

> When A and B are mutually exclusive events: P(A or B) = P(A) + P(B)

Eg 4 A box contains red, green, blue and yellow counters.
The table shows the probability of getting each colour.

Colour	Red	Green	Blue	Yellow
Probability	0.4	0.25	0.25	0.1

A counter is taken from the box at random.
What is the probability of getting a red or blue counter?

P(Red or Blue) = P(Red) + P(Blue) = 0.4 + 0.25 = 0.65

- **The probability of an event, A, not happening is: P(not A) = 1 − P(A)**

Eg 5 Kathy takes a sweet from a bag at random.
The probability that it is a toffee is 0.3.
What is the probability that it is **not** a toffee?

P(not toffee) = 1 − P(toffee) = 1 − 0.3 = 0.7

- How to find all the possible outcomes when two events are combined.
  By **listing** the outcomes systematically.
  By using a **possibility space diagram**.
  By using a **tree diagram**.

- The outcomes of **independent events** do not influence each other.

  When A and B are independent events: P(A and B) = P(A) × P(B)

Eg 6 Box A contains 3 white cubes (W) and 1 blue cube (B).
Box B contains 2 white cubes (W) and 3 blue cubes (B).
A cube is drawn from each box at random.
(a) Draw a tree diagram to show all the possible outcomes.
(b) Calculate the probability of getting two white cubes.

(a)

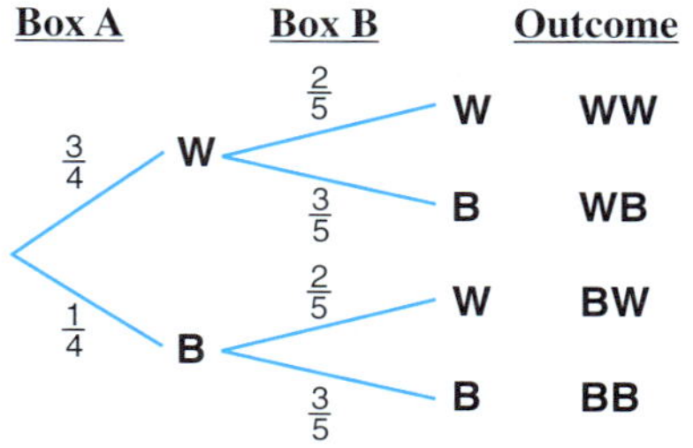

(b) To calculate P(WW), multiply the probabilities along the branches of the tree diagram.

$P(WW) = \frac{3}{4} \times \frac{2}{5}$

$= \frac{6}{20}$

$= \frac{3}{10}$

Exercise 7

1 A packet contains 5 red balloons, 3 white balloons and 4 blue balloons.
A balloon is taken from the packet at random.
(a) What is the probability that it is red?
(b) What is the probability that it is red or white?
(c) What is the probability that it is not white?

2 The letters of the word A B B E Y are written on separate cards and placed in a box.
A card is taken from the box at random.
(a) What is the probability that it is the letter B?
(b) The probability that it is a vowel is 0.4
What is the probability that it is not a vowel?

3 Petra has 5 numbered cards.
She uses the cards to do this experiment:

Shuffle the cards and then record the number on the top card.

She repeats the experiment 20 times and gets these results.
3 3 2 3 4 3 5 2 3 4 3 5 3 3 4 2 5 3 4 2
(a) What is the relative frequency of getting a 3?
(b) What numbers do you think are on the five cards? Give a reason for your answer.
(c) She repeats the experiment 500 times.
Estimate the number of times she will get a 5. Give a reason for your answer.

4 Jeff tosses a coin three times.
(a) List all the possible outcomes.
(b) What is the probability that he gets one head and two tails?

5 The table shows information about the colour and type of symbol printed on some cards.

		Colour of symbol		
		Red	**Yellow**	**Blue**
Type of symbol	**O**	9	4	5
	X	2	7	3

(a) A card is taken at random.
   (i) What is the probability that it has a red symbol?
   (ii) What is the probability that it has a blue symbol **or** an X?
(b) A yellow card is taken at random.
   What is the probability that it has the symbol X? AQA

6 A box contains counters. The counters are numbered 1, 2, 3, 4 or 5.
A counter is taken from the box at random.
(a) Copy and complete the table to show the probability of each number being chosen.

Number on counter	1	2	3	4	5
Probability	0.20	0.30	0.15		0.10

(b) Is the number on the counter chosen more likely to be odd or even?
   You must show your working. AQA

7 The table shows the probabilities of homework being set for Mathematics and English on Monday night.

	Homework set	Homework **not** set
Mathematics	$\frac{2}{3}$	
English		$\frac{3}{5}$

(a) (i) Copy and complete the table.
   (ii) There are 630 pupils in the school.
   How many will expect to have Mathematics homework on Monday night?
(b) Calculate the probability that a pupil is set Mathematics homework and is **not** set English homework on Monday night. AQA

8 On Tuesday Jim has to catch a bus and a train to get to work.
The probability that the train is late is 0.4. The probability that the bus is late is 0.7.
(a) Copy and complete the tree diagram.

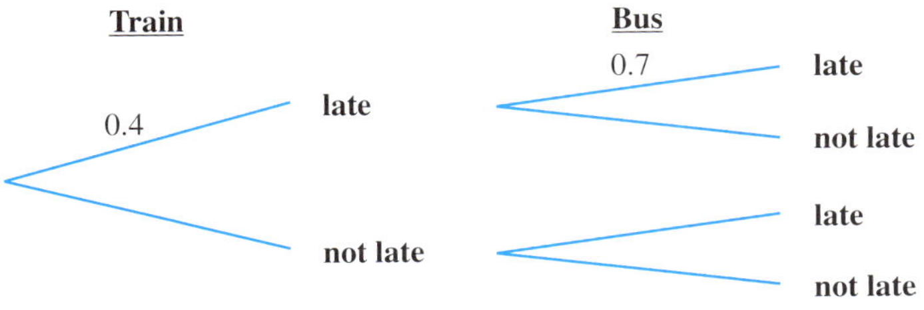

(b) What is the probability that both the bus and the train are late?
(c) What is the probability that either the train or the bus is late but not both?

9 John is taking part in a spelling test.
Words are chosen at random.
The probability that he spells a word correctly is $\frac{7}{10}$.
John is given two words to spell.
(a) What is the probability that he spells both words correctly?
(b) What is the probability that he spells only one of the words correctly? AQA

Module 1 Exam Practice Non-calculator Paper

1 The graph shows the distribution of the best height jumped by each girl in a high jump competition.

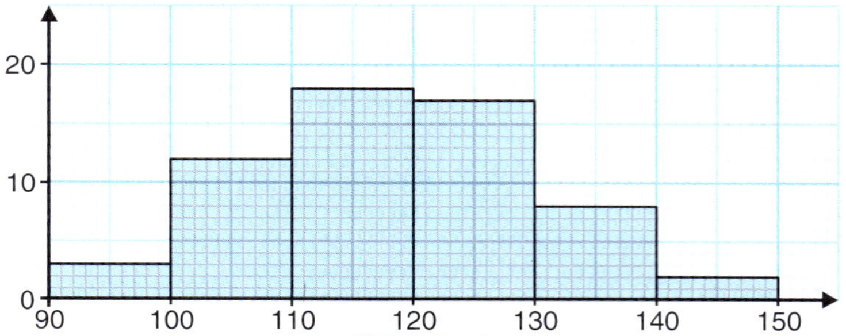

(a) (i) How many girls jumped between 100 cm and 120 cm?
(ii) How many girls took part in the competition?
(b) Which class interval contains the median height?

2 Sylvester did a survey to find the most popular pantomime.
(a) The results for children are shown in the table.

Pantomime	Aladdin	Cinderella	Jack and the Bean Stalk	Peter Pan
Number of children	45	35	25	15

(i) Draw a clearly labelled pie chart to illustrate this information.
(ii) Which pantomime is the mode?

(b) The results for adults are shown in the pie chart.
(i) 20 adults chose Aladdin.
How many adults were included in the survey?
(ii) Sylvester said, "30% of adults chose Cinderella."
Is he correct?
Explain your answer.

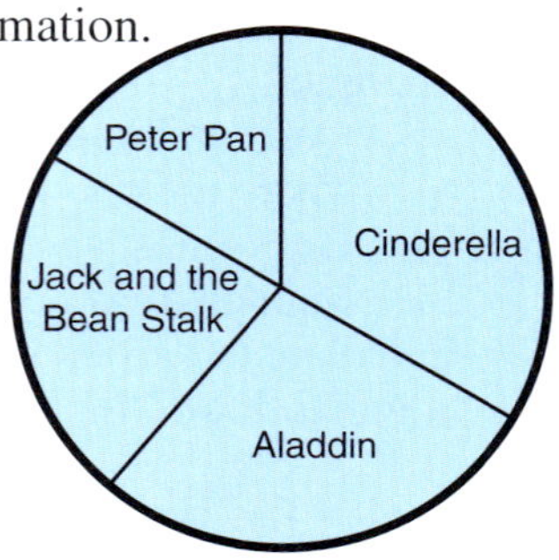

3 Karl plays a game with a spinner.
The spinner has three equal sections, coloured red, yellow and blue.
Karl spins the spinner twice.
If both spins land on the same colour, Karl wins 2 tokens.
If exactly one of the spins lands on red, Karl wins 1 token.
For any other result, Karl wins 0 tokens.

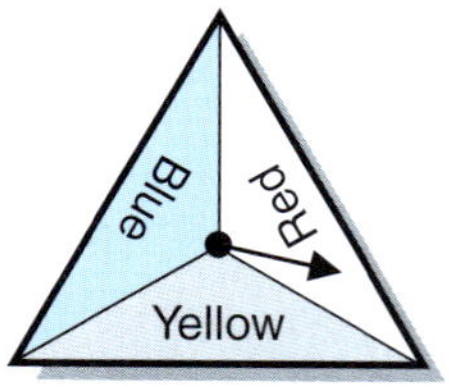

(a) Copy and complete the table to show the numbers of tokens that Karl can win.

		Second spin		
		Red	Yellow	Blue
First spin	Red			
	Yellow			
	Blue			

(b) What is the probability that Karl wins 0 tokens?
(c) Karl plays the game 70 times. How many times should he expect to win 2 tokens?

AQA

4 A teacher asked the pupils in his maths class how long they had spent revising for a maths test.
He drew a scatter graph to compare their test results and the time they had spent revising.

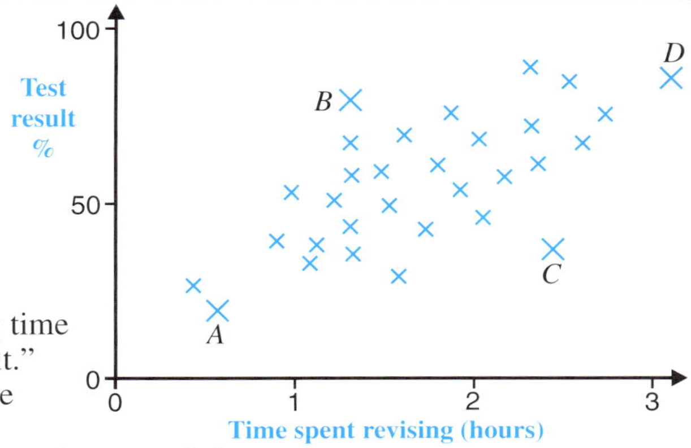

(a) State which point A, B, C or D represents the statement:
   (i) Keith, "Even though I spent a long time revising, I still got a poor test result."
   (ii) Val, "I got a good test result despite not doing much revision."
   (iii) Jane, "I revised for ages and got a good test result."

(b) Make up a statement which matches the point you have **not** used in your answer to part (a).

(c) What does the scatter graph tell you about the relationship between the time the pupils spent revising and their test results? AQA

5 Winston has designed a data collection sheet to record the number of bottles that each person puts into a bottle bank.

Number of bottles	**Tally**	**Frequency**
0 to 2		
3 to 6		
6 to 8		

(a) Give **three** criticisms of the class intervals that Winston has chosen.

Anna and Patrick watch people using the bottle bank.
Anna watches 60 people and calculates the mean to be 8.5 bottles per person.
Patrick watches 15 people and calculates the mean to be 9.2 bottles per person.

(b) Which of the two means would you expect to give the more reliable estimate of the mean number of bottles per person? Give a reason for your answer. AQA

6 The lengths of 20 bolts, in centimetres, are shown.

7.4	5.8	4.5	5.0	6.5	6.6	7.0	5.4	4.8	6.4
5.4	6.2	7.2	5.5	4.8	6.5	5.0	6.0	6.5	6.8

(a) Draw a stem and leaf diagram to illustrate this information.

(b) What is the range in the lengths of these bolts?

7 The table shows information about a group of students.

	Can speak French	Cannot speak French
Male	5	20
Female	12	38

(a) One of these students is chosen at random.
What is the probability that the student can speak French?

(b) Pru says, "If a female student is chosen at random she is more likely to be able to speak French than if a male student is chosen at random." Is she correct? Explain your answer.

8 The table shows the rainfall (cm) and the number of hours of sunshine for various towns in August one year.

Rainfall (cm)	0.1	0.1	0.2	0.5	0.8	1	1	1.5	1.5	1.9
Sunshine (hours)	200	240	210	190	170	160	130	100	120	90

(a) Use this information to draw a scatter graph.

(b) Draw a line of best fit on your diagram.

(c) Use your line of best fit to estimate the number of hours of sunshine for a town that had:
   (i) 1.4 cm of rain in August that year,   (ii) 2.5 cm of rain in August that year.

(d) Which of the answers from part (c) would you expect to be the more reliable?
Give a reason for your answer. AQA

9 To collect data for a survey on the amount of milk bought each week by families, Grant stands outside his local supermarket and asks 10 people as they leave the shop how much milk they have just bought. He repeats this each day for a week.
Write down two reasons why his results may be biased.

10 A bag contains 50 cubes of which 7 are red. A cube is taken from the bag at random.
(a) The probability that it is white is 0.3. What is the probability that it is not white?
(b) What is the probability that it is either white or red?

11 A sack contains a number of gold and silver discs.
An experiment consists of taking a disc from the sack at random, recording its colour and then replacing it.
The experiment is repeated 10, 50, 100, 150 and 200 times. The table shows the results.

Number of experiments	10	50	100	150	200
Number of gold discs	3	8	23	30	38

(a) Draw a graph to show how the relative frequency of a gold disc changes as the number of experiments increases.
(b) The sack contains 1000 discs. Estimate the number of gold discs in the sack.
Explain how you estimated your answer. AQA

12 At a fete Jessie has one go on the hoopla and one go on the darts.
The probability she wins a prize on the hoopla is 0.3.
The probability she wins a prize on the darts is 0.4.
(a) Copy and complete the tree diagram for these two events.

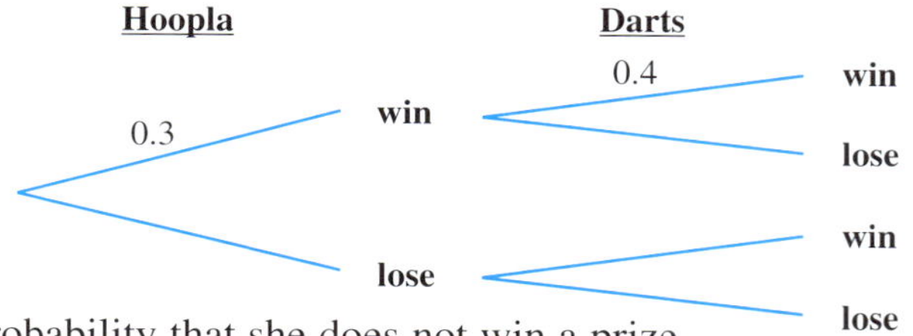

(b) Calculate the probability that she does not win a prize.
(c) Calculate the probability that she wins only one prize.

13 Students in Year 11 were asked to write an essay on "Popstars".
(a) The table shows the distribution of the times taken by male students to complete the essay.

Time (t minutes)	$10 \leqslant t < 20$	$20 \leqslant t < 30$	$30 \leqslant t < 40$	$40 \leqslant t < 50$
Frequency	8	27	19	6

(i) Draw a cumulative frequency graph for the data.
(ii) Use your graph to estimate the median and the interquartile range.
(b) The box plot illustrates the distribution of the times taken by female students to complete the essay.

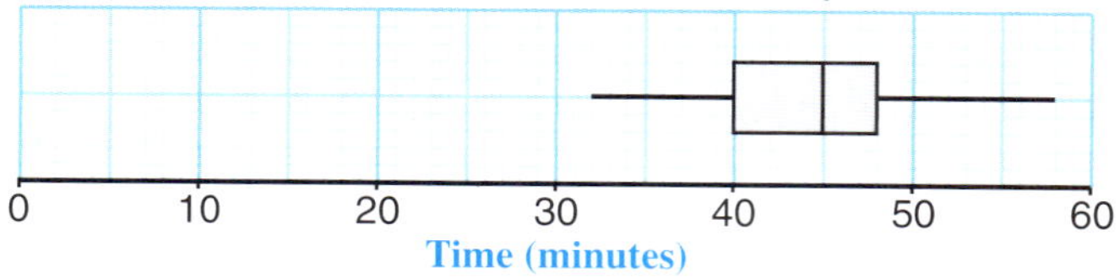

Estimate the median and the interquartile range.
(c) Compare and comment on the times taken by male students and the times taken by female students to complete the essay.

14 Giles has two chickens.
The probability that a chicken will lay an egg on any day is 0.7.
(a) What is the probability that both chickens will lay an egg on Sunday?
(b) What is the probability that only one chicken will lay an egg on Monday?

Module 1 Exam Practice Calculator Paper

1 The stem and leaf diagram shows the weights, in grams, of letters posted by a secretary.

(a) How many letters were posted?

(b) What is the median weight of one of these letters?

(c) What is the range in the weights of these letters?

(d) Calculate the mean weight of a letter.

1 | 5 means 15 grams

1	5	8				
2	0	4	5	6	8	8
3	1	2	3	5	7	
4	2	5				

2 Karina is playing a game with these cards. **X** **Y** **1** **1** **3**

One card is taken at random from the letters.
One card is taken at random from the numbers.

(a) List all the possible outcomes.

(b) Explain why the probability of getting **X** **1** is not $\frac{1}{4}$.

3 The table shows the results of asking 480 people how they travel to work.

Method of travel	**Bus**	**Train**	**Car**	**Walk**
Number of people	120	80	180	100

Draw a clearly labelled pie chart to represent this information. AQA

4 Mary has a bag in which there are 8 marbles, all green.
Tony has a bag in which there are 12 marbles, all red.
Jane has a bag in which there are some blue marbles.

(a) What is the probability of picking a red marble from Mary's bag?

(b) Mary and Tony put all their marbles into a box.
What is the probability of choosing a red marble from the box?

(c) Jane now adds her blue marbles to the box.
The probability of choosing a blue marble from the box is now $\frac{1}{2}$.
How many blue marbles does Jane put in the box? AQA

5 The numbers of people exposed to different types of radiation in the UK were recorded.
The pie chart shows the results.

If 12 000 people were exposed to Gamma radiation last year, estimate the total number of people who were exposed to any form of radiation last year.

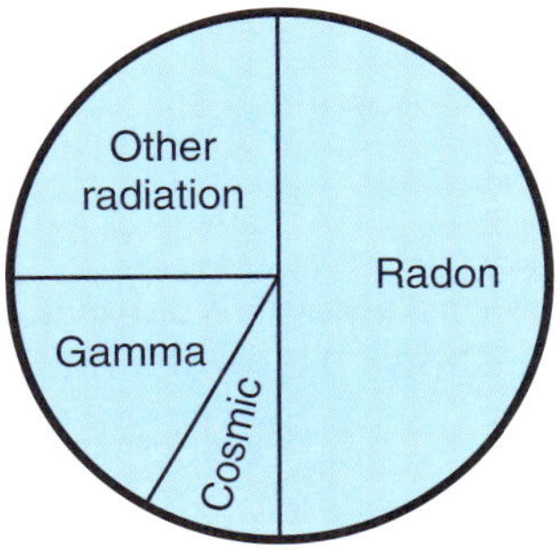

AQA

6 The mean weight of 7 netball players is 51.4 kg.

(a) Find the total weight of the players.

The mean weight of the 7 players and the reserve is 52.3 kg.

(b) Calculate the weight of the reserve. AQA

7 Corrin throws a dice 40 times. Her results are shown.

(a) Which score is the mode?
(b) Calculate the mean score.
(c) What is the median score?

Score	1	2	3	4	5	6
Frequency	7	6	7	6	6	8

8 A hospital carries out a test to compare the reaction times of patients of different ages.
The results are shown.

Age in years	17	21	24	25	31	15	18	29	20	26
Time (hundredths of a second)	29	40	45	65	66	21	33	62	32	53

(a) Plot the results as a scatter graph.
(b) What does the scatter graph tell you about the reaction times of these patients?
(c) Draw a line of best fit on the scatter graph.
(d) The hospital is worried about the reaction time of one patient.
  (i) How old is the patient?
  (ii) Using the line of best fit, what should the reaction time be for this patient?

AQA

9 The table shows the weight distribution of the fish caught in a fishing competition.

(a) Calculate an estimate of the mean weight of a fish.

(b) Draw a frequency polygon to represent this distribution.

Weight (g grams)	Frequency
$0 \leqslant g < 100$	0
$100 \leqslant g < 200$	16
$200 \leqslant g < 300$	36
$300 \leqslant g < 400$	20
$400 \leqslant g < 500$	8
$500 \leqslant g < 600$	0

AQA

10 One person is to be chosen at random from four men and two women.

Jack Trevor Eric Jeff Joan Jill

Four events are defined as

Event J: Someone with a name beginning with J is chosen.
Event M: A man is chosen.
Event N: Someone reading a newspaper is chosen.
Event W: A woman is chosen.

What is the probability that, if **one person** is chosen at random:

(a) both J and M are true, (b) both J and N are true, (c) either N or W is true?

AQA

11 The sides of a six-sided spinner are numbered from 1 to 6.
The table shows the results for 100 spins.

Number on spinner	1	2	3	4	5	6
Frequency	27	18	17	15	16	7

(a) What is the relative frequency of getting a 1?
(b) Do you think the spinner is fair?
Give a reason for your answer.
(c) The spinner is spun 3000 times.
Estimate the number of times the result is 1 or 6.

12 Here is a list of the last 8 quarterly gas bills for a householder.

Month	Jan.	Apr.	Jul.	Oct.	Jan.	Apr.	Jul.	Oct.
Amount	£67	£188	£27	£18	£139	£103	£23	£27

Calculate the first two 4-point moving averages for this data.

13 (a) Part of a cumulative frequency graph for a set of data is shown.
The lower quartile is 15.
How many values are in the set of data?

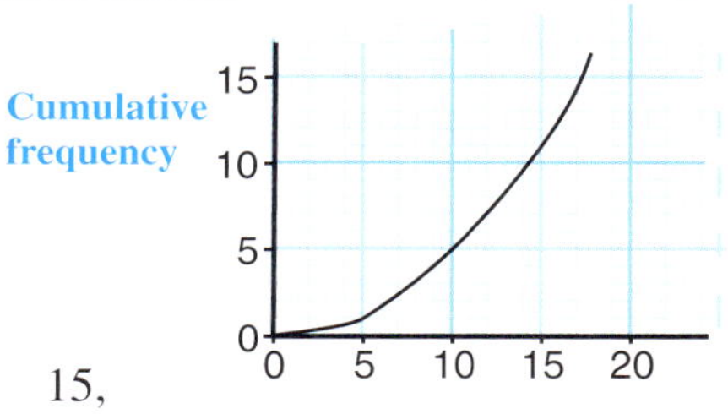

(b) **Without** doing any calculations, state which of the three averages, mean, mode or median, would best describe the following data.
Give reasons why the other two are **not** as suitable.

5, 6, 6, 6, 7, 8, 12, 12, 14, 15,
17, 18, 22, 22, 24, 26, 37, 49, 158, 196.

AQA

14 A bag contains a number of counters.
Each counter is coloured red, white or blue.
Each counter is numbered 1, 2 or 3.
The table shows the probability of colour and number for these counters.

Colour of counter

Number on counter	Red	White	Blue
1	0.2	0.1	0
2	0.1	0.3	0.1
3	0.1	0	0.1

(a) A counter is taken from the bag at random.
(i) What is the probability that the counter is red or white?
(ii) What is the probability that the counter is white or numbered 2?

(b) There are 10 blue counters in the bag.
How many counters are in the bag altogether?

A counter is taken from the bag at random.
The colour is noted and the counter is then **returned** to the bag.
Another counter is then taken from the bag at random.

(c) What is the probability that both counters are the same colour? AQA

15 (a) The frequency distribution table gives information about the distances travelled to school by pupils at a primary school.

Distance (k kilometres)	$0 \leq k < 1$	$1 \leq k < 2$	$2 \leq k < 3$	$3 \leq k < 4$	$4 \leq k < 5$
Frequency	36	76	28	12	8

(i) Draw a cumulative frequency graph to illustrate the data.
(ii) Use your graph to find the median and the interquartile range.

(b) A survey of the distances travelled to school by pupils at a secondary school gave the following information.

Shortest distance	0.2 km	Median	2.8 km
Longest distance	9.6 km	Lower quartile	2.0 km
		Upper quartile	3.4 km

Draw a box plot to illustrate the data.

(c) Compare and comment on the distances travelled to school by pupils at these schools.

16 A pupil cycles to school. On her route, there is a set of traffic lights and a railway crossing.
She will be late for school if she has to stop at the traffic lights **and** at the railway crossing.
Otherwise she will be on time.
The probability that she does **not** have to stop at the traffic lights is 0.4.
The probability that she does **not** have to stop at the railway crossing is 0.9.
Calculate the probability that she is on time for school. AQA

SECTION 8 Whole Numbers

What you need to know

- You should be able to read and write numbers expressed in figures and words.

  Eg 1 The number 8543 is written or read as, "eight thousand five hundred and forty-three".

- Be able to recognise the place value of each digit in a number.

  Eg 2 In the number 5384 the digit 8 is worth 80, but in the number 4853 the digit 8 is worth 800.

- Know the Multiplication Tables up to 10×10.
- Use mental methods to carry out addition and subtraction.
- Use non-calculator methods for addition, subtraction, multiplication and division.

Eg 3 $476 + 254$

$$\begin{array}{r} 476 \\ +\ 254 \\ \hline 730 \\ \hline \end{array}$$

Eg 4 $374 - 147$

$$\begin{array}{r} 3\,\overset{6}{\not 7}\,{}^{1}4 \\ -\ 147 \\ \hline 227 \\ \hline \end{array}$$

Addition and Subtraction
Write the numbers in columns according to place value.
You can use addition to check your subtraction.

Eg 5 324×13

$$\begin{array}{r} 324 \\ \times \quad 13 \\ \hline 972 \\ +\ 3240 \\ \hline 4212 \\ \hline \end{array}$$

Long multiplication
Multiply by the units figure, then the tens figure, and so on.
Then add these answers.

Eg 6 $343 \div 7$

$$\begin{array}{r} 49 \\ 7\overline{)343} \\ 28 \\ \hline 63 \\ 63 \\ \hline 0 \\ \hline \end{array}$$

Long division
→ ÷ (Obtain biggest answer possible.)
Calculate the remainder.
Bring down the next figure and repeat the process until there are no more figures to be brought down.

- Know the order of operations in a calculation.

First	Brackets and Division line
Second	Divide and Multiply
Third	Addition and Subtraction

Eg 7 $4 + 2 \times 6 = 4 + 12 = 16$

Eg 8 $9 \times (7 - 2) + 3 = 9 \times 5 + 3 = 45 + 3 = 48$

Exercise 8

Do not use a calculator for this exercise.

1. Work out $769 + 236$.
   (a) Give your answer in figures. (b) Give your answer in words.

2 (a) By using each of the digits 8, 5, 2 and 3 write down
(i) the smallest four-digit number, (ii) the largest four-digit number.
(b) What is the value of the 5 in the largest number?
(c) What is the value of the 5 in the smallest number?
(d) What is the answer when you subtract the smallest number from the largest number?

3 The chart shows the distances in kilometres between some towns.

Tony drives from Poole to Bath and then from Bath to Selby.
(a) How far does Tony drive?

Jean drives from Poole to Woking and then from Woking to Selby.
(b) Whose journey is longer?
How much further is it?

Bath			
104	Poole		
153	133	Woking	
362	452	367	Selby

4 Work out. (a) 200×60 (b) $40\,000 \div 80$ (c) 25×7 (d) $45 \div 3$

5 Last year Mr Alderton had the following household bills.

Gas	£364	Electricity	£158	Telephone	£187
Water	£244	Insurance	£236	Council Tax	£983

He paid the bills by 12 equal monthly payments.
How much was each monthly payment?

6 A supermarket orders one thousand two hundred tins of beans.
The beans are sold in boxes of twenty-four.
How many boxes of beans are ordered?

7 Work out. (a) $6 + 4 \times 3$ (b) $96 \div (3 + 5)$ (c) $2 \times (18 - 12) \div 4$

8 Chris is 10 cm taller than Steven. Their heights add up to 310 cm. How tall is Steven? AQA

9 The table shows the money Jayne has saved in her money box.
How much money has Jayne saved altogether?

Value of coin	5p	10p	20p	50p
Number of coins	6	12	5	3

AQA

10 A roll of wire is 500 cm long. From the roll, Debra cuts 3 pieces which each measure 75 cm and 4 pieces which each measure 40 cm. How much wire is left on the roll?

11 James packs teddy bears into boxes. He packs 283 teddy bears every hour.
James works 47 hours in one week.
How many teddy bears does James pack in this week? AQA

12 Mrs. Preece is printing an examination for all Year 11 students.
Each examination uses 14 sheets of paper.

(a) There are 235 students in Year 11.
How many sheets of paper does she need?
(b) A ream contains 500 sheets of paper.
How many reams of paper does she need to print all the examinations? AQA

13 (a) A travel company takes a party of people to a hockey match at Wembley.
17 coaches are used. Each coach has seats for 46 passengers.
There are 12 empty seats altogether.
How many people are in the party?
(b) 998 football supporters use another travel company to go to a football match at Wembley.
Each coach has seats for 53 passengers.
(i) How many coaches are needed? (ii) How many empty seats are there?
AQA

Decimals

What you need to know

- You should be able to use non-calculator methods for addition, subtraction, multiplication and division of decimals.

Eg 1 $2.8 + 0.56$

$$\begin{array}{r} 2.8 \\ +\ 0.56 \\ \hline 3.36 \end{array}$$

Eg 2 $9.5 - 0.74$

$$\begin{array}{r} \overset{8}{\cancel{9}}.\overset{14}{\cancel{5}}\overset{1}{0} \\ -\ 0.74 \\ \hline 8.76 \end{array}$$

Addition and Subtraction
Keep the decimal points in a vertical column.
9.5 can be written as 9.50.

Eg 3 0.43×5.1

$$\begin{array}{rl} 0.43 & (2\text{ d.p.}) \\ \times\ \ 5.1 & (1\text{ d.p.}) \\ \hline 43 & \leftarrow 43 \times 1 \\ +\ 2150 & \leftarrow 43 \times 50 \\ \hline 2.193 & (3\text{ d.p.}) \end{array}$$

Multiplication
Ignore the decimal points and multiply the numbers.
Count the total number of decimal places in the question.
The answer has the same total number of decimal places.

Eg 4 $1.64 \div 0.2$

$\frac{1.64}{0.2} = \frac{16.4}{2} = 8.2$

Division
It is easier to divide by a whole number than by a decimal.
So, multiply the numerator and denominator by a power of 10 (10, 100, 1000, …) to make the dividing number a whole number.

- Be able to use decimal notation for money and other measures.

The metric and common imperial units you need to know are given in Section 40.

- Be able to change decimals to fractions.

Eg 5 (a) $0.2 = \frac{2}{10} = \frac{1}{5}$ (b) $0.65 = \frac{65}{100} = \frac{13}{20}$ (c) $0.07 = \frac{7}{100}$

- Carry out a variety of calculations involving decimals.
- Know that:
  when a number is **multiplied** by a number between 0 and 1 the result will be **smaller** than the original number,
  when a number is **divided** by a number between 0 and 1 the result will be **larger** than the original number.

Exercise 9

Do not use a calculator for questions 1 to 11.

1 Look at this collection of numbers.

13.5 0.065 0.9 23.0 4.5

(a) Which number is the largest?
(b) Which number is the smallest?
(c) Write the numbers in ascending order.
(d) Two of these numbers are multiplied together.
Which two numbers will give the smallest answer?

2 (a) Multiply 3.2 by 100. (b) Divide 3.2 by 100.

3 Work out. (a) $6.8 + 4.57$ (b) $4.7 - 1.8$ (c) $5 - 2.36$

4 (a) Lucy works out 0.2×0.4. She gets the answer 0.8
Explain why her answer must be wrong.
(b) Work out (i) 0.3×0.4, (ii) 0.3×0.2.

5 Work out. (a) (i) 13.4×0.3 (ii) 4.8×2.5 (b) (i) $54.4 \div 0.4$ (ii) $0.294 \div 12$

6 Using the calculation $24 \times 26 = 624$, find the values which complete the three boxes.

$24 \times 26 = 624$

$48 \times 26 = \ldots\ldots$ $2.4 \times 2.6 = \ldots\ldots$ $62.4 \div 26 = \ldots\ldots$

AQA

7 (a) Work out the answer to this sum in your head. 900×0.6
Explain clearly the method you used.
(b) $40 \div 0.8$ Work out the answer to this sum in your head.
Explain clearly the method you used.

AQA

8 A pen costs 31p.
(a) How many pens can Alice buy with a £5 note?
(b) How much change will she receive?

AQA

9 Two pieces of wood of length 0.75 m and 2.68 m are sawn from a plank 5 m long.
What length of wood is left?

10 Joe is making sandwiches for a meeting of the Women's Institute.
He bought 25 loaves of bread from the local supermarket.
The cost was £14.
How much was each loaf?

AQA

11

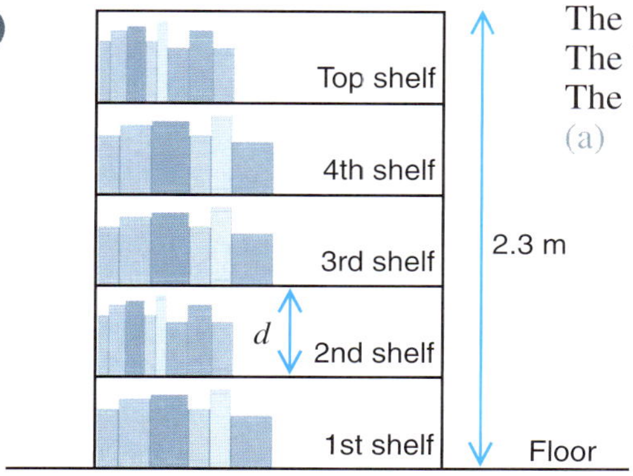

The diagram shows one of the bookcases in a public library.
The bookcase is 2.3 metres high.
The shelves are equally spaced.
(a) Calculate the distance, d, between the shelves.
(You should ignore the thickness of the shelves.)
(b) A disabled person in a wheelchair visits the public library.
This diagram shows the maximum height she can reach from her wheelchair.
Will she be able to reach the top shelf?
Show your working clearly.

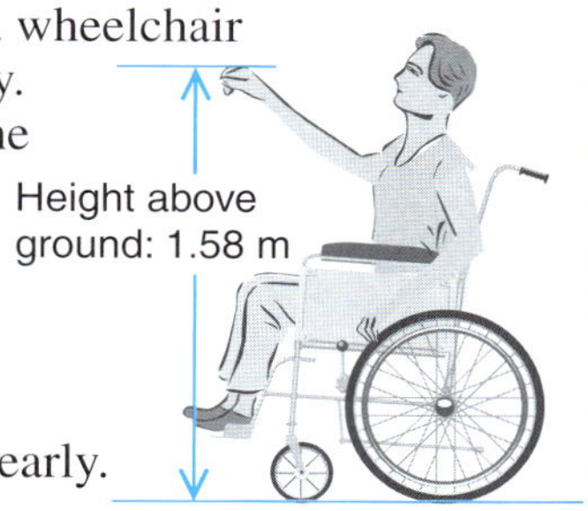

AQA

12 David buys 0.6 kg of grapes and 0.5 kg of apples.
He pays £1.36 altogether.
The grapes cost £1.45 per kilogram.
How much per kilogram are apples?

AQA

13 A shopkeeper changed from selling sweets in ounces to selling them in grams.
He used to charge 56p for 4 ounces of sweets.

1 ounce = 28.4 grams

How much should he now charge for 125 g of these sweets?

AQA

14 Work out $\dfrac{12.9 \times 7.3}{3.9 + 1.4}$. Write down your full calculator display.

SECTION 10

Approximation and Estimation

What you need to know

- How to **round** to the nearest 10, 100, 1000.

Eg 1 Write 6473 to (a) the nearest 10, (b) the nearest 100, (c) the nearest 1000.
(a) 6470 (b) 6500 (c) 6000

- How to approximate using **decimal places**.

Write the number using one more decimal place than asked for.
Look at the last decimal place and
- if the figure is 5 or more round up,
- if the figure is less than 5 round down.

Eg 2 Write the number 3.649 to
(a) 2 decimal places,
(b) 1 decimal place.

(a) 3.56
(b) 3.6

- How to approximate using **significant figures**.

Start from the most significant figure and count the required number of figures.
Look at the next figure to the right of this and
- if the figure is 5 or more round up,
- if the figure is less than 5 round down.

Add noughts, as necessary, to locate the decimal point and preserve the place value.

Eg 3 Write each of these numbers correct to 2 significant figures.
(a) 365
(b) 0.0423

(a) 370
(b) 0.042

- You should be able to choose a suitable degree of accuracy.

The result of a calculation involving measurement should not be given to a greater degree of accuracy than the measurements used in the calculation.

- Be able to use approximations to estimate that the actual answer to a calculation is of the right order of magnitude.

Estimation is done by approximating every number in the calculation to one significant figure.
The calculation is then done using the approximated values.

Eg 4 Use approximations to estimate $\frac{5.1 \times 57.2}{9.8}$

$\frac{5 \times 60}{10} = 30$

- Be able to recognise limitations on the accuracy of data and measurements.

Eg 5 Jamie said, "I have 60 friends at my party."
This figure is correct to the nearest 10.
What is the smallest and largest possible number of friends Jamie had at his party?

The smallest whole number that rounds to 60 is 55.
The largest whole number that rounds to 60 is 64.
So, smallest is 55 friends and largest is 64 friends.

Eg 6 A man weighs 57 kg, correct to the nearest kilogram.
What is the minimum weight of the man?
Minimum weight = 57 kg − 0.5 kg = 56.5 kg

Exercise 10

Do not use a calculator for questions 1 to 17.

1 Write the result shown on the calculator display

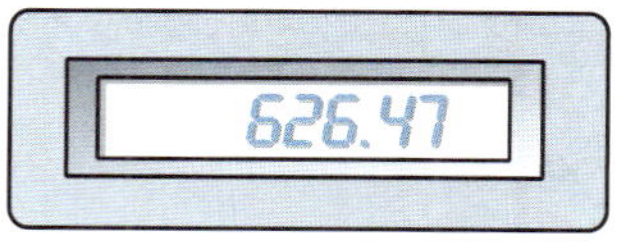

(a) to the nearest whole number,
(b) to the nearest ten,
(c) to the nearest hundred.

2 A newspaper's headline states: "20 000 people attend concert".
The number in the newspaper is given to the nearest thousand.
What is the smallest possible attendance?

3 The diagram shows the distance between towns *A*, *B* and *C*.

By rounding each of the distances given to the nearest hundred, estimate the distance between *A* and *C*.

4 A queue of cars on the motorway is 3580 metres long.
Cars use an average length of 8.13 metres of roadway.
By rounding each of these numbers to one significant figure,
estimate how many cars are in the queue. AQA

5 A snack bar sells coffee at 48 pence per cup.
In one day 838 cups are sold.
By rounding each number to one significant figure, estimate the total amount received from the sale of coffee, giving your answer in pounds. AQA

6

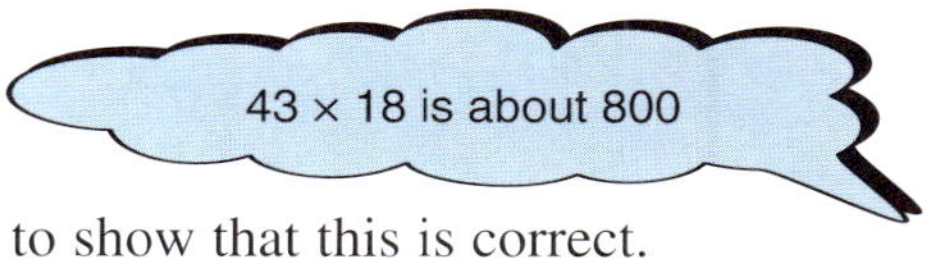

(a) Use approximation to show that this is correct.
(b) (i) Show how you could find an estimate for $2019 \div 37$.
(ii) What is your estimated answer?

7 (a) To estimate 97×49 Charlie uses the approximations 100×50.
Explain why his estimate will be larger than the actual answer.
(b) To estimate $1067 \div 48$ Patsy uses the approximations $1000 \div 50$.
Will her estimate be larger or smaller than the actual answer?
Give a reason for your answer.

8 A fence beside a motorway is 2.3 metres high and 15 miles in length.
(a) What is the height of the fence in centimetres?
(b) Estimate the length of the fence in kilometres.

9 The length of a garden is 50 m, correct to the nearest metre.
What is the minimum length of the garden?

10 Isobella pays for 68 photographs to be developed.
Each photograph costs 34 pence.
Isobella calculates the total cost to be £231.20.
(a) Which two numbers would you multiply to find a quick estimate of the total cost?
(b) Use your numbers to show whether Isobella's calculation could be correct.
Comment on your answer. AQA

11 Clint has to calculate $\frac{414 + 198}{36}$
He calculates the answer to be 419.5.
By rounding each number to one significant figure estimate whether his answer is about right.
Show all your working.

12 Sarah is 122 cm tall.
(a) Sarah's height has been given to the nearest centimetre.
What is the minimum height she could be?
(b) Estimate Sarah's height in feet. Give your answer to the nearest foot. AQA

13 Tom weighs 64 kg.
(a) Tom's weight has been given to the nearest kilogram.
What is the minimum weight he could be?
(b) What is Tom's weight in pounds? Give your answer to the nearest pound.

14 In 2001 Mr Symms drove 8873 kilometres.
His car does 11 kilometres per litre. Petrol costs 69.9 pence per litre.
Use approximations to estimate the amount he spent on petrol.

15 Melanie needs 200 crackers for an office party.
The crackers are sold in boxes of 12.
How many boxes must she buy?

16 Use approximations to estimate the value of the following.
(a) $\frac{6.12}{11.3 + 19.8}$ (b) $\frac{0.613}{297}$ (c) $\frac{897 \times 5.03}{0.304}$

17 A running track is 400 m correct to the nearest metre.
(a) What is the maximum length of the track?
(b) An athlete runs round the track four times.
What is the minimum distance he has run? AQA

18 A cabbage weighs 5 pounds.
(a) Estimate its weight in kilograms.
(b) The cabbage costs 90p per kilogram. Estimate the cost of the cabbage. AQA

19 Calculate $97.2 \div 6.5$.
Give your answer correct to (a) two decimal places, (b) one decimal place.

20 Calculate 78.4×8.7.
Give your answer correct to (a) two significant figures, (b) one significant figure.

21 Andrew says, "Answers given to two decimal places are more accurate than answers given to two significant figures."
Is he right? Explain your answer.

22 Calculate the value of $\frac{45.6}{5.3 - 2.78}$
(a) Write down your full calculator display.
(b) Give your answer correct to 3 significant figures. AQA

23 Use your calculator to evaluate the following. $\frac{13.2 + 24.7}{21.3 - 17.2}$
Give your answer correct to one decimal place. AQA

24 (a) Calculate $\frac{89.6 \times 10.3}{19.7 + 9.8}$.
(b) By using approximations show that your answer to (a) is about right.
You **must** show all your working. AQA

SECTION 11

Negative Numbers

What you need to know

- You should be able to use **negative numbers** in context, such as temperature, bank accounts.
- Realise where negative numbers come on a **number line**.

- Be able to put numbers in order (including negative numbers).

Eg 1 Write the numbers 19, -3, 7, -5 and 0 in ascending order.
-5, -3, 0, 7, 19

- Add (+), subtract (−), multiply (×) and divide (÷) with negative numbers.

To **add** or **subtract** negative numbers:
Replace double signs with a single sign.

+ + can be replaced by +
− − can be replaced by +
+ − can be replaced by −
− + can be replaced by −

Use these rules to **multiply** or **divide** negative numbers.

When multiplying:
+ × + = +
− × − = +
+ × − = −
− × + = −

When dividing:
+ ÷ + = +
− ÷ − = +
+ ÷ − = −
− ÷ + = −

Eg 2 Work out.

(a) $(-3) + (-2)$
$= -3 - 2$
$= -5$

(b) $(-5) - (-8)$
$= -5 + 8$
$= 3$

(c) $(-2) \times (-3)$
$= 6$

(d) $(-8) \div (+2)$
$= -4$

Exercise 11

Do not use a calculator for this exercise.

1. What temperatures are shown by these thermometers?

(a)
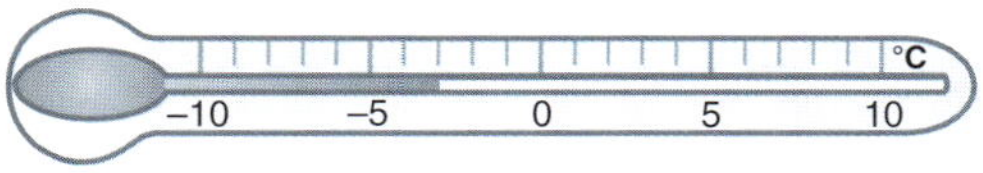

(b)
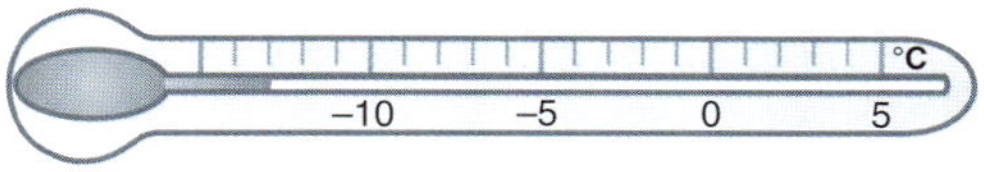

2. The midday temperatures in three different places on the same day are shown.

Moscow −7°C Oslo −9°C Warsaw −5°C

(a) (i) Which place was coldest? (ii) Which place was warmest?
(b) The temperature in Siberia is 17°C less than the temperature in Moscow.
What is the temperature in Siberia?

3. Place the following numbers in order of size, starting with the smallest.
17 −9 −3 5 0 7

4. Work out. (a) $-5 + 10$ (b) $-5 - 10$ (c) $-5 - (-10)$

5. What number must be placed in the box to complete each of the following?
(a) $-4 + \square = 2$ (b) $-2 - \square = -1$

6 The top of a cliff is 125 m above sea level.
The bottom of the lake is 15 m below sea level.
How far is the bottom of the lake below the top of the cliff?

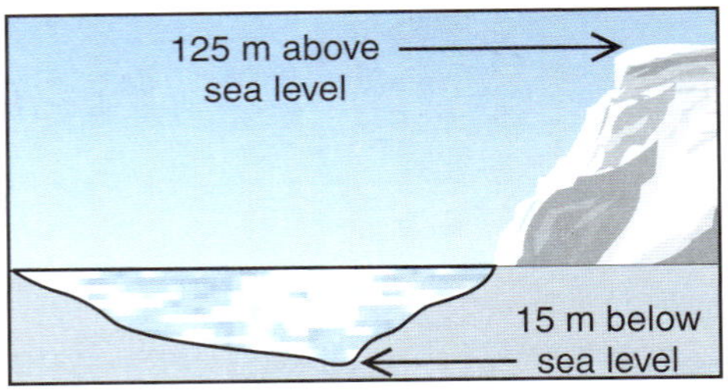

7 In Gdansk, Poland, the temperature on one day in January rose from $-7°F$ to $+22°F$.
By how many degrees did the temperature rise? AQA

8 Poppy's bank account is overdrawn by £79.
She pays in a cheque and then has a balance of £112.
How much has she paid into her bank account? AQA

9 The table shows the temperatures recorded at a ski resort one day in February.

Time	0600	1200	1800	2400
Temperature (°C)	-3	3	-2	-6

(a) By how many degrees did the temperature rise between 0600 and 1200?
(b) During which six-hourly period was the maximum drop in temperature recorded?

10 Simon took some chicken pieces out of the freezer.
The temperature of the chicken pieces was $-20°C$.
Two hours later he measured the temperature of the chicken pieces to be $-7°C$.
(a) By how many degrees had the temperature risen?
(b) After another two hours the temperature had risen by the same amount again.
What is the new temperature? AQA

11 The ice cream is stored at $-25°C$.
How many degrees is this below the required storage temperature?

12 Work out. (a) (i) $(+5) \times (-4)$ (ii) $(-7) \times (-3)$
(b) (i) $(-12) \div (+3)$ (ii) $(-15) \div (-5)$

13 This rule can be used to estimate the temperature in °F for temperatures given in °C.

> Multiply the temperature in °C by 2 and add 30.

Use this rule to estimate $-5°C$ in °F.

14 Work out. (a) $\frac{(-2) \times (-5) \times (+6)}{(-3)}$ (b) $(-3) + (-2) \times (+6)$

15 (a) Copy and complete this magic square, so that every row, column and diagonal adds up to 3.
(b) Paul says, "If I multiply each number in the square by -6, the new total for each row, column and diagonal will be -18."
Show **clearly** that this is true for the first row of numbers.

2	**–3**	**4**
3	**1**	
–2		**0**

AQA

SECTION 12

Working with Number

What you need to know

- **Multiples** of a number are found by multiplying the number by 1, 2, 3, 4, ...

  Eg 1 The multiples of 8 are $1 \times 8 = \mathbf{8}$, $2 \times 8 = \mathbf{16}$, $3 \times 8 = \mathbf{24}$, $4 \times 8 = \mathbf{32}$, ...

- **Factors** of a number are found by listing all the products that give the number.

  Eg 2 $1 \times 6 = 6$ and $2 \times 3 = 6$. So, the factors of 6 are: 1, 2, 3 and 6.

- A **prime number** is a number with only two factors, 1 and the number itself.
  The first few prime numbers are: 2, 3, 5, 7, 11, 13, 17, 19, ...
  The number 1 is not a prime number because it has only one factor.

- The **prime factors** of a number are those factors of the number which are themselves prime numbers.

  Eg 3 The factors of 18 are: 1, 2, 3, 6, 9 and 18.
  The prime factors of 18 are: 2 and 3.

- The **Least Common Multiple** of two numbers is the smallest number that is a multiple of them both.

  Eg 4 The Least Common Multiple of 4 and 5 is 20.

- The **Highest Common Factor** of two numbers is the largest number that is a factor of them both.

  Eg 5 The Highest Common Factor of 8 and 12 is 4.

- An expression such as $3 \times 3 \times 3 \times 3 \times 3$ can be written in a shorthand way as 3^5.
  This is read as '3 to the power of 5'. The number 3 is the **base** of the expression. 5 is the **power**.

- Powers can be used to help write any number as the **product of its prime factors**.

  Eg 6 $72 = 2 \times 2 \times 2 \times 3 \times 3 = 2^3 \times 3^2$

- Numbers raised to the power of 2 are **squared**.

  Squares can be calculated using the x^2 button on a calculator.

  The opposite of squaring a number is called finding the **square root**.
  Square roots can be calculated using the $\sqrt{}$ button on a calculator.

  The square root of a number can be positive or negative.

  > **Square numbers** are whole numbers squared.
  > The first few square numbers are:
  > 1, 4, 9, 16, 25, 36, ...

  Eg 7 The square root of 9 is $+3$ or -3.

- Numbers raised to the power of 3 are **cubed**.
  The opposite of cubing a number is called finding the **cube root**.

  Cube roots can be calculated using the $\sqrt[3]{}$ button on a calculator.

  > **Cube numbers** are whole numbers cubed.
  > The first few cube numbers are:
  > 1, 8, 27, 64, 125, ...

12

- **Powers**
The squares and cubes of numbers can be worked out on a calculator by using the [x^y] button.
The [x^y] button can be used to calculate the value of a number x raised to the power of y.

Eg 8 Calculate 2.6^4.
Enter the sequence: [2] [.] [6] [x^y] [4] [=]. So $2.6^4 = 45.6976$

- The **reciprocal** of a number is the value obtained when the number is divided into 1.

Eg 9 The reciprocal of 2 is $\frac{1}{2}$.

The reciprocal of a number can be found on a calculator by using the [$\frac{1}{x}$] button.

Eg 10 Find the reciprocal of 5.
The reciprocal of 5 $= 5^{-1} = \frac{1}{5} = 0.2$
Using a calculator, press: [5] [$\frac{1}{x}$]

> A number times its reciprocal equals 1.
> Zero has no reciprocal.
> The reciprocal of a number can be shown using an index of -1.

- Square roots and cube roots can be found using a method called **trial and improvement**.

> When using trial and improvement:
> Work methodically using trials first to the nearest whole number, then to one decimal place etc.
> Do at least one trial to one more decimal place than the required accuracy to be sure of your answer.

- Powers of the same base are **added** when terms are **multiplied**.
Powers of the same base are **subtracted** when terms are **divided**.

Eg 11 (a) $2^3 \times 2^2 = 2^5$ (b) $2^3 \div 2^2 = 2^1 = 2$

- Any number raised to the power zero equals 1.

> In general: $a^m \times a^n = a^{m+n}$
> $a^m \div a^n = a^{m-n}$
> $a^1 = a$
> $a^0 = 1$

- A surd is the square root of a positive integer, like $\sqrt{3}$, for which the root is not exact.

> $\sqrt{9}$ is not a surd because it has an exact root.
> To keep an exact answer it is therefore necessary to keep numbers like $\sqrt{3}$ in surd form.

- You should be able to use a calculator to solve a variety of problems.

Exercise 12

Do not use a calculator for questions 1 to 17.

1 (a) Write down all the factors of 18.
(b) Write down a multiple of 7 between 30 and 40.
(c) Explain why 15 is not a prime number.

2 Look at these numbers.

2	5	8	11	14	17	20

(a) Which of these numbers are factors of 10?
(b) Which of these numbers is a multiple of 10?
(c) Which of these numbers are prime numbers?

3 (a) What is the square of 6?
(b) What is the square root of 100?
(c) What is the cube of 3?
(d) What is the cube root of 8?

4 A number of counters can be grouped into 2's, 3's, 4's and 5's.
Find the smallest possible number of counters.

5 Look at these numbers. 2 15 27 36 44 51 64

(a) Which of these numbers is a prime number?
(b) Which of these numbers is both a square number and a cube number?

6 (a) Work out the value of (i) 5^3 (ii) $\sqrt{64}$
(b) Between which two consecutive whole numbers does $\sqrt{30}$ lie? AQA

7 (a) Find the square of 4. (b) Find the square root of 36.
(c) Find the value of 3×7^2. (d) Evaluate $(0.1)^2$. AQA

8 Find the values of (a) $\sqrt{25} + \sqrt{144}$ (b) $\sqrt{(25 \times 144)}$ AQA

9 (a) Write 36 as a product of its prime factors.
(b) Write 45 as a product of its prime factors.
(c) What is the highest common factor of 36 and 45?
(d) What is the least common multiple of 36 and 45?

10 A white light flashes every 10 seconds. A red light flashes every 6 seconds.
The two lights flash at the same time.
After how many seconds will the lights next flash at the same time?

11 (a) What is the cube root of 125? (b) What is the reciprocal of 4?

12 Work out. (a) $2^3 \times 3^2$ (b) $(\sqrt{9} \times \sqrt{25})^2$ (c) $2^3 \times \sqrt[3]{64}$

13 (a) Which is smaller $\sqrt{225}$ or 2^4? Show your working.
(b) Work out the value of $3^1 - 3^0$.

14 Find the value of x in each of the following.
(a) $7^6 \times 7^3 = 7^x$ (b) $7^6 \div 7^3 = 7^x$ (c) $(7^6)^3 = 7^x$ (d) $7^0 = x$

15 Simplify fully each of these expressions. Leave your answers in power form.
(a) $3^2 \times 3^3$ (b) $4^{-2} \times 4^5$ (c) $5^6 \div 5^3$ (d) $9^4 \div 9^{-2}$ (e) $\frac{2^3 \times 2}{2^6}$

16 Which is bigger 2^6 or 3^4? Show all your working. AQA

17 (a) **Without using a calculator**, write down an estimate of the square root of 40.
Give your estimate correct to one decimal place.
(b) Explain how you obtained your estimate to the square root of 40.
(c) Use a trial and improvement method to find the square root of 40 correct to two decimal places. Show your working clearly. AQA

18 Find the reciprocal of 7.
Give your answer correct to two decimal places.

19 Calculate $\sqrt{\frac{3.9}{(0.6)^3}}$ AQA

20 (a) Use your calculator to find $3.5^3 + \sqrt{18.4}$. Give all the figures on your calculator.
(b) Write your answer to 3 significant figures. AQA

21 (a) Calculate the value of $\sqrt{3.1 + \frac{6}{3.1} - \frac{9}{3.1^2}}$
(b) Show how to check that your answer is of the right order of magnitude. AQA

22 (a) Calculate. (i) $\sqrt{3.1 - \frac{1}{3.1}}$ (ii) $(1.1 + 2.2 + 3.3)^2 - (1.1^2 + 2.2^2 + 3.3^2)$
(b) Show how you would make a quick estimation of the answer to part (a)(ii). AQA

Standard Index Form

What you need to know

- **Standard index form**, or **standard form**, is a shorthand way of writing very large and very small numbers.
- In **standard form** a number is written as: **a number between 1 and 10 × a power of 10**
  Large numbers (ten, or more) have a **positive** power of 10.

Eg 1 Write 370 000 in standard form.
$370\,000 = 3.7 \times 100\,000 = 3.7 \times 10^5$

Eg 2 Write 5.6×10^7 as an ordinary number.
$5.6 \times 10^7 = 5.6 \times 10\,000\,000 = 56\,000\,000$

Small positive numbers (less than one) have a **negative** power of 10.

Eg 3 Write 0.000 73 in standard form.
$0.000\,73 = 7.3 \times 0.000\,1 = 7.3 \times 10^{-4}$

Eg 4 Write 2.9×10^{-6} as an ordinary number.
$2.9 \times 10^{-6} = 2.9 \times 0.000\,001 = 0.000\,002\,9$

- You should be able to interpret the display on a calculator.

Eg 5 The calculator display shows the answer to 0.007×0.09
In standard form, the answer is 6.3×10^{-4}
As an ordinary number, the answer is 0.000 63

6.3	−04

- You should be able to solve problems involving numbers given in standard form.

Exercise 13

Do not use a calculator for questions 1 to 7.

1. Write one million in standard form.

2. Look at these numbers.

2.6×10^4	6.2×10^3	9.8×10^{-4}	8.9×10^{-5}

   (a) (i) Which number is the largest? (ii) Write your answer as an ordinary number.
   (b) (i) Which number is the smallest? (ii) Write your answer as an ordinary number.

3. (a) Write 57 000 000 in standard index form. (b) Write 0.000 057 in standard index form.

4. Work out.
   (a) $(6 \times 10^3) + (5 \times 10^4)$ (b) $(6 \times 10^3) \times (5 \times 10^4)$ (c) $(6 \times 10^3) \div (5 \times 10^4)$
   Give your answers in standard form.

5. (a) A company buys 2 340 000 packs of paper.
   Write this number in standard form.
   (b) A pack of paper has a thickness of 4.8 cm.
   There are 500 sheets of paper in each pack.
   Calculate the thickness of one sheet of paper in centimetres.
   Give your answer in standard form. AQA

6 The table shows the average speed of planets that orbit the Sun.

Planet	Average speed of orbit (km/h)
Jupiter	4.7×10^4
Mercury	1.7×10^5
Neptune	1.2×10^4
Pluto	1.7×10^4
Saturn	3.5×10^4
Uranus	2.5×10^5

(a) Which planet is travelling the fastest?
(b) What is the difference between the average speeds of Neptune and Pluto? Give your answer in standard form. AQA

7 The population of Spain is 3.6×10^7 and there are 1.2×10^5 doctors in Spain. Calculate the average number of people per doctor. AQA

8 The surface area of the Earth is approximately 5.05×10^8 square kilometres. The surface area of the Earth covered by water is approximately 3.57×10^8 square kilometres.

Calculate the surface area of the Earth not covered by water. Give your answer in standard form.

9 (a) Calculate $\frac{7.2 \times 10^6}{0.0045}$.
Give your answer in standard form.

(b) Calculate $\frac{530}{6.7 \times 10^5}$.
Give your answer as an ordinary number correct to two significant figures.

10 In England £1.012×10^{10} is spent on healthcare per year. There are 4.71×10^7 people in England. How much per person is spent on healthcare in England per year? AQA

11 Very large distances in the Universe are measured in **parsecs** and **light-years**. One parsec is 3.0857×10^{13} kilometres. One parsec is 3.26 light-years. How many kilometres are in 1 light-year? Give your answer in standard form to an appropriate degree of accuracy. AQA

12 A publisher prints 1.25×10^6 copies of a magazine. Each magazine consists of 18 sheets of paper.
(a) Calculate the number of sheets of paper needed to print all the magazines. Give your answer in standard form.

To make the magazine, the sheets of paper are folded as shown.

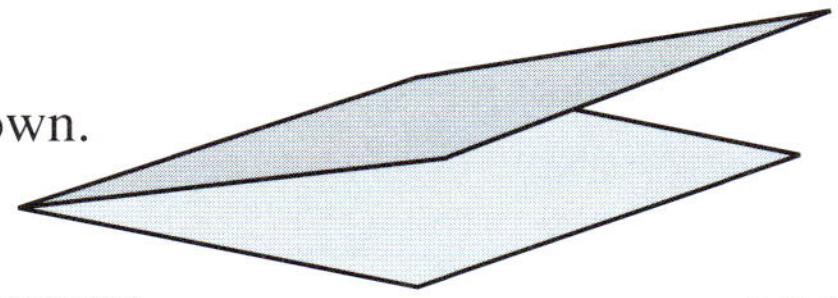

(b) The height of a pile of magazines is 79.1 cm. The pile contains 232 magazines. Calculate, in centimetres, the thickness of one sheet of paper. AQA

13 Work out $\frac{3.5 \times 10^{-3}}{4.1 \times 10^2}$.
Give your answer as an ordinary number correct to 2 significant figures.

SECTION 14

Fractions

What you need to know

- The top number of a fraction is called the **numerator**, the bottom number is called the **denominator**.
- Fractions which are equal are called **equivalent fractions**.

To write an equivalent fraction:
Multiply the numerator and denominator by the **same** number.

Eg 1 $\frac{1}{4} = \frac{1 \times 3}{4 \times 3} = \frac{1 \times 5}{4 \times 5}$

$\frac{1}{4} = \frac{3}{12} = \frac{5}{20}$

- In its **simplest form**, the numerator and denominator of a fraction have no common factor, other than 1.
- $2\frac{1}{2}$ is an example of a **mixed number**. It is a mixture of whole numbers and fractions.
- $\frac{5}{2}$ is an **improper** (or '**top heavy**') fraction.
- Fractions must have the **same denominator** before **adding** or **subtracting**.

Eg 2 Work out.

(a) $\frac{3}{4} + \frac{2}{3} = \frac{9}{12} + \frac{8}{12} = \frac{17}{12} = 1\frac{5}{12}$

(b) $\frac{4}{5} - \frac{1}{2} = \frac{8}{10} - \frac{5}{10} = \frac{3}{10}$

Add (or subtract) the numerators only. When the answer is an improper fraction change it into a mixed number.

- Mixed numbers must be changed to **improper fractions** before **multiplying** or **dividing**.

Eg 3 Work out.

(a) $1\frac{1}{4} \times 2\frac{1}{5} = \frac{\cancel{5}^{1}}{4} \times \frac{11}{\cancel{5}_{1}} = \frac{11}{4} = 2\frac{3}{4}$

(b) $1\frac{1}{3} \div 1\frac{3}{5} = \frac{4}{3} \div \frac{8}{5} = \frac{\cancel{4}^{1}}{3} \times \frac{5}{\cancel{8}_{2}} = \frac{5}{6}$

The working can be simplified by dividing a numerator and a denominator by the same number.

Notice that dividing by $\frac{8}{5}$ is the same as multiplying by $\frac{5}{8}$.

- All fractions can be written as decimals.

To change a fraction to a decimal divide the **numerator** by the **denominator**.

Eg 4 Change $\frac{4}{5}$ to a decimal.

$\frac{4}{5} = 4 \div 5 = 0.8$

- Some decimals have **recurring digits**. These are shown by:

a single dot above a single recurring digit, **Eg 5** $\frac{2}{3} = 0.6666\ldots = 0.\dot{6}$

a dot above the first and last digit of a set of recurring digits. **Eg 6** $\frac{5}{11} = 0.454545\ldots = 0.\dot{4}\dot{5}$

Exercise 14

Do not use a calculator for this exercise.

1. Each of these pairs of fractions are equivalent. In each case find the value of n.

(a) $\frac{3}{5}$ and $\frac{n}{15}$ (b) $\frac{n}{3}$ and $\frac{8}{12}$ (c) $\frac{6}{8}$ and $\frac{15}{n}$

2 (a) Which of the fractions $\frac{7}{10}$ or $\frac{4}{5}$ is the smaller? Explain why.
(b) Write down a fraction that lies halfway between $\frac{1}{3}$ and $\frac{1}{2}$.

3 Which of the following fractions is nearest to $\frac{1}{2}$?

$\frac{4}{10}$ $\frac{9}{20}$ $\frac{14}{30}$ $\frac{19}{40}$

Show how you decide. AQA

4 Write these fractions in order of size, with the smallest first. $\frac{2}{3}$ $\frac{5}{8}$ $\frac{7}{12}$ $\frac{3}{4}$ AQA

5 This rule can be used to change kilometres into miles.

Multiply the number of kilometres by $\frac{5}{8}$

Flik cycles 24 kilometres. How many miles is this?

6 Alec's cat eats $\frac{2}{3}$ of a tin of food each day.
What is the least number of tins Alec needs to buy to feed his cat for 7 days? AQA

7 An examination is marked out of 48.
Ashley scored 32 marks.
What fraction of the total did he score?
Give your answer in its simplest form.

8 A garden centre buys 1000 Christmas trees. It sells $\frac{3}{5}$ of them at £8 each.
The remaining trees are then reduced to £5 each and all except 30 are sold.
These 30 trees are thrown away.
How much money does the garden centre get from selling the trees? AQA

9 Elaine buys 0.4 kg of Edam cheese at £4.80 per kilogram and $\frac{1}{4}$ kg of Cheddar cheese.
She pays £2.73 altogether.
How much per kilogram is Cheddar cheese? AQA

10 (a) Change $\frac{1}{6}$ to a decimal. Give the answer correct to 3 d.p.
(b) Write these numbers in order of size, starting with the largest.

1.067 1.7 1.66 $1\frac{1}{6}$ 1.67

11 (a) Work out $\frac{2}{3} \times \frac{1}{4}$ (b) Work out $\frac{2}{3} - \frac{1}{4}$ AQA

12 Income tax and national insurance take $\frac{1}{5}$ of Phillip's pay.
He gives $\frac{2}{5}$ of what he has left to his parents for housekeeping.
What fraction of his pay does Phillip have left for himself?

13 Three-fifths of the people at a party are boys. Three-quarters of the boys are wearing fancy dress.
What fraction of the people at the party are boys wearing fancy dress?

14 Evaluate (a) $3 - 1\frac{1}{5}$ (b) $4 \times 1\frac{1}{3}$ (c) $7\frac{1}{2} \div 1\frac{1}{2}$ AQA

15 Work out $\dfrac{81 \times \frac{1}{3}}{\frac{1}{16} \times 8}$. AQA

16 In a sale the price of a microwave is reduced by $\frac{1}{5}$.
The sale price is £96.
What was the price of the microwave before the sale?

SECTION 15

Percentages

What you need to know

- 10% is read as '10 percent'. 'Per cent' means out of 100. 10% means 10 out of 100.
- A percentage can be written as a fraction, 10% can be written as $\frac{10}{100}$.
- To change a decimal or a fraction to a percentage: **multiply by 100**.

Eg 1 Write as a percentage (a) 0.12 (b) $\frac{8}{25}$

(a) $0.12 \times 100 = 12\%$ (b) $\frac{8}{25} \times 100 = 32\%$

- To change a percentage to a fraction or a decimal: **divide by 100**.

Eg 2 Write 18% as (a) a decimal, (b) a fraction.

(a) $18\% = 18 \div 100 = 0.18$ (b) $18\% = \frac{18}{100} = \frac{9}{50}$

- How to express one quantity as a percentage of another.

Eg 3 Write 30p as a percentage of £2.

$\frac{30}{200} \times 100 = 30 \times 100 \div 200 = 15\%$

> Write the numbers as a fraction, using the same units.
> Change the fraction to a percentage.

- You should be able to use percentages to solve a variety of problems.
- Be able to find a percentage of a quantity.

Eg 4 Find 20% of £64.

£64 ÷ 100 = £0.64

£0.64 × 20 = £12.80

> 1. Divide by 100 to find 1%.
> 2. Multiply by the percentage to be found.

- Be able to find a percentage increase (or decrease).

Eg 5 Find the percentage loss on a micro-scooter bought for £25 and sold for £18.

Percentage loss $= \frac{7}{25} \times 100 = 28\%$

$$\text{Percentage decrease} = \frac{\text{actual decrease}}{\text{initial value}} \times 100\%$$

$$\text{Percentage increase} = \frac{\text{actual increase}}{\text{initial value}} \times 100\%$$

- Be able to solve reverse percentage problems.

Eg 6 Find the original price of a car which is sold at a loss of 20% for £1200.

80% of original price = £1200

1% of original price = £1200 ÷ 80 = £15

Original price = £15 × 100 = £1500

> First find 1% of the original value by dividing the selling price by (100 − % loss), then multiply by 100.

Exercise 15

Do not use a calculator for questions 1 to 7.

1. Write 0.4, $\frac{9}{20}$ and 42% in order of size, smallest first.
2. Work out (a) 25% of 60 kg, (b) 5% of £900.

3 In an examination Felicity scored 75% of the marks and Daisy scored $\frac{4}{5}$ of the marks.
Who has the better score?
Give a reason for your answer.

4 What is (a) 60 pence as a percentage of £3, (b) 15 seconds as a percentage of 1 minute?

5 An athletics stadium has 35 000 seats.
4% of the seats are fitted with headphones to help people hear the announcements.
How many headphones are there in the stadium? AQA

6 Jayne is given £5 for her birthday. She spends 30% of it.
How much of her birthday money does she spend? AQA

7 A dress normally costs £35. The price is reduced by 15% in a sale.
What is the price of the dress in the sale? AQA

8 Harvey sees this advertisement.
Calculate the actual price of the language course.

9 A pogo stick is bought for £12.50 and sold for £8.
What is the percentage loss?

10 A farmer has 200 sheep.
90% of the sheep have lambs.
Of the sheep which have lambs 45% have two lambs.
How many of the sheep have two lambs?

11 At the beginning of the year the value of car A was £3000 and the value of car B was £15 000.
At the end of the year the value of car A is £2400 and the value of car B is £12 150.
Which car has the larger percentage loss?
Show your working.

12

(a) The original price of a tennis racket was £35.
What is the sale price of the tennis racket?
(b) The sale price of a pair of roller blades is £48.
What was the original price of the roller blades? AQA

13 In the United Kingdom there are 26 million vehicles.
Approximately 5.8 million vehicles are 10 years old or more.
What percentage of vehicles are less than 10 years old?
Give your answer to an appropriate degree of accuracy. AQA

14 The land area of a farm is 385 acres.
96 acres is pasture.
What percentage of the total land is pasture?
Give your answer to the nearest 1%. AQA

15 When a ball is dropped onto the floor, it bounces and then rises.
This is shown in the diagram.

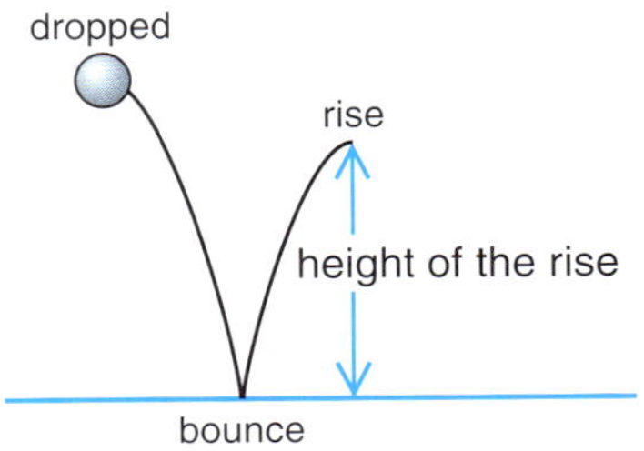

The ball rises to 80% of the height from which it was dropped.
It was dropped from a height of 3 metres.

(a) Calculate the height of the rise after the first bounce.

The ball bounces a second time.
It rises to 80% of the height of the first rise.

(b) Calculate the height of the second rise.

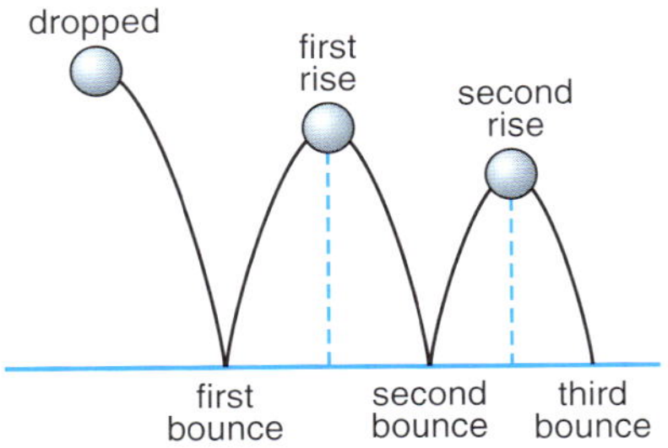

(c) The ball carries on bouncing in this way.
Each time it rises to 80% of the last rise.
For how many bounces does it rise to a height greater than 1 metre? AQA

16

1st STOP Car Insurance

Typical insurance:
Vauxhall Corsa - £650 per year
No Claims Discount Available

(a) Vanessa has a Vauxhall Corsa. She is given a no claims discount.
After taking off her no claims discount she has to pay £390 to insure her car.
Calculate her no claims discount as a percentage of £650.

(b) Cedric has a BMW car. He is given a 65% no claims discount.
After the discount he has to pay £336 to insure his car.
Calculate the price of the insurance before the discount.

17 This report appeared in a motoring magazine.

> In the first year of ownership a new car loses 20% of its value and in the second year it loses 15% of its one-year old value.

If this report is true, what is the percentage loss in the value of a new car in its first 2 years?

18 Questionnaires were sent to a number of people.
72 people replied.
This was only 18% of all the people that had been sent questionnaires.
How many people had been sent questionnaires?

19 A garden centre buys plants and resells them at a profit of 28%.
How much was the original price of a rose bush which is sold for £4.80? AQA

SECTION 16

Time and Money

What you need to know

- Time can be given using either the **12-hour clock** or the **24-hour clock**.

Eg 1 (a) 1120 is equivalent to 11.20 am.
(b) 1645 is equivalent to 4.45 pm.

> When using the 12-hour clock:
> times **before** midday are given as am,
> times **after** midday are given as pm.

- **Timetables** are usually given using the 24-hour clock.
- **Hourly pay** is paid at a **basic rate** for a fixed number of hours.
Overtime pay is usually paid at a higher rate such as time and a half, which means each hour's work is worth 1.5 times the basic rate.
- Everyone is allowed to earn some money which is not taxed. This is called a **tax allowance**.
- Tax is only paid on income earned in excess of the tax allowance. This is called **taxable income**.

Eg 2 Tom earns £5800 per year. His tax allowance is £4615 per year and he pays tax at 10p in the £ on his taxable income. Find how much income tax Tom pays per year.

Taxable income = £5800 − £4615 = £1185
Income tax payable = £1185 × 0.10 = £118.50

> First find the taxable income, then multiply taxable income by rate in £.

- **Value added tax**, or **VAT**, is a tax on some goods and services and is added to the bill.
- When considering a **best buy**, compare quantities by using the same units.

Eg 3 Peanut butter is available in small or large jars.
Small jar: 250 grams for 68 pence Large jar: 454 grams for £1.25
Which size is the better value for money?

Small jar: 250 ÷ 68 = 3.67... grams per penny
Large jar: 454 ÷ 125 = 3.63... grams per penny
The small jar gives more grams per penny and is better value.

> Compare the number of grams per penny for each size.

- Money invested in a savings account at a bank or building society earns **interest**.
- With **Simple Interest**, the interest is paid out each year and not added to your account.

> Simple Interest = Amount invested × Time in years × Rate of interest per year

Eg 4 Find the Simple Interest paid on £600 invested for 6 months at 8% per year.

Simple Interest = $600 \times \frac{6}{12} \times \frac{8}{100} = 600 \times 0.5 \times 0.08 =$ £24

- With **Compound Interest**, the interest earned each year is added to your account and also earns interest the following year.

Eg 5 Find the **Compound Interest** paid on £600 invested for 2 years at 6% per year.

1st year
Investment = £600
Interest: £600 × 0.06 = £ 36
Value after one year = £636

2nd year
Investment = £636
Interest: £636 × 0.06 = £ 38.16
Value after two years = £674.16

Compound Interest = Final value − Original value = £674.16 − £600 = £74.16

- **Exchange rates** are used to show what £1 will buy in foreign currencies.

Exercise 16

Do not use a calculator for questions 1 to 7.

1 The times of rail journeys from Guildford to Waterloo are shown.

Guildford	0703	0722	0730	0733	0749	0752
Worplesdon	0708	0727	—	0739	—	0757
Clapham Junction	0752	—	0800	0822	—	—
Waterloo	0800	0815	0808	0830	0823	0844

(a) Karen catches the 0722 from Guildford to Waterloo.
How many minutes does the journey take?

(b) Graham arrives at Worplesdon station at 0715.
What is the time of the next train to Clapham Junction?

2 Last year Harry paid the following gas bills.

£146.32	£42.87	£36.55	£133.06

This year he will pay his gas bills by 12 equal monthly payments.
Use last year's gas bills to calculate his monthly payments.

3 Felix is paid at time and a half for overtime. His overtime rate of pay is £8.40 per hour.
What is his basic rate of pay?

4 Amrit pays his council tax by 10 instalments.
His first instalment is £143.25 and the other 9 instalments are £137 each.
How much is his total council tax?

5 Nick is on holiday in Spain.
He hires a car at the rates shown.

There are 1.60 euros to £1.

Nick hires the car for 5 days and drives it for a total of 720 kilometres.
Calculate the total cost of hiring the car.
Give your answer in pounds.

CAR HIRE

Daily rate	54 euros
Free kilometres per day	120
Excess kilometre charge	0.60 euros

6 Joe insures his house for £90 000 and its contents for £7000.
The premiums for the insurance are:

House: . . . . 23p per annum for every £100 of cover,
Contents: . . . . £1.30 per annum for every £100 of cover.

What is the total cost of Joe's insurance? AQA

7 Steve receives his electricity bill.
The charge for the electricity he has used is £70 plus VAT at 5%.

(a) Calculate the VAT charged.

(b) Hence find the total amount Steve has to pay.

AQA

8 Mrs Tilsed wishes to buy a car priced at £2400.

Two options are available.
Option 1 – A deposit of 20% of £2400 and 24 monthly payments of £95.
Option 2 – For a single payment the dealer offers a discount of 5% on £2400.

How much more does it cost to buy the car if option 1 is chosen rather than option 2?

9 Angela is paid £5.40 per hour for a basic 35-hour week. Overtime is paid at time and a half.
One week Angela worked $37\frac{1}{2}$ hours.
How much did Angela earn that week?

10 Leroy earns £13 600 per year.
He has a tax allowance of £4615 and pays tax at the rate of 10p in the £ on the first £1920 of his taxable income and 22p in the £ on the remainder.
How much income tax does he pay each year?

11 The table below shows the cost of hiring a ladder.

Cost for the first day	Extra cost per day for each additional day
£13.75	£7.25

A family hires the ladder.
The total cost of hiring the ladder was £50.
How many days did the family hire it for?
AQA

12 William saw two identical sweatshirts.
Work out which sweatshirt will cost less to buy.
You must show all your working.

In the shop they said, "You can have it at $\frac{2}{3}$ of the marked price."

At the market they said, "You can have it 20% off the marked price."

AQA

13 Reg travels to Ireland. The exchange rate is 1.60 euros to the £.
(a) He changes £40 into euros.
How many euros does he receive?
(b) A taxi fare costs 10 euros.
What is the cost of the taxi fare in pounds and pence?

14 Toffee is sold in bars of two sizes.
A large bar weighs 450 g and costs £1.69.
A small bar weighs 275 g and costs 99p.
Which size of bar is better value for money?
You must show all your working.

15 Terry receives a bill for £284 for repairs to his car. VAT at $17\frac{1}{2}\%$ is then added to this amount.
Calculate the total amount which Terry pays.
AQA

16 Simon invests £360 at 6.4% per annum simple interest.
How much interest does he get at the end of 6 months?
AQA

17 Nadia invests £400 in an account which pays 6.5% interest per year.
The interest is added to her investment at the end of each year.
Nadia does not withdraw any money.
Calculate the number of years Nadia must invest her money so that the total investment has a value of more than £480.
You must show all your working.
AQA

18 (a) Mike invests £3000 at 5% per annum compound interest.
What is the value of his investment after 3 years?
(b) Jayne invests her money at 6% per annum compound interest.
What is the percentage increase in the value of her investment after 3 years?

SECTION 17

Ratio

What you need to know

- The ratio 3 : 2 is read '3 to 2'.
- A ratio is used only to **compare** quantities.
  A ratio does not give information about the exact values of quantities being compared.
- Different forms of the **same ratio**, such as 2 : 1 and 6 : 3, are called **equivalent ratios**.
- In its **simplest form**, a ratio contains whole numbers which have no common factor other than 1.

Eg 1 Write £2.40 : 40p in its simplest form.
£2.40 : 40p = 240p : 40p
= 240 : 40
= 6 : 1

> All quantities in a ratio must be in the **same units** before the ratio can be simplified.

- You should be able to solve a variety of problems involving ratio.

Eg 2 The ratio of bats to balls in a box is 3 : 5.
There are 12 bats in the box.
How many balls are there?

12 ÷ 3 = 4
3 × 4 : 5 × 4 = 12 : 20
There are 20 balls in the box.

> For every 3 bats there are 5 balls.
> To find an equivalent ratio to 3 : 5, in which the first number is 12, multiply each number in the ratio by 4.

Eg 3 A wall costs £660 to build.
The costs of materials to labour are in the ratio 4 : 7.
What is the cost of labour?

4 + 7 = 11
£660 ÷ 11 = £60
Cost of labour = £60 × 7 = £420

> The numbers in the ratio add to 11.
> For every £11 of the total cost, £4 pays for materials and £7 pays for labour.
> So, **divide** by 11 and then **multiply** by 7.

- When two different quantities are always in the **same ratio** the two quantities are in **direct proportion**.

Eg 4 20 litres of petrol cost £14.
Find the cost of 25 litres of petrol.

20 litres cost £14
1 litre costs £14 ÷ 20 = £0.70
25 litres cost £0.70 × 25 = £17.50

> This is sometimes called the **unitary method**.
> **Divide** by 20 to find the cost of 1 litre.
> **Multiply** by 25 to find the cost of 25 litres.

Exercise 17

Do not use a calculator for questions 1 to 6.

1. A toy box contains large bricks and small bricks in the ratio 1 : 4.
   The box contains 40 bricks. How many large bricks are in the box?
2. To make mortar a builder mixes sand and cement in the ratio 3 : 1.
   The builder uses 2.5 kg of cement. How much sand does he use?
3. In a drama club the ratio of boys to girls is 2 : 3.
   What fraction of club members are girls?

4 This magnifying glass makes things look larger.
It enlarges in the ratio 1 : 4.

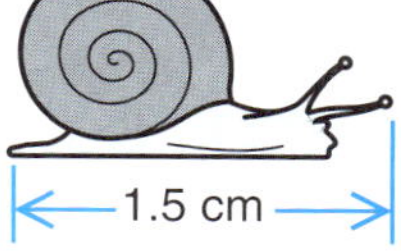

(a) How long will the snail look under the magnifying glass?

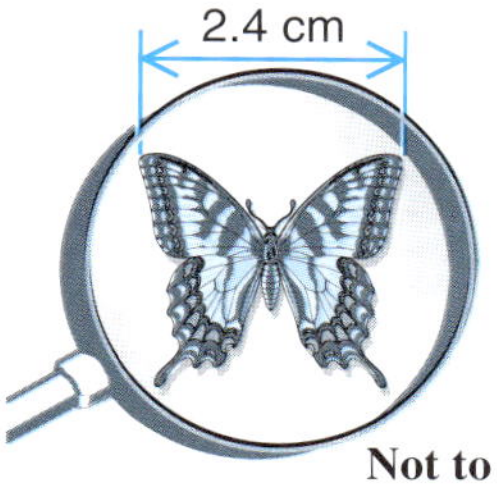

Not to scale

The moth looks 2.4 cm wide under the magnifying glass.

(b) What is the actual width of the moth? AQA

5 The ratio of men to women playing golf one day is 5 : 3.
There are 20 men playing. How many women are playing?

6 A gardener wants to make a display of red and yellow tulips.
He orders red and yellow tulip bulbs in the ratio of 3 : 5. He orders a total of 2000 bulbs.
How many of each colour bulb will he get? AQA

7 Dec shares a prize of £435 with Annabel in the ratio 3 : 2.
What is the difference in the amount of money they each receive?

8 A town has a population of 45 000 people.
1 in every 180 people are disabled.
How many disabled people are there in the town? AQA

9 This is a list of ingredients to make 12 rock cakes.
You have plenty of margarine, sugar, fruit and spice but only half a kilogram of flour.
What is the largest number of rock cakes you can make?

Rock cakes (makes 12)

240 g flour
75 g margarine
125 g sugar
150 g fruit
$\frac{1}{4}$ teaspoon spice

AQA

10 Two students are talking about their school outing.

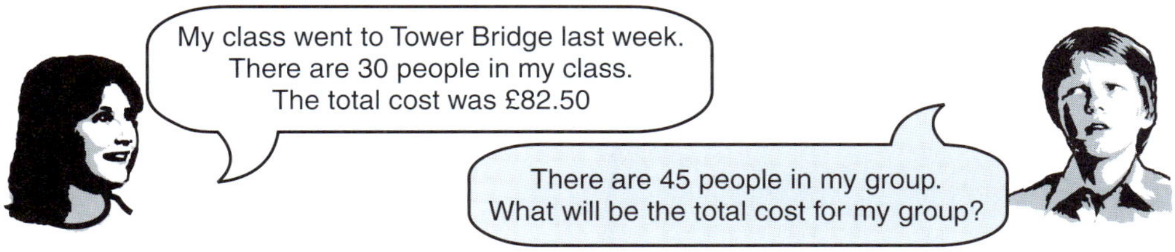

11 A Munch Crunch bar weighs 21 g.
The table shows the nutrients that each bar contains.

(a) What percentage of the bar is fat?
Give your answer to an appropriate degree of accuracy.

(b) What is the ratio of protein to carbohydrate?
Give your answer in the form 1 : n.

Protein	1.9 g
Fat	4.7 g
Carbohydrate	13.3 g
Fibre	1.1 g

AQA

12 On a map the distance between two towns is 5 cm.
The actual distance between the towns is 1 kilometre.
What is the scale of the map in the form of 1 : n?

13 Three friends agree to buy a hi-fi set for £792. Lauren contributes £110, Jack contributes £250 and Chloe contributes the rest. Three years later, they sell the hi-fi for £352.
They agree to divide the money in the ratio in which they contributed.
How much does Chloe receive? AQA

SECTION 18

Speed and Other Compound Measures

What you need to know

- **Speed** is a compound measure because it involves **two** other measures.
- **Speed** is a measurement of how fast something is travelling.
  It involves two other measures, **distance** and **time**.
  In situations where speed is not constant, **average speed** is used.

$$\text{Speed} = \frac{\text{Distance}}{\text{Time}} \qquad \text{Average speed} = \frac{\text{Total distance travelled}}{\text{Total time taken}}$$

The formula linking speed, distance and time can be rearranged and remembered as:
$S = D \div T$
$D = S \times T$
$T = D \div S$

- You should be able to solve problems involving speed, distance and time.

Eg 1 A greyhound takes 32 seconds to run 400 metres.
Calculate its speed in metres per second.

$\text{Speed} = \frac{\text{Distance}}{\text{Time}} = \frac{400}{32} = 12.5$ metres per second

Eg 2 Norrie says, "If I drive at an average speed of 60 km/h it will take me $2\frac{1}{2}$ hours to complete my journey." What distance is his journey?

$\text{Distance} = \text{Speed} \times \text{Time} = 60 \times 2\frac{1}{2} = 150\,\text{km}$

Eg 3 Ellen cycles 5 km at an average speed of 12 km/h.
How many minutes does she take?

$\text{Time} = \frac{\text{Distance}}{\text{Speed}} = \frac{5}{12}\ \text{hours} = \frac{5}{12} \times 60 = 25$ minutes

To change hours to minutes:
multiply by 60

- **Density** is a compound measure which involves the measures **mass** and **volume**.

Eg 4 A block of metal has mass 500 g and volume 400 cm³.

$\text{Density} = \frac{\text{Mass}}{\text{Volume}} = \frac{500}{400} = 1.25\,\text{g/cm}^3$

$$\text{Density} = \frac{\text{Mass}}{\text{Volume}}$$

- **Population density** is a measure of how populated an area is.

Eg 5 The population of Cumbria is 489 700.
The area of Cumbria is 6824 km².

$\text{Population density} = \frac{\text{Population}}{\text{Area}} = \frac{489\,700}{6824} = 71.8\ \text{people/km}^2.$

$$\text{Population density} = \frac{\text{Population}}{\text{Area}}$$

Exercise 18

Do not use a calculator for questions 1 to 5.

1. Norma travels 128 km in 2 hours.
   Calculate her average speed in kilometres per hour.

2. Sean cycled 24 km at an average speed of 16 km/h.
   How long did he take to complete the journey?

3. Ahmed takes $2\frac{1}{2}$ hours to drive from New Milton to London.
   He averages 66 km/h. What distance does he drive?

4. Nigel runs 4 km at an average speed of 6 km/h.
   How many minutes does he take?

5. The distance between Heysham and the Isle of Man is 80 km.
A hovercraft travels at 50 km per hour. How long does the journey take? AQA

6. A bus travels 12 miles in 45 minutes.
Calculate the average speed in miles per hour. AQA

7. A motorist travels a distance of 156 miles in $3\frac{1}{4}$ hours.
Calculate the average speed of the motorist in miles per hour.

8. Kay walks 2.5 km in 50 minutes.
Calculate her average walking speed in kilometres per hour.

9. Sheila lives 6 kilometres from the beach.
She jogs from her home to the beach at an average speed of 10 km/h.
She gets to the beach at 1000. Calculate the time when she left home. AQA

10. The diagram shows the distances, in miles, between some junctions on a motorway.

A coach is travelling west. At 1040 it passes junction 27 and at 1052 it passes junction 26.
(a) Calculate the average speed of the coach in miles per hour.

Between junctions 26 and 25 the coach travels at an average speed of 30 miles per hour.
(b) Calculate the time when the coach passes junction 25.

11. A train travels at an average speed of 80 miles per hour.
At 0940 the train is 65 miles from Glasgow.
The train is due to arrive in Glasgow at 1030.
Will it arrive on time? Show your working.

12. On Monday it took Helen 40 minutes to drive to work.
On Tuesday it took Helen 25 minutes to drive to work.
Her average speed on Monday was 18 miles per hour.
What was her average speed on Tuesday?

13. Henry completes a 200 m race in 25 seconds. What is his average speed in kilometres per hour? AQA

14. A jet-ski travels 0.9 kilometres in 1.5 minutes.
Calculate the average speed of the jet-ski in metres per second.

15. A copper statue has a mass of 1080 g and a volume of 120 cm^3.
Work out the density of copper.

16. A silver medal has a mass of 200 g. The density of silver is 10.5 g/cm^3.
What is the volume of the medal?

17. The population of Jamaica is 2.8 million people. The area of Jamaica is 10 800 km^2.
What is the population density of Jamaica?

18. The table gives some information about North America.

Country	Area (km^2)	Population	Population density (people/km^2)
Canada	9 860 000		2.98
United States		2.68×10^8	28.9

(a) Calculate the population of Canada.
(b) Calculate the area of the United States.
Give your answers to 3 significant figures.

Module 3 Exam Practice Non-calculator Paper

Do not use a calculator for this exercise.

1. Work out $40 \times 50 \times 500$. Give your answer in words.

2. Alison worked for 2 hours 40 minutes and was paid £6 per hour. How much did Alison earn? AQA

3. Here is a way to multiply a number by 25.

   STEP 1: Divide the number by 4
   STEP 2: Multiply the answer by 100

   (a) Use **this** way to multiply 84 by 25.
   (b) Explain how you would use your answer to part (a) to work out 85×25.
   (c) How would you change the steps if you wanted a way to **divide** by 25? AQA

4. (a) 4 litres of milk costs £1.96. How much is 1 litre of milk?
   (b) Apples cost 84 pence per kilogram. What is the cost of 5 kilograms of apples?

5. Use these numbers to answer the following questions:

2	12	27	36	80	88

   (a) Which number is a factor of 16?
   (b) Which number is a multiple of 16?
   (c) Which number is a prime number?
   (d) Which number is a square number?
   (e) Which number is a cube number?

6. To buy a car, Ricky has to pay 24 monthly payments of £198.
   How much does he have to pay altogether to buy the car?

7. A group of 106 students travel to London by minibuses to watch an international hockey match.
   Each minibus can carry 15 passengers. What is the smallest number of minibuses needed? AQA

8. The temperature at 6 am is -3°C. The temperature at 6 pm is 5°C.
   How many degrees warmer is it at 6 pm than at 6 am?

9. Work out. (a) 5^3 (b) $(-3) \times (-4)$ (c) $2 + 6 \times 3$

10. (a) Write these decimals in order, from smallest to largest.

    0.345 0.35 -0.4 0.355 -0.35

    (b) Write down a decimal that lies halfway between 0.4 and 0.5.
    (c) Work out (i) $5 - 0.26$, (ii) 0.2×0.4, (iii) $24 \div 0.3$.
    (d) A turkey costs £2.40 per kilogram.
    What is the cost of a turkey which weighs 6.5 kilograms?

11. A plank of wood is 225 cm in length. It is cut into two pieces.
    One piece is 37 cm longer than the other.
    What is the length of the shorter piece of wood? AQA

12. (a) Work out (i) 10^5, (ii) $10^2 - 2^5$, (iii) $2^3 \times 3^2$, (iv) $30^2 \div 10^3$.
    (b) Which is smaller, 5^4 or 4^5? Show **all** your working.
    (c) Work out $\sqrt{25} \times \sqrt{100}$.

13. (a) Write $\frac{4}{5}$ as a percentage.
    (b) Find 25% of £500.
    (c) Nora gets 26 out of 40 in a test. What percentage of the marks did she get?

14. Gavin wins £48.
    He gives his son one quarter of his winnings. He gives half of the remainder to his wife.
    What fraction of his winnings does he keep for himself?

15 (a) Write these fractions in ascending order: $\frac{1}{2}$ $\frac{2}{3}$ $\frac{3}{5}$ $\frac{5}{8}$ $\frac{3}{4}$

(b) Write down a fraction that lies halfway between $\frac{1}{5}$ and $\frac{1}{4}$.

(c) Work out (i) $\frac{1}{4} + \frac{2}{5}$, (ii) $\frac{2}{3} - \frac{1}{2}$, (iii) $\frac{4}{5} \times \frac{2}{3}$.

(d) Work out $\frac{2}{5}$ of 12.

16 A crowd of 54 000 people watch a carnival.
(a) 15% of the crowd are men. How many men watch the carnival?
(b) Two-thirds of the crowd are children. How many children watch the carnival?

17 (a) Given that $59 \times 347 = 20\,473$, find the exact value of $\frac{20\,473}{590}$.
(b) Use approximations to estimate the value of 49×302.
Show all your working.

18 Strawberries cost 90p per pound.
(a) Estimate, to the nearest £, the cost of buying 2 kg of strawberries.
(b) Gooseberries cost 30% per pound more than strawberries.
Calculate the cost of a pound of gooseberries.
(c) John buys 500 g of strawberries.
The weight of the strawberries is correct to the nearest 10 g.
What is the minimum weight of the strawberries? AQA

19 (a) Diesel costs £0.75 per litre in England. Calculate the cost of 45 litres of diesel.
(b) In France, diesel is 20% cheaper than in England.
Calculate the cost of 45 litres of diesel in France.

20 Colin buys two cups of tea and three cups of coffee. He pays £4.65 altogether.
The price of a cup of tea is 84 pence. What is the price of a cup of coffee? AQA

21 The cost of 6 medium eggs is 48 pence.
(a) How much will 10 medium eggs cost?
(b) Small eggs cost $\frac{7}{8}$ of the price of medium eggs. How much will 6 small eggs cost?
(c) Large eggs cost 25% more than medium eggs. How much will 6 large eggs cost? AQA

22 (a) A machine stamps 120 letters per minute.
How long will it take to stamp 300 letters?
Give your answer in minutes and seconds.
(b) A machine sorts 2000 letters per hour at normal speed.
At high speed it sorts 15% more letters per hour.
How many letters per hour does it sort at high speed? AQA

23 Four cabbages cost £2.88. How much will five cabbages cost? AQA

24 (a) 7 *Arctic* ice creams cost a total of £3.85. How much will 12 *Arctic* ice creams cost?
(b) A large box of ice cream cones contains 750 cones to the nearest 10.
(i) What is the smallest possible number of cones in the box?
(ii) What is the largest possible number of cones in the box? AQA

25 (a) Conrad cycles 24 km in $1\frac{1}{2}$ hours. What is his cycling speed in kilometres per hour?
(b) Cas cycles 24 km at 15 km/h. She sets off at 0930. At what time does she finish?

26 A quiz has 40 questions.
(a) Lenny gets 34 questions right. What percentage of the questions did he get right?
(b) 12 boys took part in the quiz.
The ratio of boys to girls taking part in the quiz is 3 : 5.
How many girls took part?

27 (a) Which of these numbers are prime? 25 29 33 37 48

(b) Work out $2^3 \times 5^2$.

(c) Evaluate $\frac{3}{4} - \frac{2}{5}$, giving your answer as a fraction.

(d) Given that $56 \times 473 = 26\,488$, find the exact value of $\frac{264.88}{5.6}$.

(e) Find an approximate value of $\frac{29.7 \times 5.98}{0.32}$. You **must** show all your working. AQA

28 A train travels from Basingstoke to London in 40 minutes.
The distance is 50 miles.
Find the average speed of the train in miles per hour. AQA

29 Trevor did a sponsored walk.
The length of the walk, to the nearest kilometre, was 12 km.
Trevor's time was 110 minutes to the nearest minute.

(a) What was the longest length the walk could have been?

(b) What was Trevor's shortest possible time? AQA

30 Shelley wants to buy a minidisc player which is on sale at £239.99.
She can pay by cash or credit.
Shelley buys the minidisc player on credit, and pays a deposit of £79.99.
She must also pay 36 monthly payments of £6.

(a) Find the total credit price.

Shelley needs a loan of £160 to buy the minidisc player on credit.

(b) Express the extra amount paid for credit, compared with cash, as a percentage of the loan. AQA

31 Here are the first four terms of a sequence of numbers written in standard form.

6×10^{-1}, 6×10^{-3}, 6×10^{-5}, 6×10^{-7}, ...

(a) Write down the 10th term of the sequence.

(b) (i) Write down the 1st term of the sequence as a decimal.

(ii) Write down the **sum** of the first four terms as a decimal. AQA

32 A youth club organises a skiing holiday for 45 children.
The ratio of boys to girls is 5 : 4.
40% of the boys have skied before.
How many boys have skied before?

33 (a) Write 48 as a product of its prime factors.

(b) Write 108 as a product of its prime factors.

(c) Hence find the least common multiple of 48 and 108.

34 $u = 5 \times 10^3$ $v = 7 \times 10^6$
Evaluate uv. Give your answer in standard form. AQA

35 Hugh buys a box of fireworks.
After lighting 40% of the fireworks he has 24 fireworks left.
How many fireworks did he buy?

36 (a) Work out. (i) $2\frac{1}{2} - 1\frac{2}{3}$ (ii) $2\frac{1}{2} \div 1\frac{2}{3}$ (b) What is the reciprocal of $1\frac{1}{4}$?

37 (a) Use approximations to estimate $\sqrt{\frac{40\,095}{(9.87^2)}}$

(b) Work out $3 \times 10^5 \times 5 \times 10^{-2}$. Give your answer in standard form.

(c) The value of a house has increased by 10% in one year. It is now valued at £55 000.
What was the value of the house a year ago? AQA

Module 3 Exam Practice Calculator Paper

You may use a calculator for this exercise.

1 Use these numbers to answer the following questions.

3 7 11 15 19 23 27

(a) Which number in the list is a factor of another number in the list?
(b) Which number is a cube number?
(c) (i) Which numbers are not prime numbers? Give a reason for your answer.
(ii) The numbers are part of a sequence.
What is the next number in the sequence which is not a prime number?

2 (a) Write $\frac{7}{9}$ as a decimal. Give your answer correct to two decimal places.
(b) Write 33%, 0.3, $\frac{8}{25}$ and $\frac{1}{3}$ in order of size, smallest first.

3 Bruce buys two packets of baby wipes on special offer.
Calculate the actual cost of each baby wipe.

4 A packet of washing powder costs £3.96 and weighs 1.5 kg.
The packet has enough powder for 22 washes.
(a) What is the cost of powder for one wash?
(b) How much powder is needed for one wash?
Give your answer in grams correct to one decimal place. AQA

5 (a) (i) Calculate $\sqrt{3}$. Give your answer correct to two decimal places.
(ii) Calculate $(0.6)^3$.
(b) What is the value of m, if $47.6 \div m = 0.\dot{3}$?

6 A quiz consists of ten questions.
Beth, John and Sue take part.
These are their results.

	Beth	John	Sue
Number of answers correct	4	6	5
Number of answers incorrect	4	3	1
Number of questions not attempted	2	1	4

A correct answer scores 3 points.
An incorrect answer scores −2 points.
A question not attempted scores 0 points.
Who scores the most points? Show your working. AQA

7 Cheri is paid a basic rate of £5.40 per hour for a 35-hour week.
Overtime is paid at $1\frac{1}{2}$ times the basic rate.
Last week she worked 41 hours.
Calculate her pay for last week.

8 Calculate the value of (a) $\frac{7.89 + 13.56}{5}$, (b) $2.6^2 - \sqrt{6.2}$.

9 Jacob is 3.7 kg heavier than Isaac. The sum of their weights is 44.5 kg. How heavy is Jacob?

10 Work out (a) $\frac{2}{5} - \frac{1}{3}$, (b) $1\frac{1}{4} + \frac{2}{3}$, giving your answers as fractions.

11 A shop sells 4000 items in a week.
5% are returned. $\frac{1}{4}$ of the returned items are faulty. How many items are faulty? AQA

12 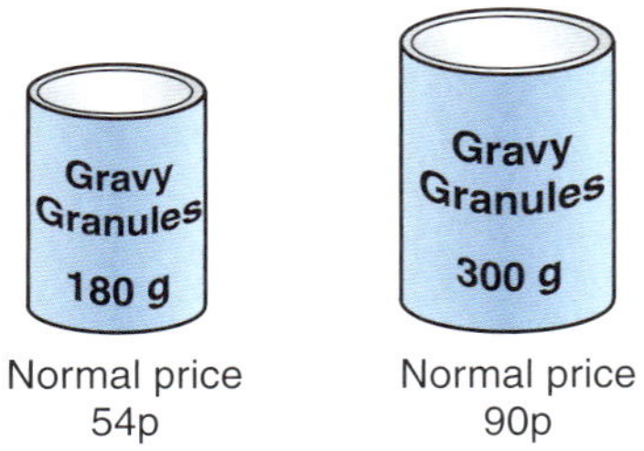

The diagram shows the weights and prices of two packets of gravy granules.
This week both packets are on special offer.
The smaller packet has one third off the normal price.
The larger packet has 30% off the normal price.
Which packet is better value this week?
Show your working.

13 In America a camera costs \$110.
In England an identical camera costs £65.
The exchange rate is £1 = \$1.62
In which country is the camera cheaper and by how much?
You must show all your working.

AQA

14 Petrol costs 78.9 pence per litre.
A car can travel 8.5 miles on one litre of petrol.
Calculate the cost of travelling 1000 miles in the car.
Give your answer to a suitable degree of accuracy.

AQA

15 Kelly states that $a^2 + b^2$ is always an even number when a and b are prime numbers.
By means of an example, show that Kelly is **not** correct.

AQA

16 Harvey lives 3 kilometres from school. He walks to school at an average speed of 5 km/h.
The school day starts at 0900.
What is the latest time Harvey can leave home and still get to school on time?

17 (a) What is the reciprocal of 0.25? (b) Work out $\dfrac{3.2^2}{\sqrt{0.04}}$.

18 A caravan is for sale at £7200. Stuart buys the caravan on credit.
The credit terms are:

deposit 25% of sale price and 36 monthly payments of £175.

Express the extra amount paid for credit, compared with the cash price, as a percentage of the cash price.

19 A puppy weighed 1.50 kg when it was born.
(a) Its weight increased by 28% during the first month.
Calculate the puppy's weight at the end of the first month.
(b) In the second month the puppy's weight increased by 15% of its **new** weight.
Calculate its weight at the end of the second month.
(c) The puppy's weight continues to increase by 15% each month.
How many months old is the puppy when it has doubled its birth weight?
Show your working.

AQA

20 (a) Gerald invests £4000 at 4.5% per annum compound interest.
Calculate the interest on his investment at the end of 3 years.
(b) Steff invests her money at 5% per annum compound interest.
Calculate the percentage increase in the value of her investment after 3 years.

21 (a) Express the following numbers as products of their prime factors. (i) 72 (ii) 80
(b) Two cars go round a race track. The first car takes 1 minute 12 seconds to complete a circuit and the other car takes 1 minute 20 seconds.
They start together on the starting line.
Find the length of time, in minutes, before they are together again.

AQA

22 £1 can buy 1.54 euros. £1 can buy 1.37 dollars.
How many dollars can be bought with 1000 euros?

23 Use your calculator to find the value of $\frac{29.7 + 17.3}{1.54 \times 68.5}$.
Give your answer to a suitable degree of accuracy **and** give a reason for your choice.

24 Hannah wishes to insure the contents of her house for £7500.
She is quoted a premium of £1.30 for every £100 of contents.
(a) Find the premium which she is quoted.
(b) Hannah can receive a 20% discount for agreeing to pay the first £100 of any claim.
She can then receive a further 8% discount because her house is in a neighbourhood watch area.
Find the premium which Hannah actually pays. AQA

25 (a) Place the following numbers in descending order.

$\sqrt{6.9}$	2.58	1.6^2	$2\frac{4}{7}$

(b) (i) Calculate $\frac{612 \times 29.6}{81.3 - 18.9}$.
Give your answer correct to 3 significant figures.
(ii) Use approximations to show that your answer is about right.
Show all your working.

26 $p = 3^2 \times 5 \times 7$ and $q = 2 \times 3 \times 5^2$. Find the least common multiple of p and q.

27 (a) You are given the formula $k = \frac{3}{4}m^2$.
Calculate the exact value of k, when $m = 4.8 \times 10^3$. Give your answer in standard form.
(b) Calculate $\sqrt{\frac{5.2 \times 10^{-3}}{(0.039)^2}}$, correct to two decimal places.

28

SALE "30% Off All Prices".
A suitcase costs £44.66 in the sale.
How much was the suitcase before the sale?

29 (a) Jools invests £2000 at 6.5% per annum compound interest.
Calculate the value of his investment at the end of 3 years.
(b) Jennifer gets 6% per annum on her investment.
After one year the value of her investment is £1272.
How much did she invest?

30 Last year Alf had a tax allowance of £4615 and paid £4328 in tax.
The rates of tax were:

10p in the £ on the first £1920 of taxable income and
22p in the £ on all the remaining taxable income.

How much did Alf earn last year?

31 In 1998 the average cost of printing 24 photographs was £3.42.
(a) In 1998 British tourists took 1.6×10^6 photographs.
Calculate the cost of printing all these photographs.
(b) The price of printing photographs in 1998 was 5% less than in 1988.
Calculate the cost of printing 24 photographs in 1988. AQA

32 The world harvest of garlic is 20 000 tonnes every day.
(a) How much garlic is harvested in one year? Take a year to be 365 days.
Give your answer in standard form.

France produces 5.29×10^4 tonnes of garlic in a year.
(b) What percentage of the world total is produced by France? AQA

SECTION 19

Introduction to Algebra

What you need to know

- You should be able to write **algebraic expressions**.

Eg 1 An expression for the cost of 6 pens at n pence each is $6n$ pence.

Eg 2 An expression for 2 pence more than n pence is $n + 2$ pence.

- Be able to **simplify expressions** by collecting **like terms** together.

Eg 3 (a) $2d + 3d = 5d$ (b) $3x + 2 - x + 4 = 2x + 6$ (c) $x + 2x + x^2 = 3x + x^2$

- Be able to **multiply expressions** together.

Eg 4 (a) $2a \times a = 2a^2$ (b) $y \times y \times y = y^3$ (c) $3m \times 2n = 6mn$

- Recall and use these properties of powers:
Powers of the same base are **added** when terms are **multiplied**.
Powers of the same base are **subtracted** when terms are **divided**.
Powers are **multiplied** when a power is raised to a power.

$$a^m \times a^n = a^{m+n}$$
$$a^m \div a^n = a^{m-n}$$
$$(a^m)^n = a^{m \times n}$$

Eg 5 (a) $x^3 \times x^2 = x^5$ (b) $a^5 \div a^2 = a^3$
(c) $6m^6 \div 2m^2 = 3m^4$ (d) $(x^2)^3 = x^6$

- How to **multiply out brackets**.

Eg 6 (a) $2(x - 5) = 2x - 10$ (b) $x(x - 5) = x^2 - 5x$ (c) $2m(m + 3) = 2m^2 + 6m$

- How to **factorise expressions**.

Eg 7 (a) $3x - 6 = 3(x - 2)$ (b) $m^2 + 5m = m(m + 5)$ (c) $3a^2 - 6a = 3a(a - 2)$

Exercise 19

1. A calculator costs £9.
Write an expression for the cost of k calculators.

2. Godfrey is 5 years older than Mary.
Write expressions for the following.
(a) Godfrey's age when Mary is t years old.
(b) Mary's age when Godfrey is x years old.

3. A cup of coffee costs x pence and a cup of tea costs y pence.
Write an expression for the cost of 3 cups of coffee and 2 cups of tea.

4. Simplify (a) $m + 2m + 3m$, (b) $2m + 2 - m$, (c) $m \times m \times m$.

5. (a) A pen costs x pence. How much will 4 pens cost?
(b) Simplify $3m + 2 + m - 3$. AQA

6. A muffin costs $d + 3$ pence.
Write an expression for the cost of 5 muffins.

7 Write an expression, in terms of x, for the sum of the angles in this shape.

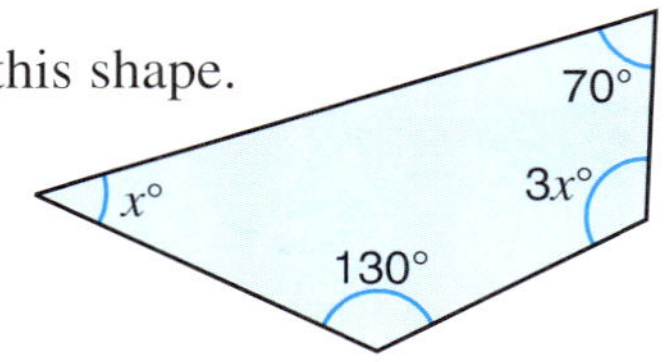

8 A man leads a string of n donkeys.

(a) How many heads are there?
(b) How many legs are there?

AQA

9 Simplify (a) $5a \times 2a$, (b) $3g \times 2h$, (c) $6k \div 3$, (d) $3m \div m$.

10 Which algebraic expressions are equivalent?

$2y$	y^2	$2(y+1)$	$y \times y$	$y + y$
$2y + 2$	$2y + y$	$2y^2$	$3y$	$2y + 1$

AQA

11
(a) Simplify (i) $2x + 3 + x$, (ii) $2x + y - x + y$.
(b) Multiply out (i) $2(x + 3)$, (ii) $x(x - 1)$.
(c) Multiply out and simplify (i) $2(x - 1) - 3$, (ii) $7 + 3(2 + x)$.
(d) Factorise (i) $2a - 6$, (ii) $x^2 + 2x$.

12
(a) Ken works x hours a week for £y per hour.
Write an expression for the amount he earns each week.
(b) Sue works 5 hours less than Ken each week and earns £y per hour.
Write an expression for the amount Sue earns each week.

13
(a) Simplify $8a + ab - a + 2b + 3ab$.
(b) Expand and simplify $5(x + 3) - x$.

AQA

14 Multiply out and simplify $3(4x - 1) + 2x - 6$.

AQA

15 Simplify. (a) $y^3 \times y^2$ (b) $x^6 \div x^3$ (c) $\frac{z^4 \times z}{z^3}$ (d) $\frac{x^2y}{xy^2}$

16
(a) Simplify (i) $2a^5 \times 3a^2$, (ii) $36a^6 \div 9a^2$.
(b) Factorise completely $3x^2 - 9x$.

AQA

17
(a) Simplify $5 - 3(2n - 1)$.
(b) Multiply out $(-3m) \times (-2m)$.
(c) Factorise fully $8mn - 2m$.

18 Expand and simplify $3(2x + 3) - 2(5 + x)$.

19 Simplify (a) $2a^3 \times 3a$, (b) $6x^8 \div 3x^2$, (c) $\frac{3m^2 \times 4n^6}{6mn^2}$, (d) $4x^3y \times 5x^2y$.

20
(a) Expand the brackets. (i) $2x(x - 3y)$ (ii) $3a(3a + a^2)$
(b) Factorise. (i) $4xy - 2y^2$ (ii) $3m^2 - 12m$
(c) Simplify. $2x^2 - x(1 + x)$

21 Simplify fully $\frac{2a^3b^2 \times 6a^4b^2}{4ab^3}$.

AQA

22
(a) Multiply out $2x(2y - xy)$.
(b) Factorise $6pq - 3pq^2$.
(c) Simplify $21m^6 \div 7m^3$.

SECTION 20

Solving Equations

What you need to know

- The solution of an equation is the value of the unknown letter that fits the equation.
- You should be able to solve simple equations by **inspection**.

Eg 1 (a) $a + 2 = 5$, $a = 3$ (b) $m - 3 = 7$, $m = 10$ (c) $2x = 10$, $x = 5$

- Be able to solve simple problems by **working backwards**.

Eg 2 I think of a number, multiply it by 3 and add 4. The answer is 19.

x → multiply by 3 → add 4 → Answer 19

5 ← divide by 3 ← 15 ← subtract 4 ← 19

The number I thought of is 5.

- Be able to use the **balance method** to solve equations.

Eg 3 Solve these equations.

(a) $d - 13 = -5$
$d = -5 + 13$
$d = 8$

(b) $-4a = 20$
$a = \frac{20}{-4}$
$a = -5$

(c) $5 - 4n = -1$
$-4n = -6$
$n = 1.5$

- Be able to solve equations with unknowns on both sides of the equals sign.

Eg 4 Solve $3x + 1 = x + 7$.
$3x = x + 6$
$2x = 6$
$x = 3$

- Be able to solve equations which include brackets.

Eg 5 Solve $4(3 + 2x) = 5(x + 2)$.
$12 + 8x = 5x + 10$
$8x = 5x - 2$
$3x = -2$
$x = -\frac{2}{3}$

- Be able to solve equations which involve fractions.

Eg 6 Solve $\frac{x}{2} + \frac{2x}{3} = 7$.
$6 \times \frac{x}{2} + 6 \times \frac{2x}{3} = 6 \times 7$
$3x + 4x = 42$
$7x = 42$
$x = 6$

Eg 7 Solve $\frac{x - 1}{3} = \frac{x + 1}{4}$.
$4(x - 1) = 3(x + 1)$
$4x - 4 = 3x + 3$
$4x = 3x + 7$
$x = 7$

- You should be able to write, or form, equations using the information given in a problem.

Exercise 20

1 What number should be put in the box to make each of these statements correct?

(a) $\square - 6 = 9$ (b) $2 + \square = 11$ (c) $4 \times \square = 20$ (d) $\square \times 3 - 5 = 7$

2 Solve these equations.

(a) $7 + x = 12$ (b) $5 - x = 3$ (c) $5x - 9 = 11$

3 Jaspel says to his friends:

> "Think of a number, add 5, then divide by 2. Tell me your answer."

(a) Huw thinks of the number 7. What is his answer?
(b) Gary says his answer is 11. What number did he start with? AQA

4 (a) I think of a number, add 3, and then multiply by 2.
The answer is 16. What is my number?
(b) I think of a number, double it and then subtract 3.
The answer is 5. What is my number?

5 Solve these equations.
(a) $3x - 7 = 23$ (b) $5 + 7x = 47$ (c) $5(x - 2) = 20$ (d) $3x - 7 = x + 15$

6 The lengths of these rods are given, in centimetres, in terms of n.

The total length of the rods is 30 cm.
By forming an equation, find the value of n.

7 Mandy buys a small box of chocolates and a large box of chocolates.
The diagram shows the number of chocolates in each box.

Altogether there are 47 chocolates.
By forming an equation, find the number of chocolates in the larger box.

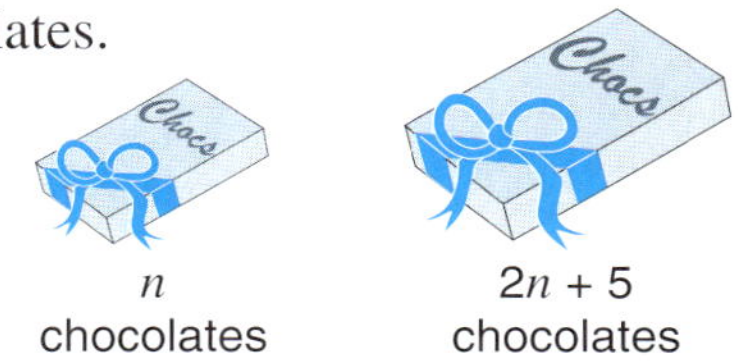

8 Solve these equations.
(a) $7x + 4 = 60$ (b) $3x - 7 = -4$ (c) $2(x + 3) = -2$ (d) $3x - 4 = 1 + x$

9 Solve the equations (a) $2x + 3 = 15$, (b) $3(x - 1) = 6$, (c) $x + 2 = 5 - x$. AQA

10 Solve these equations.
(a) $\frac{x}{3} = -7$ (b) $2(x - 1) = 3$ (c) $5 - 2x = 3x + 2$ (d) $\frac{1}{4}x + 5 = 2$

11 Solve the equations (a) $\frac{x - 7}{5} = 2$, (b) $5x + 6 = 24 - 10x$. AQA

12 Solve these equations.
(a) $\frac{x + 5}{2} = 3$ (b) $\frac{1 - 2x}{3} = 2$ (c) $\frac{3}{2} = \frac{3x}{5}$ (d) $\frac{x}{2} + \frac{x}{3} = 5$

13 The diagram shows a rectangle and a right-angled triangle.

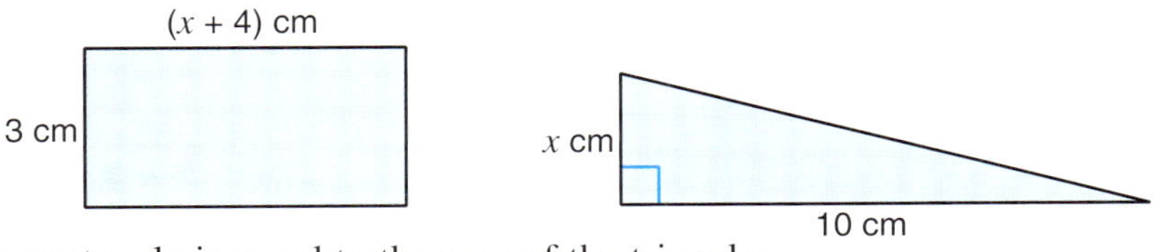

Not drawn accurately

The area of the rectangle is equal to the area of the triangle.
By forming an equation work out the value of x. AQA

14 Solve these equations.
(a) $2(x - 3) + 3(x + 1) = 2$ (b) $3(2 + 3a) = 5(a - 2)$ (c) $x - 3(x + 1) = 2(5 - 2x)$

15 Solve the equations (a) $\frac{x - 3}{4} = 1 - x$, (b) $\frac{x - 3}{2} = \frac{2x + 1}{3}$.

SECTION 21

Formulae

What you need to know

- An **expression** is just an answer using letters and numbers.
  A **formula** is an algebraic rule. It always has an equals sign.
- You should be able to **write simple formulae**.

Eg 1 A packet of crisps weighs 25 grams. Write a formula for the total weight, W grams, of n packets of crisps.

$W = 25n$

Eg 2 Start with t, add 5 and then multiply by 3. The result is p. Write a formula for p in terms of t.

$p = 3(t + 5)$

- Be able to **substitute** values into given expressions and formulae.

Eg 3 (a) Find the value of $4x - y$ when $x = 5$ and $y = 7$.

$4x - y = 4 \times 5 - 7$
$= 20 - 7$
$= 13$

(b) $A = pq - r$
Find the value of A when $p = 2$, $q = -2$ and $r = 3$.

$A = pq - r$
$= 2 \times (-2) - 3$
$= -4 - 3$
$= -7$

(c) $M = 2n^2$
Find the value of M when $n = 3$.

$M = 2n^2$
$= 2 \times 3^2$
$= 2 \times 9$
$= 18$

- Be able to **rearrange** a given formula to make another letter (variable) the subject.

Eg 4 $y = 2x + a$
Make x the subject of the formula.

$y = 2x + a$
$y - a = 2x$
$\frac{y - a}{2} = x$
So, $x = \frac{y - a}{2}$

Eg 5 $T = a + \sqrt{b}$
Rearrange the formula to give b in terms of T and a.

$T = a + \sqrt{b}$
$T - a = \sqrt{b}$
$(T - a)^2 = b$
So, $b = (T - a)^2$

Exercise 21

Do not use a calculator for questions 1 to 10.

1. What is the value of $a - 3b$ when $a = 10$ and $b = 2$?
2. What is the value of $2x + y$ when $x = -3$ and $y = 5$?
3. $H = ab - c$. Find the value of H when $a = 2$, $b = -5$ and $c = 3$.
4. Given that $m = -3$ and $n = 5$, find the value of
   (a) $m + n$, (b) $m - n$, (c) $n - m$, (d) mn.
5. If $p = 4$ and $q = -5$ find the value of (a) $3pq$, (b) $p^2 + 2q$.
6. $L = 5(p + q)$. Find the value of L when $p = 2$ and $q = -0.4$.
7. $A = b - cd$. Find the value of A when $b = -3$, $c = 2$ and $d = 4$.

8. What is the value of $10y^2$ when $y = 3$?

9. What is the value of $3x^3$ when $x = 2$?

10. $T = ab^2$. Find the value of T when $a = 4$ and $b = -5$.

11. A boat is hired. The cost, in £, is given by: Cost = 6 × Number of hours + 5
    (a) Calculate the cost of hiring the boat for 2 hours.
    (b) The boat was hired at a cost of £29.
    For how many hours was it hired?
    AQA

12. Each year the High School has a disco for Year 7.
    A teacher works out the number of cans of drink to buy,
    using this rule: 3 cans for every 2 tickets sold, plus 20 spare cans.

    (a) This year, 160 tickets have been sold. How many cans will he buy?
    (b) Using N for the number of cans and T for the number of tickets, write down the teacher's formula for N in terms of T.
    (c) Last year, he bought 215 cans. How many tickets were sold last year?
    AQA

13. The formula $F = \frac{9}{5}C + 32$ is used to change temperatures in degrees Centigrade (C) to temperatures in degrees Fahrenheit (F).
    A thermometer reads a temperature of 15°C.
    What is the equivalent temperature in degrees Fahrenheit?
    AQA

14. Given that $m = \frac{1}{2}$, $p = \frac{3}{4}$, $t = -2$, calculate (a) $mp + t$ (b) $\frac{(m + p)}{t}$
    AQA

15. A formula is given as $c = 3t - 5$. Rearrange the formula to give t in terms of c.

16. (a) Make c the subject of the formula $P = 2a + 2b + 2c$.
    (b) Find the value of c when $P = 46$, $a = 7.7$ and $b = 10.8$.
    AQA

17. A formula for calculating distance is $d = \frac{(u + v)t}{2}$.
    (a) Find the value of d when $u = 9.4$, $v = 6.3$ and $t = 8$.
    (b) Make t the subject of the formula.
    (c) Find the value of t when $d = 60$, $u = 5.8$ and $v = 10.2$
    AQA

18. $m = \frac{3}{5}(n - 17)$. Find the value of n when $m = -9$.

19. Make r the subject of the formula $p = \frac{gr}{s}$.

20. You are given the formula $v = u + at$.
    (a) Find v when $u = 17$, $a = -8$ and $t = \frac{3}{5}$.
    (b) Rearrange the formula to give a in terms of v, u and t.

21. Make s the subject of the formula $t = s^2 + 5$.

22. You are given the formula $V = \sqrt{PR}$.
    Rearrange the formula to give P in terms of V and R.
    AQA

23. s is given by the formula $s = ut + \frac{1}{2}at^2$.
    Find the value of s when $u = 2.8$, $t = 2$ and $a = -1.7$.
    AQA

24. Make h the subject of the formula $g = \frac{3}{5}h^2$.

SECTION 22

Sequences

What you need to know

- A **sequence** is a list of numbers made according to some rule.
  The numbers in a sequence are called **terms**.
- You should be able to draw and continue number sequences represented by patterns of shapes.

Eg 1 This pattern represents the sequence:
3, 5, 7, ...

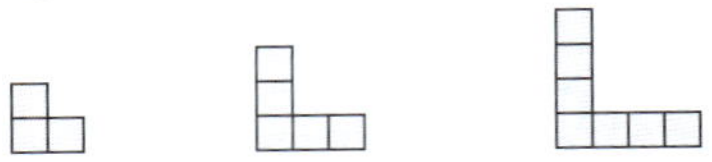

- Be able to continue a sequence by following a given rule.

Eg 2 The sequence 2, 7, 22, ... is made using the rule:

Multiply the last number by 3, then add 1.

The next term in the sequence $= (22 \times 3) + 1 = 66 + 1 = 67$

- Be able to find a rule, and then use it, to continue a sequence.

> **To continue a sequence:**
> 1. Work out the rule to get from one term to the next.
> 2. Apply the same rule to find further terms in the sequence.

Eg 3 Describe the rule used to make the following sequences.
Then use the rule to find the next term of each sequence.

(a) 5, 8, 11, 14, ...
Rule:
add 3 to last term
Next term: 17

(b) 2, 4, 8, 16, ...
Rule:
multiply last term by 2
Next term: 32

(c) 1, 1, 2, 3, 5, 8, ...
Rule:
add the last two terms
Next term: 13

- Find an expression for the nth term of a sequence.

> A number sequence which increases (or decreases) by the same amount from one term to the next is called a **linear sequence**.
> The sequence 2, 8, 14, 20, 26, ... has a **common difference** of 6.

Eg 4 Find the nth term of the sequence: 3, 5, 7, 9, ...
The sequence is linear, common difference = 2.
To find the nth term add one to the multiples of 2.
So, the nth term is $2n + 1$.

> **Special sequences - Square numbers:** 1, 4, 9, 16, 25, ...
> **Triangular numbers:** 1, 3, 6, 10, 15, ...

Exercise 22

1 What is the next number in each of these sequences?
(a) 1, 2, 5, 10, ...
(b) 1, 3, 9, 27, ...
(c) 1, $\frac{1}{2}$, $\frac{1}{4}$, $\frac{1}{8}$, ...

2 The first six terms of a sequence are shown. 1, 4, 5, 9, 14, 23, ...
Write down the next two terms.

3 Look at this sequence of numbers. 2, 5, 8, 11, ...
(a) What is the next number in the sequence?
(b) Is 30 a number in this sequence? Give a reason for your answer.

4 The rule for a sequence is:

Add the last two numbers and divide by 2.

Write down the next three terms when the sequence begins: 3, 7, ...

5 A sequence begins: 5, 15, 45, 135, ...
(a) Write down the rule, in words, used to get from one term to the next in the sequence.
(b) Use your rule to find the next term in the sequence.

6 A sequence begins: 1, −2, ...
The next number in the sequence is found by using the rule:

ADD THE PREVIOUS TWO NUMBERS AND MULTIPLY BY TWO

Use the rule to find the next **two** numbers in the sequence. AQA

7 Ahmed writes down the first four numbers of a sequence: 10, 8, 4, −2, ...
(a) What is the next number in this sequence? (b) Explain how you found your answer. AQA

8 A sequence begins: 1, 6, 10, 8, ...
The rule to continue the sequence is:
double the difference between the last two numbers.
Ravi says if you continue the sequence it will end in 0. Is he correct? Explain your answer.

9 The first three patterns in a sequence are shown.

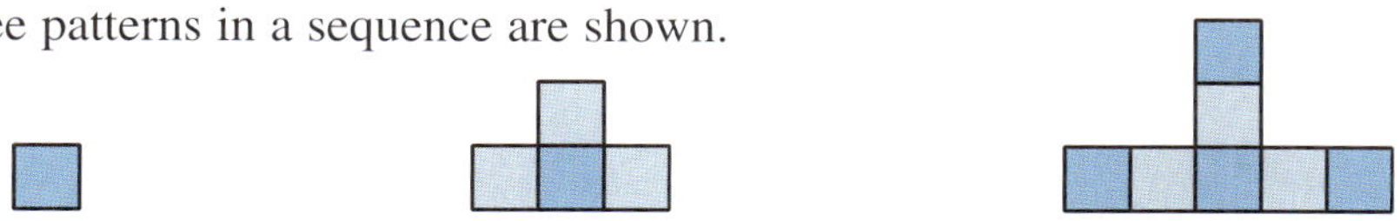

(a) How many squares are in pattern 20?
Explain how you found your answer.
(b) Write an expression for the number of squares in the nth pattern.

10 A sequence is given by 5, 12, 19, 26, 33, ...
(a) What is the next term in this sequence? Explain how you got your answer.
(b) Write down the nth term for the sequence. AQA

11 Find the nth term of the following sequences.
(a) 5, 7, 9, 11, ... (b) 1, 5, 9, 13, ...

12 (a) Write down the first **three** terms of the sequence whose nth term is given by $n^2 + 4$.
(b) Will the number 106 be in this sequence? Explain your answer. AQA

13 The nth term of a sequence is $\frac{5n}{4n+5}$.
(a) Write down the first two terms of this sequence.
(b) Which term of the sequence has the value 1? AQA

14 A sequence begins: 3, 6, 11, 18, 27, ...
(a) Find the next two terms in this sequence.
(b) Explain why this is not a linear sequence.
(c) Explain how you can find the 20th term in the sequence without writing down all the previous terms.

SECTION 23

Graphs

What you need to know

- **Coordinates** (involving positive and negative numbers) are used to describe the position of a point on a graph.

Eg 1 The coordinates of A are $(-3, 2)$.

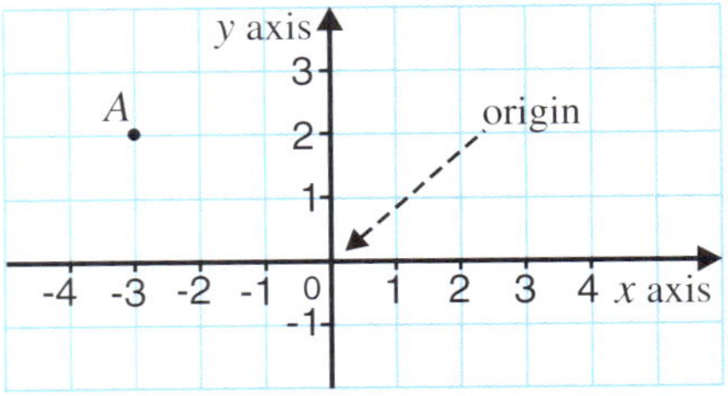

- The x axis is the line $y = 0$.
  The y axis is the line $x = 0$.

- The **gradient** of a line can be found by drawing a right-angled triangle.

$$\text{Gradient} = \frac{\text{distance up}}{\text{distance along}}$$

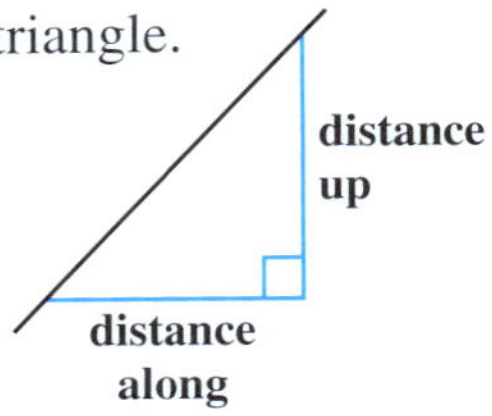

Gradients can be positive, zero or negative.

- You should be able to find the equation for a given line.

In general, the equation of any straight line can be written in the form

$$y = mx + c$$

where m is the **gradient** of the line
and c is the ***y*-intercept**.

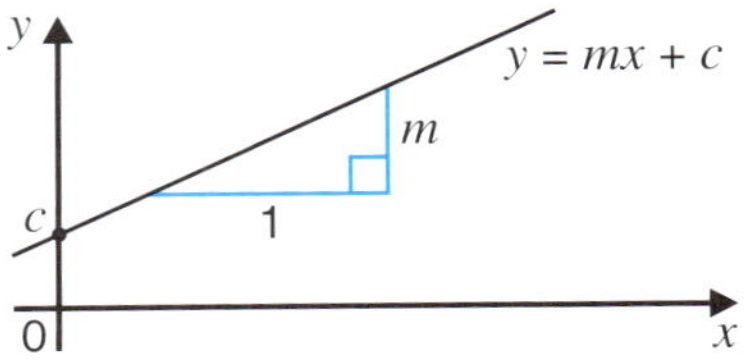

Eg 2 Find the equation of the line shown on this graph.

Gradient of line $= \frac{\text{distance up}}{\text{distance along}} = \frac{2}{1} = 2$

The graph crosses the y axis at the point $(0, -3)$,
so the y-intercept is -3.
The equation of the line is $y = 2x - 3$.

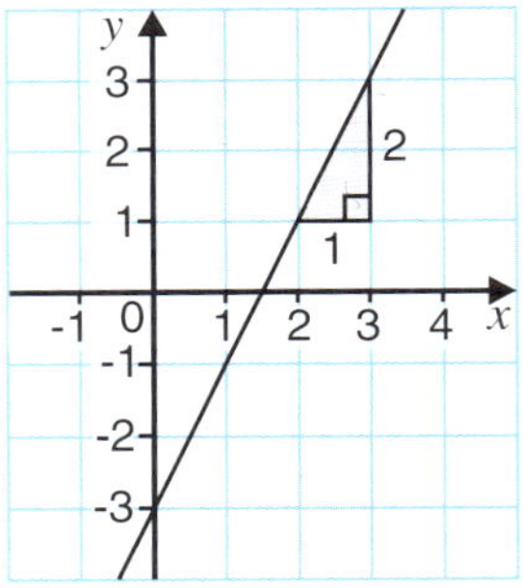

- The points where a line crosses the axes can be found:
  by reading the coordinates from a graph,
  by substituting $x = 0$ and $y = 0$ into the equation of the line.

Eg 3 The diagram shows a sketch of the line $2y = x + 3$.
Find the coordinates of the points P and Q.

When $x = 0$, $2y = 0 + 3$, $2y = 3$, $y = 1\frac{1}{2}$.
When $y = 0$, $0 = x + 3$, $x = -3$.

The points are $P\left(0, 1\frac{1}{2}\right)$ and $Q(-3, 0)$.

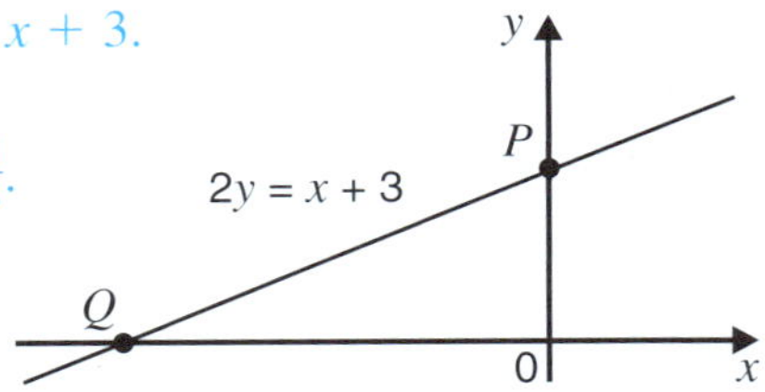

- Equations of the form $px + qy = r$ can be **rearranged** to the form $y = mx + c$.

Eg 4 The graph of a straight line is given by the equation $4y - 3x = 8$.
Write this equation in the form $y = mx + c$.

$4y - 3x = 8$
$4y = 3x + 8$
$y = \frac{3}{4}x + 2$

The line has gradient $\frac{3}{4}$ and y-intercept 2.

- You should be able to solve equations and problems involving straight line graphs.

- You should be able to draw and interpret graphs which represent real-life situations.
- A **gradient** measures the **rate of change** of one quantity with respect to another.
  A **positive** gradient represents a **rate of increase**.
  A **negative** gradient represents a **rate of decrease**.
- The gradient of a **distance-time graph** gives the speed.

Speed is the rate of change of distance with respect to time.
When the distance-time graph is **linear** the **speed is constant**.
When the distance-time graph is **horizontal** the **speed is zero**.

Eg 5 The graph shows a car journey.
(a) Between what times does the car travel fastest? Explain your answer.
(b) What is the speed of the car during this part of the journey?

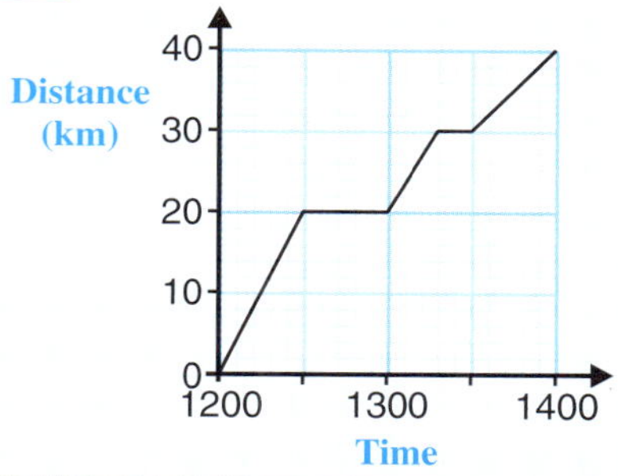

(a) 1200 to 1230. Steepest gradient.

(b) Speed $= \frac{\text{Distance}}{\text{Time}} = \frac{20\text{ km}}{\frac{1}{2}\text{ hour}} = 40$ km/h

Exercise 23

1 Draw and label x and y axes from -5 to 4.
(a) On your diagram plot $A(4, 3)$ and $B(-5, -3)$.
(b) $C(p, -1)$ is on the line segment AB.
What is the value of p?

2 (a) Copy and complete the table of values for $y = 1 - 2x$.

x	-3	0	3
y		1	

(b) Draw the line $y = 1 - 2x$ for values of x from -3 to 3.
(c) Use your graph to find the value of y when $x = -1.5$.

3 On the same diagram, draw and label the lines: $y = x + 1$ and $y = 1 - x$. AQA

4 (a) On the same axes, draw the graphs of $y = -2$, $y = x$ and $x + y = 5$.
(b) Which of these lines has a negative gradient?

5 The diagram shows a sketch of the line $2y = 6 - x$.
(a) Find the coordinates of the points P and Q.
(b) The line $2y = 6 - x$ goes through $R(-5, m)$.
What is the value of m?

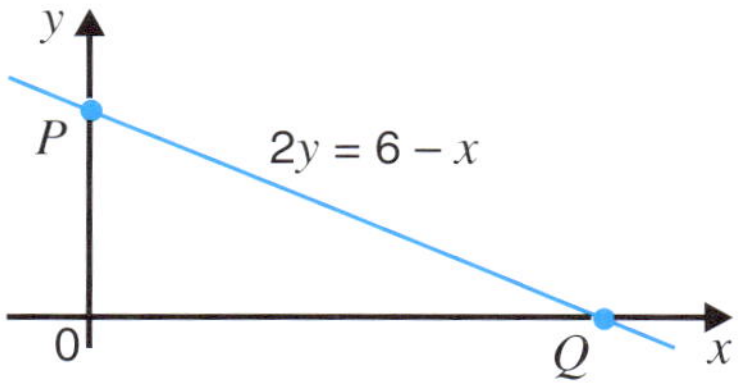

6 Points A, B and C are shown on the grid.
(a) Write down the equation of the line AB.
(b) (i) Use the grid to work out the gradient of the line CB.
(ii) Write down the equation of the line CB.

AQA

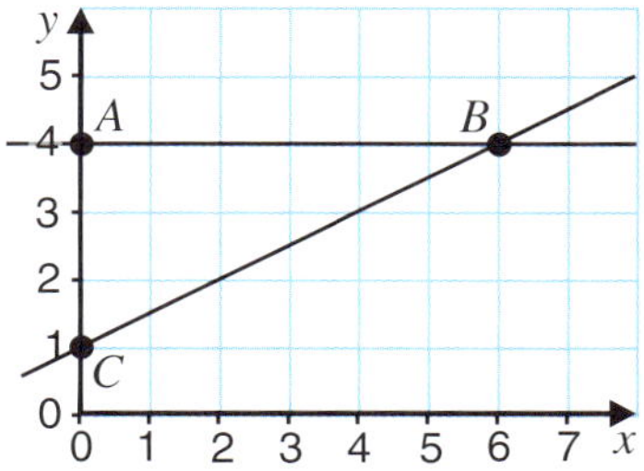

7 Match these equations to their graphs.

1 $y = 2x$
2 $y - x = 2$
3 $y + x = 2$
4 $2y = x$

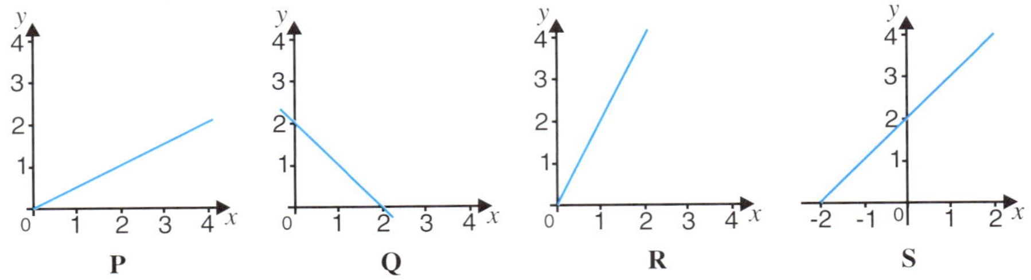

8 (a) Copy and complete the table of values for $2y = 3x - 6$.

x	-2	0	4
y		-3	

(b) Draw the graph of $2y = 3x - 6$ for values of x from -2 to 4.
(c) What is the gradient of the line $2y = 3x - 6$?
(d) Use your graph to find the value of x when $y = 1.5$.

9 The equation of a line is $5y - 2x = 10$.
(a) Write this equation in the form $y = mx + c$.
(b) Write down the equation of the line, parallel to $5y - 2x = 10$, which passes through the point $(0, -1)$.

10 The table shows the largest quantity of salt, w grams, which can be dissolved in a beaker of water at temperature t°C.

t°C	10	20	25	30	40	50	60
w grams	54	58	60	62	66	70	74

(a) Draw a graph to illustrate this information.
(b) Use your graph to find
(i) the lowest temperature at which 63 g of salt will dissolve in the water,
(ii) the largest amount of salt that will dissolve in the water at 44°C.
(c) (i) The equation of the graph is of the form $w = at + b$.
Use your graph to estimate the values of the constants a and b.
(ii) Use the equation to calculate the largest amount of salt which will dissolve in the water at 95°C. AQA

11 The straight line on the graph shows how the monthly pay of a salesman depends on his sales.

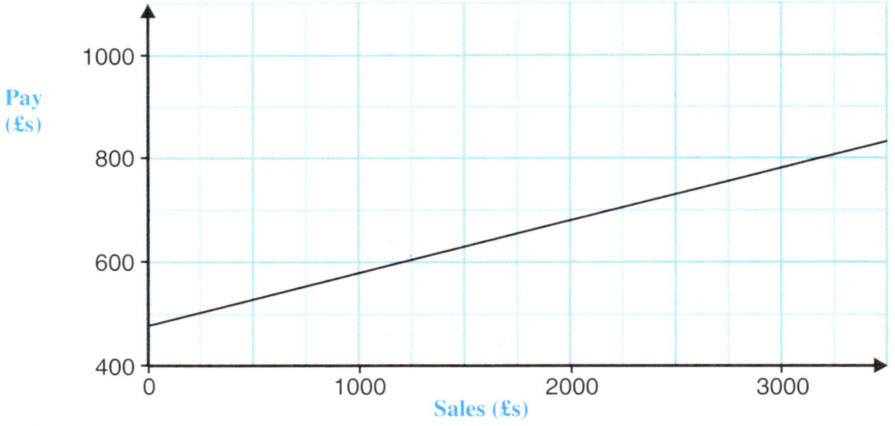

(a) Find the equation of the line in the form $y = mx + c$.
(b) Calculate the monthly pay of the salesman when his sales are £5400. AQA

12 The distance by boat from Poole Quay to Wareham is 12 miles.
The distance-time graph shows a boat trip from Poole Quay to Wareham and back.

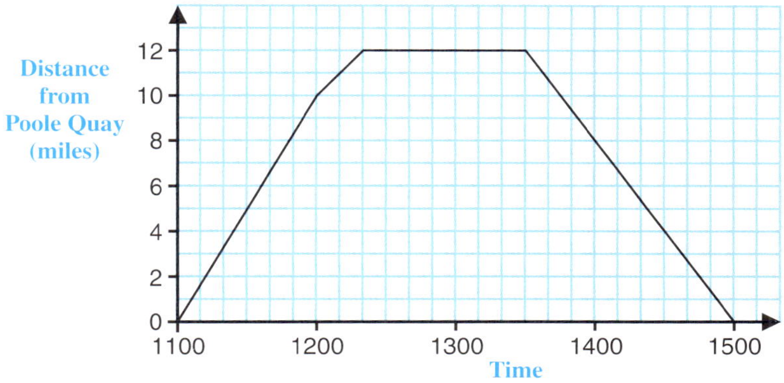

(a) Describe what happened to the speed of the boat at 1200 hours.
(b) How long did the boat stay in Wareham?
(c) What was the average speed of the boat on the return journey from Wareham to Poole Quay?

AQA

13 Ken drives from his home to the city centre.
The graph represents his journey.

(a) How long did Ken take to reach the city centre?
(b) How far from the city centre does Ken live?
(c) What is his average speed for the journey in kilometres per hour?

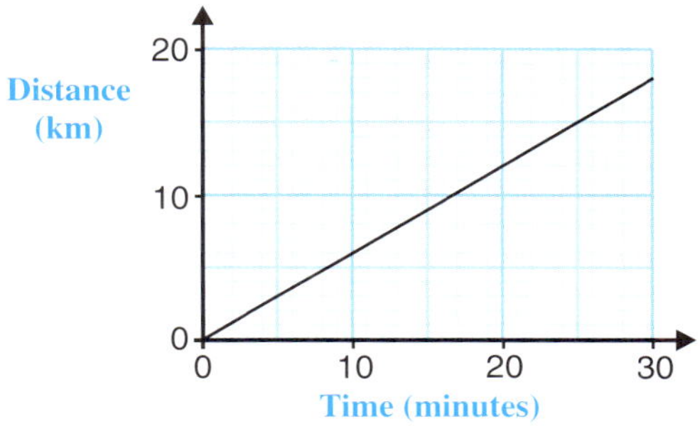

14 A coach leaves Gateshead at 0830 to travel to London.
It completes the first 270 km of the journey at 90 km/hour before stopping at a service station.
The coach stops at the service station for 30 minutes.
After leaving the service station the coach travels a further 180 km, arriving in London at 1500.

(a) Draw a distance-time graph for the coach journey.
Use a scale of 2 cm for 1 hour on the horizontal axis and 1 cm for 50 km on the vertical axis.
(b) What is the average speed of the coach from the service station to London?

Travis leaves London at 1000 and travels by car to Gateshead on the same route.

(c) Travis gets to the service station as the coach is about to leave.
At what average speed is Travis driving?

15 Water is poured at a constant rate into each of the three containers shown.

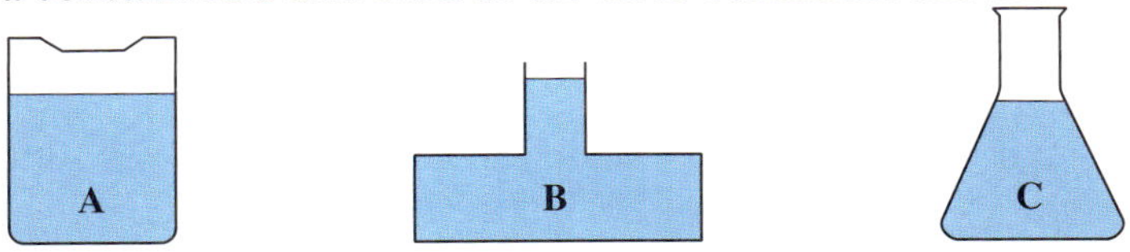

The graphs show the height of water in the containers as they are being filled.

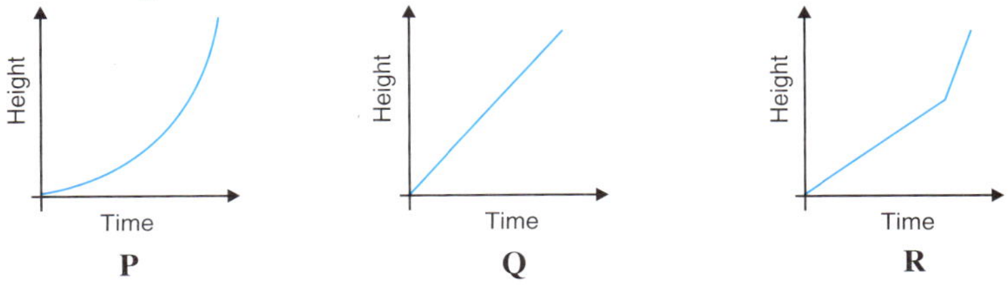

Write down the letter of the graph that matches each container.

AQA

SECTION 24

Simultaneous Equations

What you need to know

- A pair of **simultaneous equations** has the same unknown letters in each equation.
- To solve a pair of simultaneous equations find values for the unknown letters that fit **both** equations.
- Simultaneous equations can be solved either **graphically** or **algebraically**.
- Solving simultaneous equations **graphically** involves:
  drawing the graphs of both equations,
  finding the point where the graphs cross.

  When the graphs of both equations are parallel, the equations have no solution.

Eg 1 Solve the simultaneous equations $x + 2y = 5$ and $x - 2y = 1$ graphically.

For $x + 2y = 5$:
When $x = 1$, $y = 2$.
When $x = 5$, $y = 0$.
Draw a line through the points (1, 2) and (5, 0).

For $x - 2y = 1$:
When $x = 1$, $y = 0$.
When $x = 5$, $y = 2$.
Draw a line through the points (1, 0) and (5, 2).

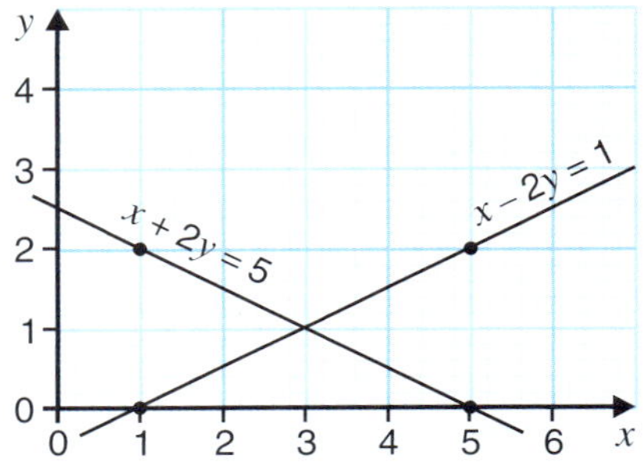

The values of x and y at the point where the lines cross give the solution to the simultaneous equations.
The lines cross at the point (3, 1). This gives the solution $x = 3$ and $y = 1$.

- Solving simultaneous equations **algebraically** involves using either:
  the **elimination** method, or
  the **substitution** method.

Eg 2 Solve the simultaneous equations $5x + 2y = 11$ and $3x - 4y = 4$ algebraically.

$5x + 2y = 11$ A
$3x - 4y = 4$ B

> To make the number of y's the same we can multiply equation A by 2.

A × 2 gives $10x + 4y = 22$ C
$3x - 4y = 4$ D

> The number of y's is the **same** but the **signs** are **different**. To eliminate the y's the equations must be **added**.

C + D gives $13x = 26$
$x = 2$

Substitute $x = 2$ into $5x + 2y = 11$.
$10 + 2y = 11$
$2y = 1$
$y = 0.5$

The solution is $x = 2$ and $y = 0.5$.

> You can check the solution by substituting $x = 2$ and $y = 0.5$ into $3x - 4y = 4$.

- You should be able to find solutions to problems which involve forming and then solving simultaneous equations.

Exercise 24

1 (a) On the same axes, draw the graphs of $y = 2x$ and $y = 6 - x$.
(b) Explain how you could use your graphs to solve the equation $2x = 6 - x$.

2 The graph of the equation $3y = x + 1$ is drawn on the grid.
Copy the diagram.

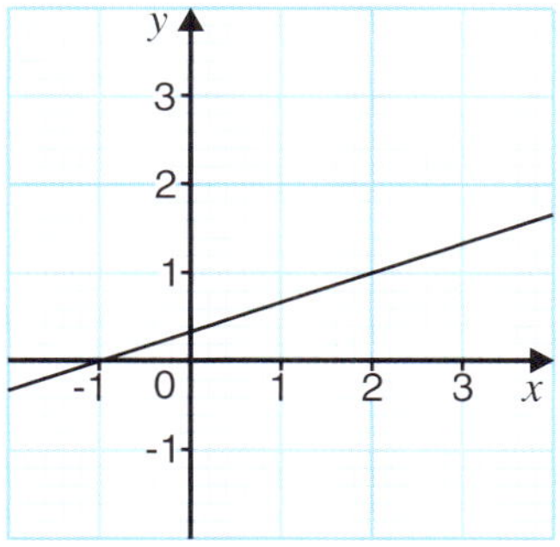

(a) On your diagram, draw the graph of the equation $y = 1 - x$.
(b) Use your graphs to solve the simultaneous equations $y = 1 - x$ and $3y = x + 1$.

AQA

3 (a) On the same axes, draw the graphs of $y + x = 4$ and $y - 3x = 2$ for values of x from -2 to 2.
(b) Hence, solve the simultaneous equations $y + x = 4$ and $y - 3x = 2$.

4 Solve graphically the simultaneous equations $y = 3 - x$ and $y = x - 2$.

5 (a) Draw the graph of $2y = 3x - 6$ and $2y = 6 - x$, on the same axes.
(b) Solve the simultaneous equations: $2y = 3x - 6$ and $2y = 6 - x$.
AQA

6 The sketch shows the graph of $y = 2x - 1$.
Copy the diagram.

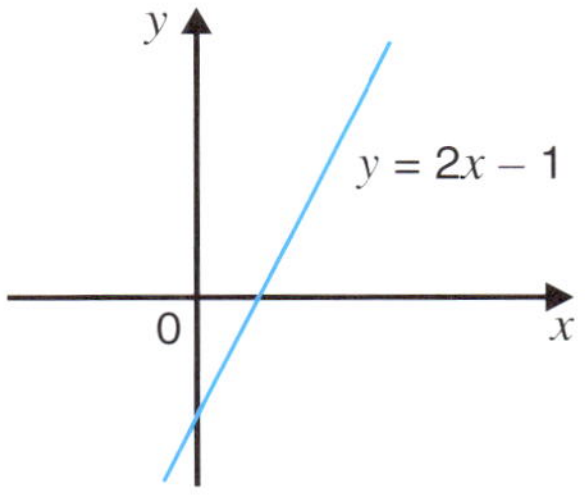

(a) On your diagram, sketch the graph of $y = 2x + 1$.
(b) Explain why the equations $y = 2x - 1$ and $y = 2x + 1$ cannot be solved simultaneously.

7 Solve these simultaneous equations.
$$6x + y = 15$$
$$8x - y = 6$$
AQA

8 Solve the simultaneous equations $x + 3y = 13$ and $4x + 2y = 2$.

9 Solve the simultaneous equations.
$$2x + y = 2$$
$$4x - 3y = 9$$
AQA

10 Heather sold 40 boxes of cards to raise money for charity.
She sold x small boxes at £4 each and y large boxes at £7 each.
She raised £184 altogether.
(a) Write down two equations connecting x and y.
(b) Solve these simultaneous equations to find how many of each size of box she sold.

11 Micro-scooters costs £x each and pogo sticks cost £y each.
2 micro-scooters and 4 pogo sticks cost £65.
1 micro-scooter and 3 pogo sticks cost £40.
(a) Write down two equations connecting x and y.
(b) Solve these simultaneous equations to find the cost of a micro-scooter and a pogo stick.

12 Solve these simultaneous equations. $4x - 3y = 17$ and $6x - 4y = 23$ AQA

13 Solve the simultaneous equations. $4x - 3y = 11$ and $6x + 2y = 10$ AQA

SECTION 25

More or Less

What you need to know

- **Inequalities** can be described using words or numbers and symbols.

Sign	Meaning
$<$	is less than
$\leqslant$	is less than or equal to

Sign	Meaning
$>$	is greater than
$\geqslant$	is greater than or equal to

- Inequalities can be shown on a **number line**.

Eg 1 This diagram shows the inequality: $-2 < x \leqslant 3$

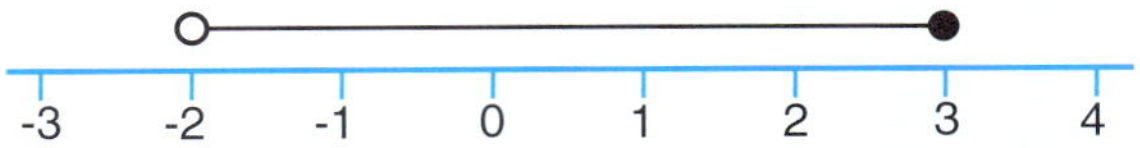

The circle is: **filled** if the inequality is **included** (i.e. $\leqslant$ or $\geqslant$),
not filled if the inequality is **not included** (i.e. $<$ or $>$).

- **Solving inequalities** means finding the values of x which make the inequality true.

The same rules for equations can be applied to inequalities, with one exception:
When you **multiply** (or **divide**) both sides of an inequality by a negative number the inequality is reversed. For example, if $-3x < 6$ then $x > -2$.

Eg 2 Solve these inequalities.

(a) $7a \geqslant a + 9$
$6a \geqslant 9$
$a \geqslant 1.5$

(b) $-3x < 6$
$x > -2$

Divide both sides by -3.
Because we are dividing by a negative number the inequality is reversed.

Eg 3 Find the integer values of n for which $-1 \leqslant 2n + 3 < 7$.

$-1 \leqslant 2n + 3 < 7$
$-4 \leqslant 2n < 4$
$-2 \leqslant n < 2$

Integer values which satisfy the inequality $-1 \leqslant 2n + 3 < 7$ are: $-2, -1, 0, 1$

- Inequalities can be shown on a graph. A line divides the graph into two **regions**.

To show an inequality on a graph: Replace the inequality by '=' and draw the line.
For $>$ and $<$ the line is **broken**. For $\geqslant$ and $\leqslant$ the line is **solid**.
Test a point on each side of the line to see whether its coordinates satisfy the inequality.
Label the required region.

Eg 4 Show the region which satisfies these inequalities:
$y < 3$, $1 < x < 4$ and $2y > x$.

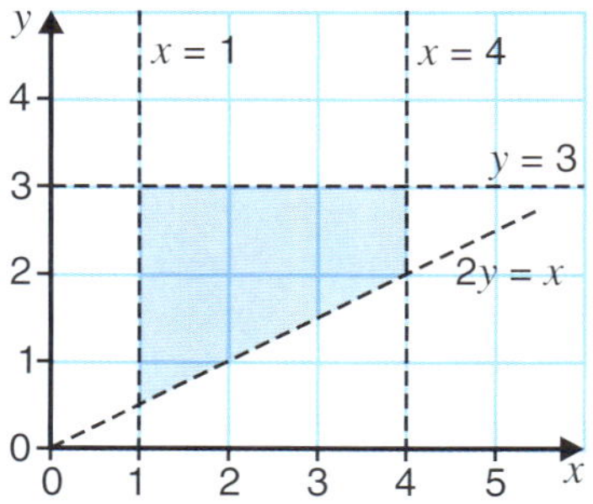

Eg 5 Use inequalities to describe the shaded region in this diagram.

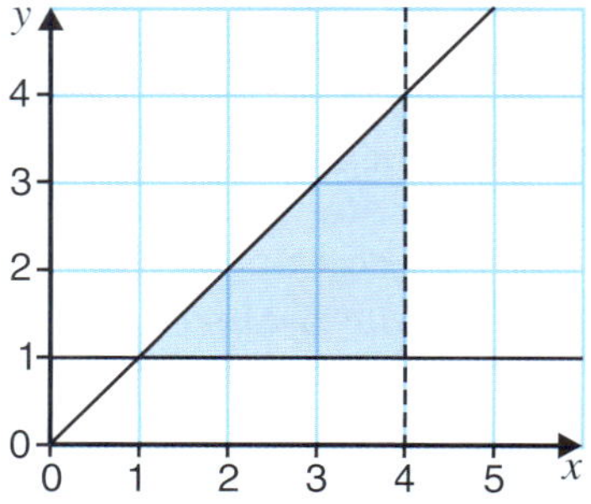

$x < 4$, $y \geqslant 1$ and $y \leqslant x$.

Exercise 25

1 Solve these inequalities.
(a) $5x > 15$ (b) $x + 3 \geqslant 1$ (c) $2x \leqslant 6 - x$ (d) $3 - 2x > 7$

2 Draw number lines to show each of these inequalities.
(a) $x \geqslant -2$ (b) $\frac{x}{3} < -1$ (c) $-1 < x \leqslant 3$ (d) $x \leqslant -1$ **and** $x > 3$

3 List the values of n, where n is an integer such that:
(a) $-2 \leqslant 2n < 6$ (b) $-3 < n - 3 \leqslant -1$ (c) $-5 \leqslant 2n - 3 < 1$

4 Solve the inequalities. (a) $2x - 5 > x + 2$ (b) $-9 < 5x + 1 \leqslant 6$

5 Solve the inequality $x + 20 < 12 - 3x$. AQA

6 Solve the inequality $3(x - 2) < x + 7$. AQA

7 Match each of the inequalities to its **unshaded** region.

1 $x + y < 2$
2 $y > 2$
3 $y > x$
4 $x < 2$

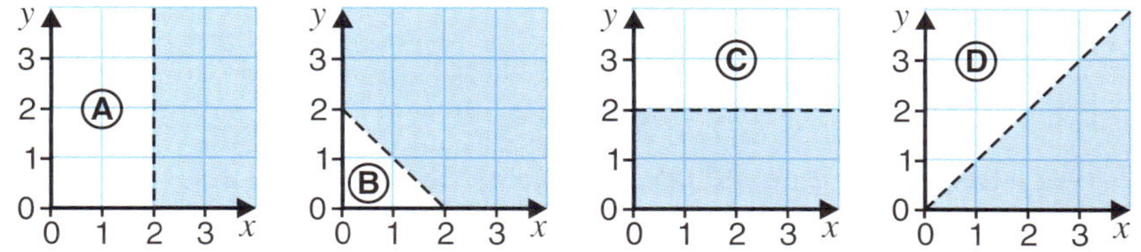

8 Draw and label axes for both x and y from 0 to 5.
(a) On your diagram draw and label the lines $x = 1$ and $x + y = 4$.
(b) Show clearly on the diagram the single region that is satisfied by all of these inequalities.
$y \geqslant 0$ $x \geqslant 1$ $x + y \leqslant 4$. Label this region R. AQA

9 (a) Draw and label axes for x from -1 to 6 and for y from -2 to 6.
On your diagram draw and label the following lines. $y = 2x$ and $x + y = 5$
(b) Show clearly the single region that is satisfied by **all** of these inequalities.
$x + y \leqslant 5$ $y \geqslant 2x$ $x \geqslant 0$. Label this region R. AQA

10 Write down three inequalities which describe the shaded region.

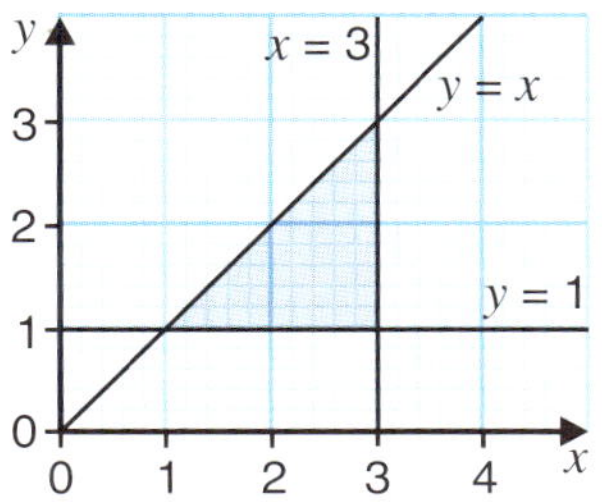

AQA

11 (a) x is an integer such that $-4 \leqslant x < 2$.
(i) Make a list of all the possible values of x.
(ii) What is the largest possible value of x^2?
(b) Every week Rucci has a test in Mathematics. It is marked out of 20.
Rucci has always scored at least half the marks available.
She has never quite managed to score full marks.
Using x to represent Rucci's marks, write this information in the form of two inequalities.
AQA

12 (a) Solve each of the following inequalities. (i) $5x - 4 \leqslant 2x + 8$ (ii) $2(2x - 1) > 6$
(b) Write down the whole number values of x which satisfy both of the above inequalities simultaneously. AQA

13 Solve the following inequalities. (a) $2 > x - 4$ (b) $2(x + 3) > 3(2 - x)$ AQA

SECTION 26

Quadratic and Other Equations

What you need to know

- Brackets, such as $(x + 2)(x + 3)$, can be multiplied out using the **diagram method**, or by **expanding**.

Eg 1 Multiply out $(x + 2)(x + 3)$.

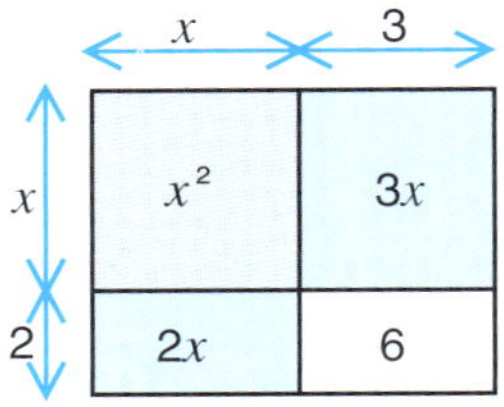

$(x + 2)(x + 3) = x^2 + 3x + 2x + 6$
$= x^2 + 5x + 6$

Eg 2 Expand $(x - 3)(2x + 1)$.

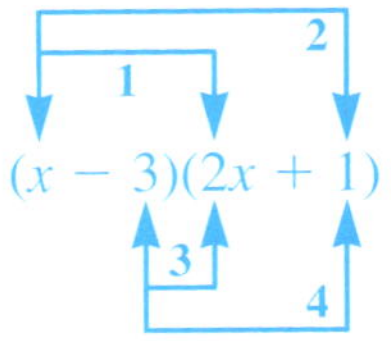

1 $x \times 2x = 2x^2$
2 $x \times 1 = x$
3 $-3 \times 2x = -6x$
4 $-3 \times 1 = -3$

$(x - 3)(2x + 1) = 2x^2 + x - 6x - 3$
$= 2x^2 - 5x - 3$

- **Factorising** is the opposite operation to removing brackets.

Eg 3 Factorise the following.
(a) $x^2 + 3x = x(x + 3)$
(b) $x^2 - 25 = (x - 5)(x + 5)$
(c) $x^2 + 3x - 10 = (x + 5)(x - 2)$

When factorising, work logically.
1. Does the expression have a **common factor**?
2. Is the expression a **difference of two squares**?
$a^2 - b^2 = (a - b)(a + b)$
3. Will the expression factorise into **two brackets**?

- To write an algebraic fraction in its **simplest form**:
factorise the numerator and denominator of the fraction,
divide the numerator and denominator by their highest common factor.

Eg 4 Simplify. (a) $\frac{5x - 10}{5} = \frac{5(x - 2)}{5} = x - 2$ (b) $\frac{2x - 4}{x^2 - 2x} = \frac{2(x - 2)}{x(x - 2)} = \frac{2}{x}$

- **Quadratic equations** can be solved by factorising.

Eg 5 Solve these equations.
(a) $x^2 - 5x = 0$
$x(x - 5) = 0$
$x = 0$ or $x = 5$
(b) $a^2 - 4a + 3 = 0$
$(a - 1)(a - 3) = 0$
$a = 1$ or $a = 3$
(c) $m^2 + m - 6 = 0$
$(m - 2)(m + 3) = 0$
$m = 2$ or $m = -3$

- **Quadratic equations** can be solved graphically.

Eg 6 (a) Draw the graph of $y = x^2 - 2x - 5$ for values of x from -2 to 4.
(b) Use your graph to solve the equation $x^2 - 2x - 5 = 0$.

(a)

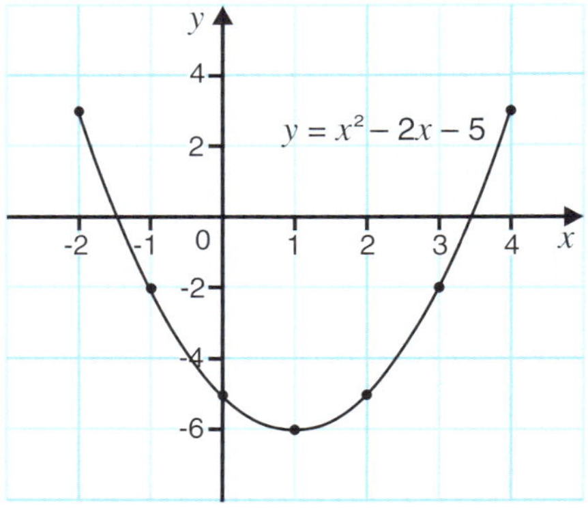

To draw a quadratic graph:
Make a table of values connecting x and y.
Plot the points.
Join the points with a smooth curve.

x	-2	-1	0	1	2	3	4
y	3	-2	-5	-6	-5	-2	3

To solve the equation, read the values of x where the graph of $y = x^2 - 2x - 5$ crosses the x axis ($y = 0$).

(b) $x = -1.4$ and 3.4, correct to one decimal place.

- The general form for a **quadratic function** is $y = ax^2 + bx + c$, where a cannot be zero. The graph of a quadratic function is symmetrical and has a **maximum** or **minimum** value.

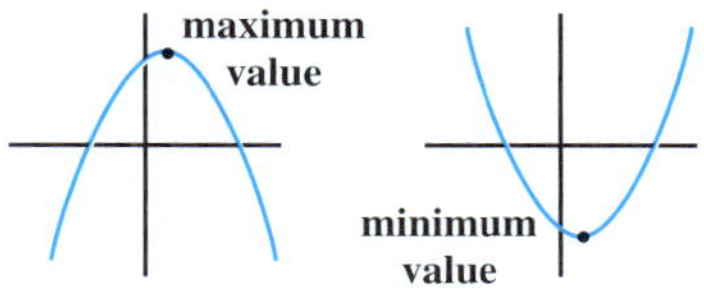

- The general form of a **cubic function** is $y = ax^3 + bx^2 + cx + d$, where a cannot be zero. **Cubic equations** can be solved graphically or by trial and improvement.
- **Trial and improvement** is a method used to solve equations. The accuracy of the value of the unknown letter is improved until the required degree of accuracy is obtained.

Eg 7 Use a trial and improvement method to find a solution to the equation $x^3 + x = 40$, correct to one decimal place.

x	$x^3 + x$	Comment
3	$27 + 3 = 30$	Too small
4	$64 + 4 = 68$	Too big
3.5	$42.8\ldots + 3.5 = 46.3\ldots$	Too big
3.3	$35.9\ldots + 3.3 = 39.2\ldots$	Too small
3.35	$37.5\ldots + 3.35 = 40.9\ldots$	Too big

For accuracy to 1 d.p. check the second decimal place. The solution lies between 3.3 and 3.35.

$x = 3.3$, correct to 1 d.p.

Exercise 26

1 Multiply out and simplify.
(a) $x(x - 7)$ (b) $(x - 2)(x + 5)$ (c) $(x + 3)(x - 5)$ (d) $(2x - 1)(x + 3)$

2 (a) (i) Multiply out $4x(x + 3)$.
(ii) Multiply out and simplify $(2x + 3)(2x + 3)$.
(b) Four identical rectangular tiles are placed around a square tile as shown in the diagram. Find the area of the square tile.

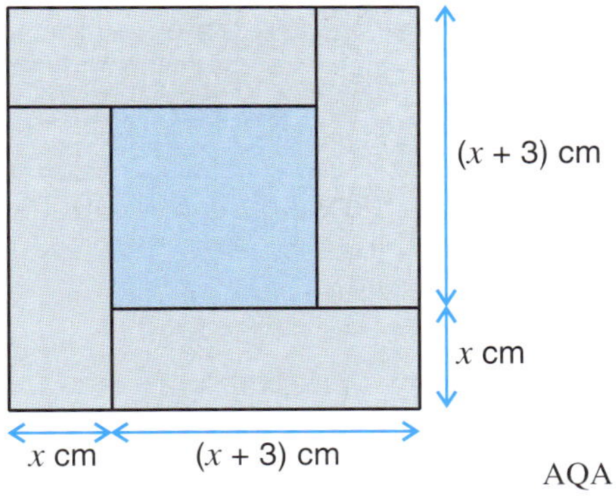

AQA

3 Expand and simplify $(3x + 2y)^2$.

4 Factorise.
(a) $x^2 - 6x$ (b) $x^2 + 6x + 9$ (c) $x^2 + 2x - 15$ (d) $x^2 - 4x + 3$

5 Factorise $x^2 - 9$.

6 Simplify. (a) $\dfrac{3a + 12}{3}$ (b) $\dfrac{x^2 - 3x}{x}$ (c) $\dfrac{x^2 + 2x}{5x + 10}$ (d) $\dfrac{2x^2 - 6x}{4x - 12}$

7 Solve these equations.
(a) $x(x + 5) = 0$ (b) $(x - 3)(x + 2) = 0$ (c) $(2x + 3)(x - 1) = 0$

8 (a) Factorise $a^2 - 2a - 8$. (b) Solve $y^2 + 4y = 0$. AQA

9 (a) Factorise $x^2 - x - 12$.
(b) Hence solve the equation $x^2 - x - 12 = 0$. AQA

10 Solve these equations.
(a) $x^2 - 3x = 0$ (b) $x^2 - 3x + 2 = 0$ (c) $x^2 - x - 6 = 0$

11 Solve the equation $x^2 - 11x + 28 = 0$.

12 (a) Factorise $2x^2 - 5x - 3 = 0$.
(b) Hence solve the equation $2x^2 - 5x - 3 = 0$.

13 Match these equations to their graphs.

1 $y = 1 - x^2$
2 $y = x^3$
3 $y = x^2 - 1$
4 $y = 1 - 2x$

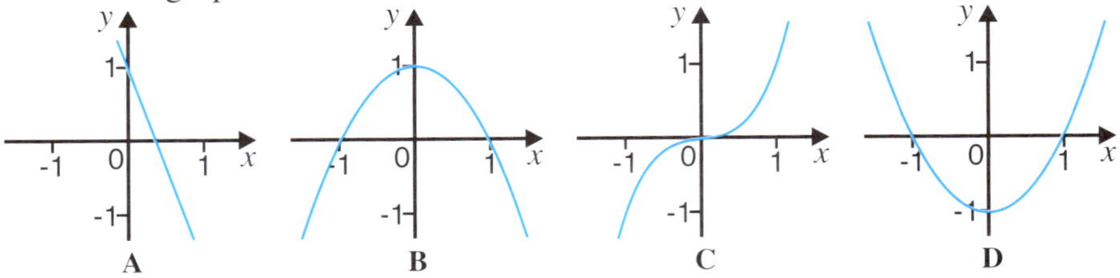

14 (a) Draw the graph for $y = 5 - x^2$ for values of x from -3 to 3.
(b) State the maximum value of y.
(c) Use your graph to solve the equation $5 - x^2 = 0$.

15 (a) Copy and complete the table of values for $y = 2x^2 - 3x + 2$.

x	-2	-1	0	1	2	3
y	16		2		4	

(b) Draw the graph of $y = 2x^2 - 3x + 2$ for values of x from -2 to 3.
(c) Explain how the graph shows that there are no values of x for which $2x^2 - 3x + 2 = 0$.
(d) State the minimum value of y.

16 A sky diver jumps from a plane. The table shows the distance he falls, d metres, in t seconds.

t (seconds)	0	0.5	1.5	2.5	3.5
d (metres)	0	1	11	31	61

(a) Plot these points and join them with a smooth curve.
(b) Use your graph to find how many seconds he takes to fall 50 m.
(c) Use your graph to estimate how far he has fallen after 4 seconds. AQA

17 (a) Draw the graph of $y = x^3 - x$ for $-3 \leqslant x \leqslant 3$.
(b) Use your graph to find the value of x when $y = 10$.
(c) Use your graph to solve the equation $x^3 - x = 0$.

18 Draw the graph of $y = \frac{1}{x}$ for values of x from -4 to 4.

19 The dimensions of a rectangle are shown.
The rectangle has an area of 32 cm².
Form an equation, in terms of x, for the area of the rectangle.
Show that it can be written in the form $x^2 + 2x - 35 = 0$.

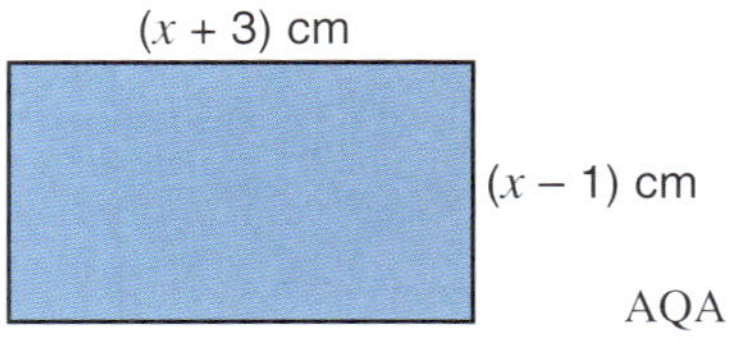

AQA

20 Aisha is using trial and improvement to find a solution to the equation $x^3 - 2x = 14$.
The table shows her first try.

x	$x^3 - 2x$	Comment
2	4	too small

Copy and continue the table to find a solution to the equation, correct to 1 decimal place. AQA

Section Review - Algebra

1 Simplify (a) $7x - 5x + 3x$, (b) $a - 3b + 2a - b$, (c) $3 \times m \times m$.

2 In this 'algebraic' magic square, every row, column and diagonal should add up and simplify to $15a + 12b + 6c$.

(a) Copy and complete the magic square.

(b) Calculate the value of $15a + 12b + 6c$ if $a = 1$, $b = 2$ and $c = 3$.

$8a + 5b + 5c$	$a + 6b - 2c$	$6a + b + 3c$
	$5a + 4b + 2c$	$7a + 8b + 4c$
$4a + 7b + c$		$2a + 3b - c$

AQA

3 (a) Find the value of $\frac{3(m + 9)}{n}$ when $m = -5$ and $n = 24$.

(b) Find the value of $3p + q$ when $p = -2$ and $q = 5$.

4 (a) On graph paper, plot the points $A(-3, -2)$ and $B(1, 4)$.
(b) What are the coordinates of the midpoint of AB?

5 A jam doughnut costs t pence.
(a) Write an expression for the cost of 5 jam doughnuts.

A cream doughnut costs 5 pence more than a jam doughnut.
(b) Write an expression for the cost of a cream doughnut.

6 Solve (a) $x - 3 = 7$, (b) $3x = 6$, (c) $5x + 4 = 19$.

7 Nick thinks of a number.
He doubles it and then subtracts 3. The answer is 17.
What is his number?

8 (a) What is the next term in this sequence? 2, 9, 16, 23, ...
(b) Will the 50th term in the sequence be an odd number or an even number?
Give a reason for your answer.

9 A sequence begins: 1, 2, 6, 16, ...
This is the rule continuing the sequence.

ADD THE PREVIOUS TWO NUMBERS TOGETHER AND THEN MULTIPLY BY TWO

Deepak says the next term in the sequence is 22.
Is he correct? **Explain your answer.** AQA

10 Here is a rule for working out a sequence of numbers.

Choose a starting number S → **Multiply by 3** → **Subtract 4** → **Write down the final number F.**

Write down an **equation** connecting the final number, F, and the starting number, S. AQA

11 (a) Draw the line $y = 2x + 1$ for values of x from -1 to 2.
(b) The line $y = 2x + 1$ crosses the line $x = -5$ at P.
Give the coordinates of P.

12 Solve (a) $x + 7 = 4$, (b) $4x = 10$, (c) $2x + 5 = 11$.

13 I think of a number. If I double my number and add 1, my answer is 35.
(a) Write down an equation to describe this.
(b) What number am I thinking of? AQA

14 (a) Simplify $3n - n + 5$.
(b) Work out the value of $2x + y^3$ when $x = -3$ and $y = 2$. AQA

15 Here is a flow diagram.

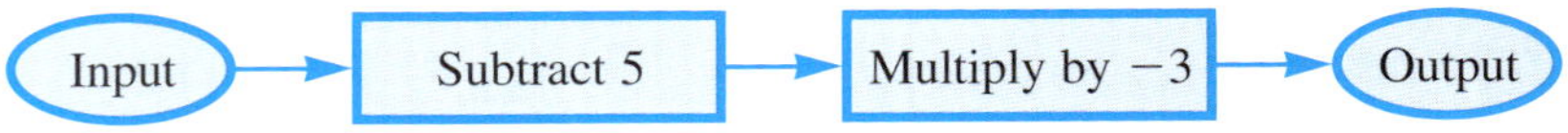

(a) What is the output when the input is 3?
(b) What is the input when the output is −21? AQA

16 The travel graph shows the journey of a train from London to Manchester.
Calculate the average speed of the train in miles per hour.

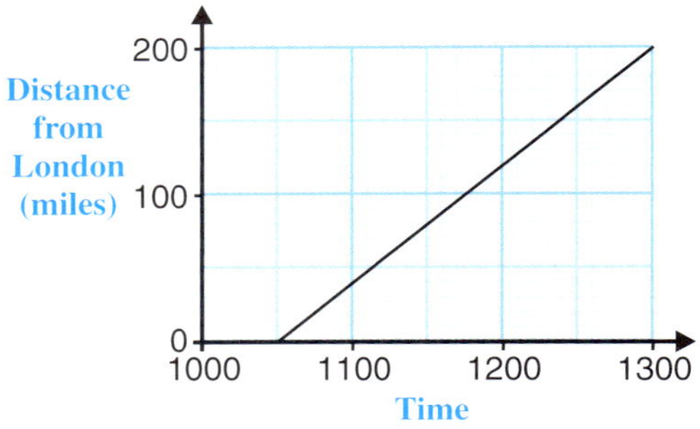

AQA

17 Find the value of $3x + y^3$ when $x = -1$ and $y = -2$.

18 Hannah is x years old.
(a) Her sister Louisa is 3 years younger than Hannah.
Write an expression, in terms of x, for Louisa's age.
(b) Their mother is four times as old as Hannah.
Write an expression, in terms of x, for their mother's age.
(c) The total of their ages is 45 years.
By forming an equation in x, find their ages.

19 (a) Solve the equations (i) $4(a - 2) = 6$, (ii) $5t + 3 = -1 + t$.
(b) The sum of the numbers x, $x - 3$ and $x + 7$ is 25.
By forming an equation in x, find the value of x.

20 Part of a number grid is shown.
The shaded shape is called $\mathbf{P}_2$ because it has the number 2 in the top left-hand corner.
The sum of the numbers in $\mathbf{P}_2$ is 17.

1	2	3	4	5	6	7	8	9	10
11	12	13	14	15	16	17	18	19	20
21	22	23	24	25	26	27	28	29	30

(a) Calculate the sum of the numbers in $\mathbf{P}_{14}$.
(b) Copy and complete the shape $\mathbf{P}_n$.

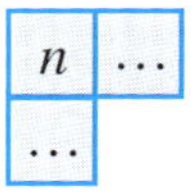

(c) Write down an expression, in terms of n, for the sum of the numbers in $\mathbf{P}_n$.
Simplify your expression.
(d) If the sum of the numbers in $\mathbf{P}_n$ is 149, find the value of n. AQA

21 (a) Factorise (i) $3a - 6$, (ii) $k^2 - 2k$.
(b) Multiply out (i) $5(x + 3)$, (ii) $m(m - 4)$.
(c) Solve (i) $\frac{3x + 5}{2} = 7$, (ii) $3(2x + 1) = 6$.

22 (a) On the same diagram draw the graphs $2y = x + 4$ and $y = \frac{1}{2}x + 1$.
(b) What do you notice about the two lines you have drawn?

23 A pencil costs x pence. A crayon costs $x + 3$ pence.
(a) Write an expression in terms of x for the cost of 5 crayons.

One pencil and 5 crayons cost 87 pence.
(b) By forming an equation in x, find the cost of the pencil. AQA

24 (a) Simplify $3(x - 2) + 5$.
(b) Solve $3 - 4x = x + 8$.

25 The graph shows the journey of a group of walkers.

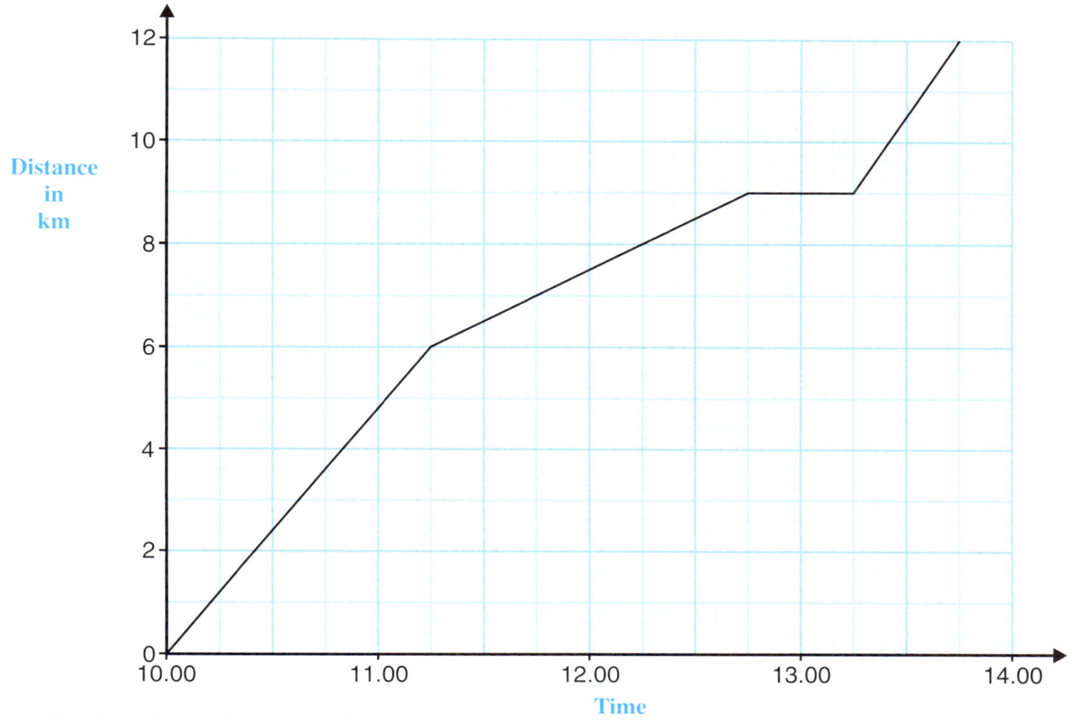

(a) For how long did the walkers stop?
(b) What was the speed for the first part of the journey?
(c) The slowest part of the journey was across boggy ground.
How far did they walk across the boggy ground?
(d) What was the average speed for the whole journey?

AQA

26 (a) This rule is used to produce a sequence of numbers.

MULTIPLY THE LAST NUMBER BY 3 AND SUBTRACT 1.

The second number in the sequence is 20. What is the first number?
(b) Another sequence begins 2, 5, 8, 11, …
(i) One number in the sequence is x.
Write, in terms of x, the next number in the sequence.
(ii) Write, in terms of n, the nth term of the sequence.

AQA

27 (a) Copy and complete the table of values for $y = x^2 - 3$.

x	-2	-1	0	1	2	3
y		-2	-3			6

(b) Draw the graph of $y = x^2 - 3$ for values of x from -2 to 3.
(c) Use your graph to solve the equation $x^2 - 3 = 0$.

28 Matches are arranged to form a sequence of diagrams as shown.

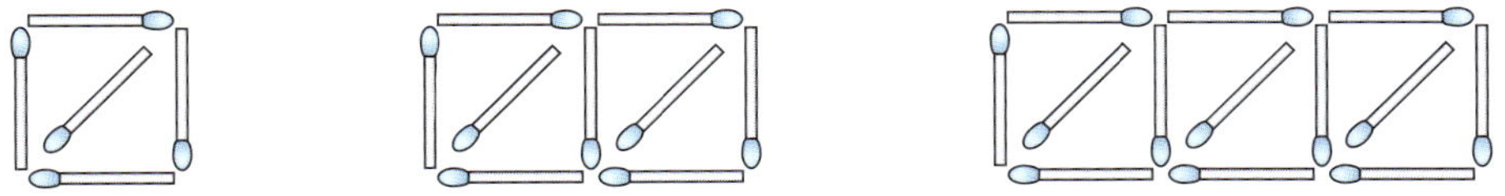

Diagram 1 **Diagram 2** **Diagram 3**

Write an expression, in terms of n, for the number of matches needed to form the nth diagram.

AQA

29 Use trial and improvement to find the solution to the equation $x^3 - 3x = 9$.

x	$x^3 - 3x$	Comment
2	2	Too low
3	18	Too high

Copy and complete the table. Give your answer to one decimal place. AQA

30 (a) Solve the inequality $3x < 6 - x$.
(b) List all the values of n, where n is an integer, such that $-3 < 2x + 1 \leqslant 3$.

31 Match these equations to their graphs.

A $y = x$
B $y + x = 1$
C $y = x^2$
D $y = x^3$

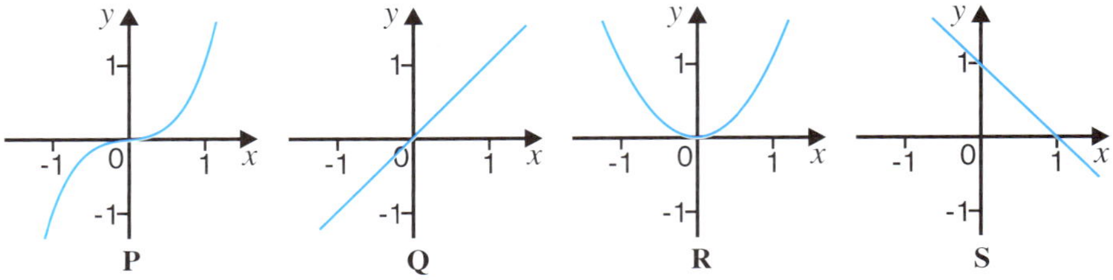

32 (a) Solve the equation $x - 4 = 3(x + 1)$.
(b) Simplify $5y^3 \times 3y^5$. AQA

33 (a) A sequence begins: -2, 1, 4, 7, 10, …
Write, in terms of n, the nth term of the sequence.
(b) Make x the subject of the formula $y = 2x - 5$.

34 (a) Write down the equations of the lines labelled **A**, **B** and **C** in the diagram.
(b) Write down three inequalities to describe the shaded region.

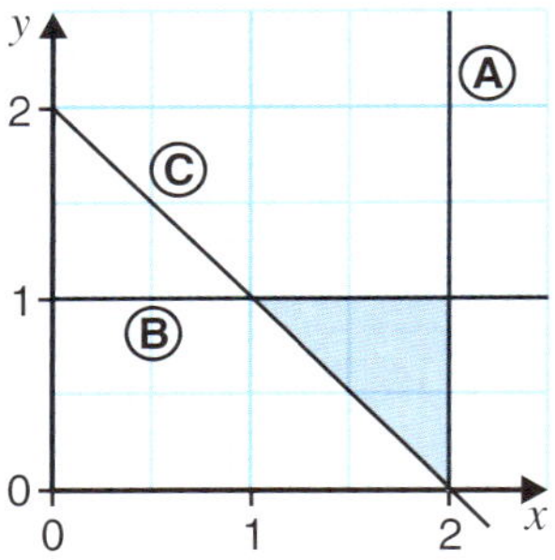

35 (a) Draw the graph of $y = x^2 - 2x + 1$ for values of x from -1 to 3.
(b) Use your graph to solve the equation $x^2 - 2x + 1 = 0$.
(c) Use your graph to solve the equation $x^2 - 2x + 1 = 2$.

36 Water is poured into some containers at a constant rate.
Copy the axes given and sketch the graph of the depth of the water against time for each container as it is filled.

(a)

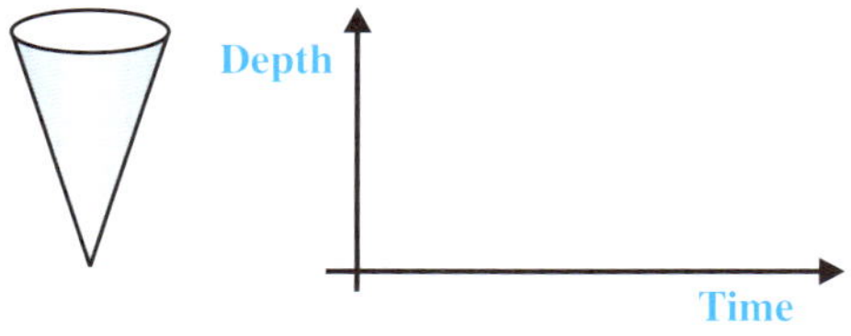

(b)

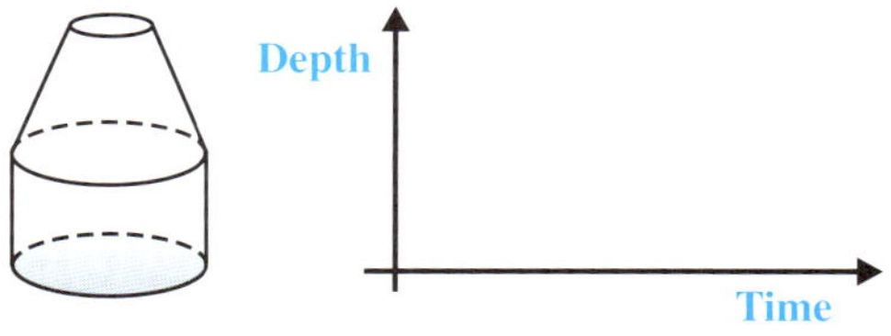

37 (a) Work out the value of $x^2 - 5x + 6$ when $x = -2$.
(b) (i) Factorise $x^2 - 5x + 6$.
(ii) Hence solve the equation $x^2 - 5x + 6 = 0$.

38 (a) Factorise (i) $2st - 4t$, (ii) $3y^2 + 6y$, (iii) $d^2 - 2d - 24$.
(b) Solve the equations (i) $x(x + 2) = 0$, (ii) $y^2 - 3y + 2 = 0$.

39 (a) Find the gradients of these lines.

(i)

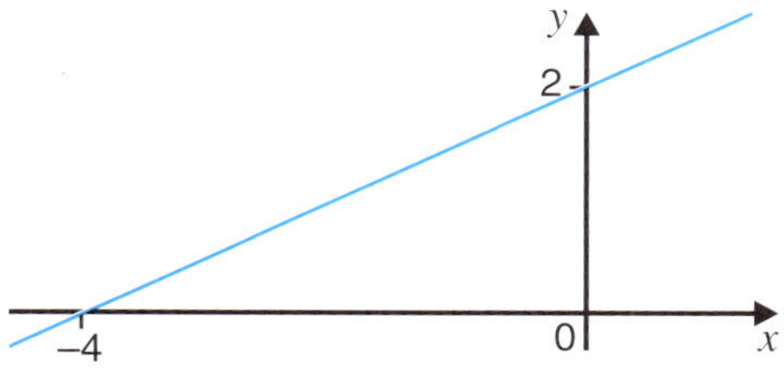

(ii)

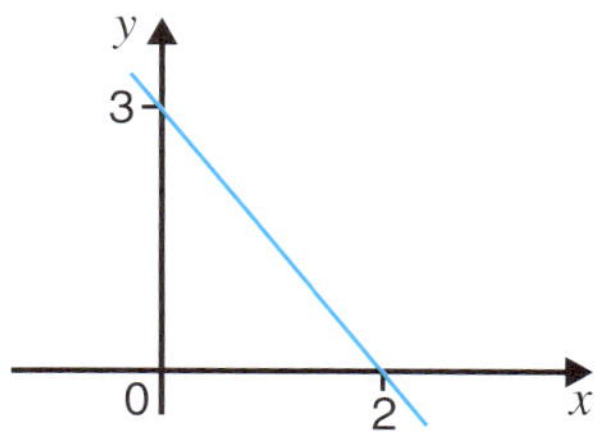

(b) The equation of a different line is $4y - 3x = 8$.
What is the gradient of this line?

40 (a) Expand and simplify. $3(2x - 1) + 2(4x - 5)$
(b) Expand and simplify. $(3x + 2)(x + 4)$ AQA

41 A quick but approximate rule for converting degrees Centigrade (C) into degrees Fahrenheit (F) is $F = 2C + 30$. The exact rule is given by this equation: $5F = 9C + 160$.
(a) (i) Solve the two simultaneous equations: $F = 2C + 30$ and $5F = 9C + 160$.
(ii) Explain what your solution to these equations tells you about the two rules for converting temperatures.
(b) (i) Write the equation $5F = 9C + 160$ in the form $F = \ldots$
(ii) Compare this equation with the equation $F = 2C + 30$.
Explain why the quick rule is a reasonable approximation for the exact rule. AQA

42 (a) Simplify, giving your answer in index form. (i) $\frac{a^8}{a^4}$ (ii) $(a^2)^3$
(b) Make q the subject of the formula $p = q^2 + r$. AQA

43 (a) Solve the inequality $3x - 5 \leqslant 16$.
(b) Multiply out and simplify $(y - 7)^2$.
(c) Simplify $2x^4 \times 3x^3$.
(d) Factorise $p^2 + p - 12$. AQA

44 (a) List all the values of n, where n is an integer, such that $-2 \leqslant n - 3 < 1$.
(b) Solve the simultaneous equations $x + 4y = 15$ and $3x - 2y = 10$.
(c) Factorise $xy - y^2$.
(d) Solve the equation $x^2 - 7x + 10 = 0$. AQA

45 The graph of a straight line is shown.
What is the equation of the line?

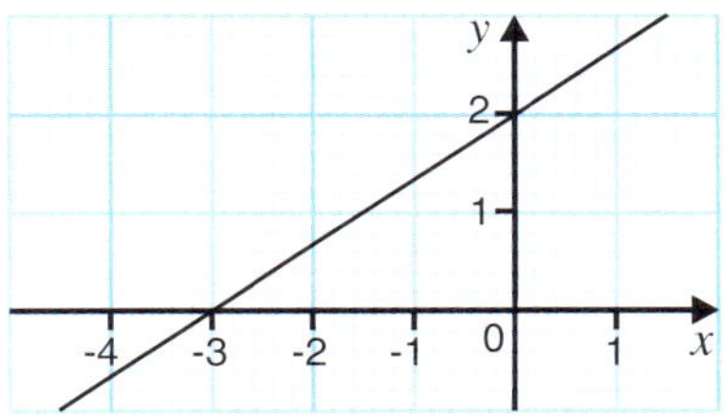

46 (a) Simplify $\frac{x^2 - 3x}{3x - 9}$.
(b) Factorise fully $3x^2 - 12$.

47 The dimensions of a rectangle are shown.
The rectangle has an area of $104\,\text{cm}^2$.
Form an equation for the area of the rectangle and show that it can be written in the form $2x^2 + x - 105 = 0$.

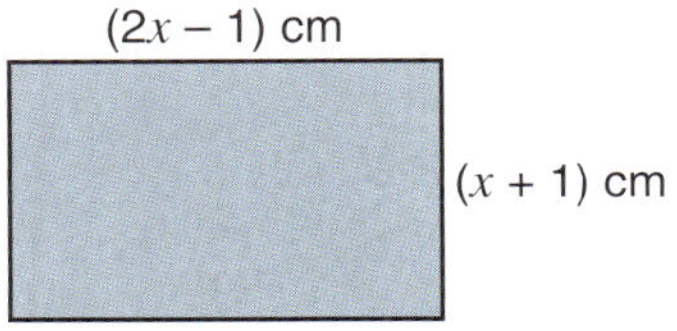

SR Section Review . . . Section Review . . .

SECTION 27

Angles

What you need to know

- Types and names of angles.

Acute angle

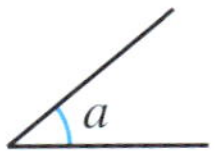

$0° < a < 90°$

Right angle

$a = 90°$

Obtuse angle

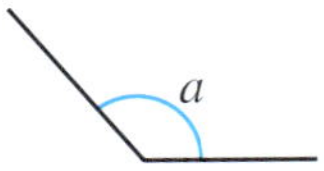

$90° < a < 180°$

Reflex angle

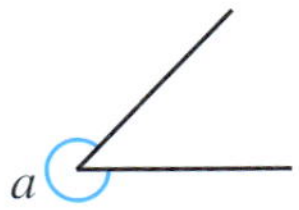

$180° < a < 360°$

- Angle properties.

Angles at a point

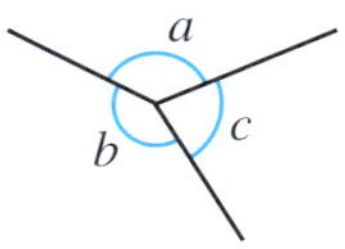

$a + b + c = 360°$

Complementary angles

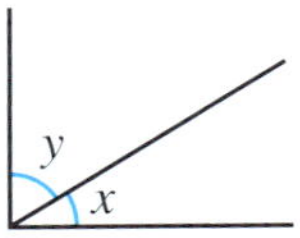

$x + y = 90°$

Supplementary angles

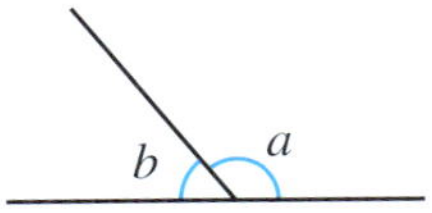

$a + b = 180°$

Vertically opposite angles

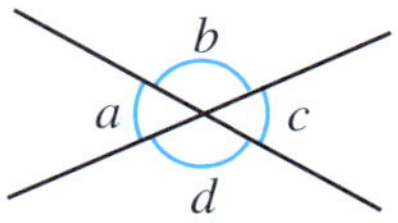

$a = c$ and $b = d$

- Lines which meet at right angles are **perpendicular** to each other.
- A straight line joining two points is called a **line segment**.
- Lines which never meet and are always the same distance apart are **parallel**.
- When two parallel lines are crossed by a **transversal** the following pairs of angles are formed.

Corresponding angles

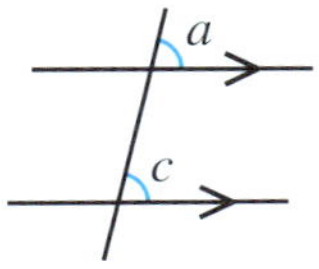

$a = c$

Alternate angles

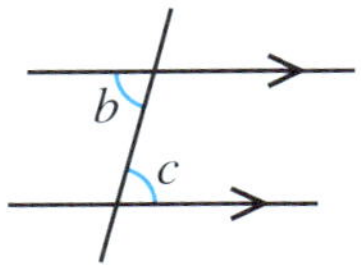

$b = c$

Allied angles

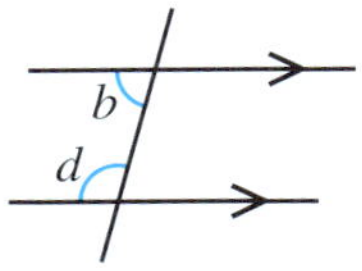

$b + d = 180°$

Arrowheads are used to show that lines are **parallel**.

- You should be able to use angle properties to solve problems involving lines and angles.
- **Bearings** are used to describe the direction in which you must travel to get from one place to another.
- A bearing is an angle measured from the North line in a clockwise direction.
  A bearing can be any angle from 0° to 360° and is written as a three-figure number.

To find a bearing:
measure angle a to find the bearing of Y from X,
measure angle b to find the bearing of X from Y.

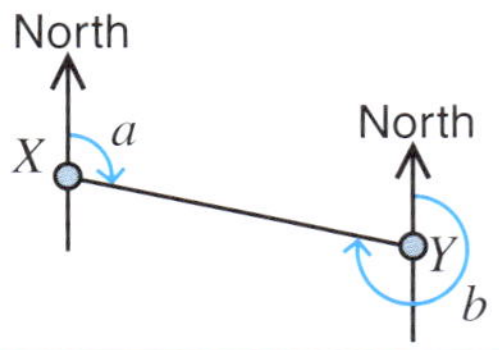

- Be able to use **scales** and **bearings** to interpret and draw accurate diagrams.

There are two ways to describe a scale.
1. A scale of 1 cm to 10 km means that a distance of 1 cm on the map represents an actual distance of 10 km.
2. A scale of 1 : 10 000 means that all distances measured on the map have to be multiplied by 10 000 to find the real distance.

1 Find the size of the lettered angles. Give a reason for each answer.

(a)

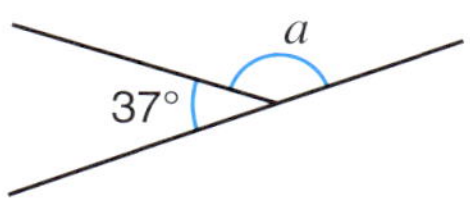

(b)

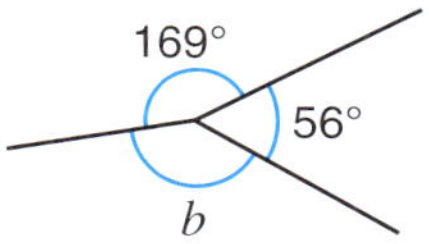

(c)

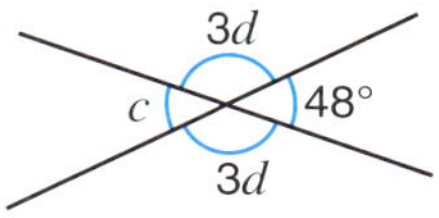

2 AB is parallel to DC.

(a) Work out the size of angle x.
Give a reason for your answer.

(b) Work out the size of angle y.
Give a reason for your answer.

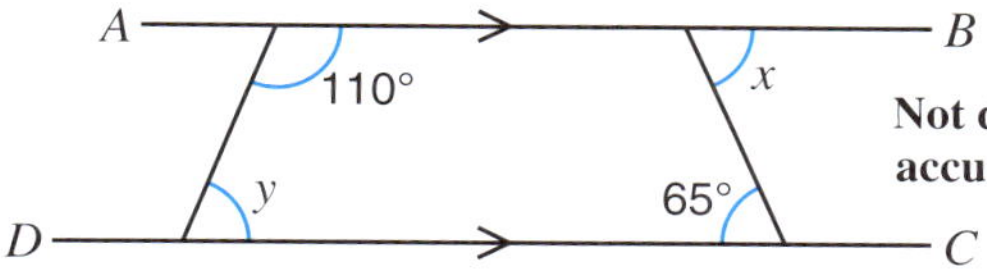

Not drawn accurately

AQA

3 In the diagram, the lines PQ and RS are parallel.

(a) What is the size of angle x?
Give a reason for your answer.

(b) Find the size of angle y.

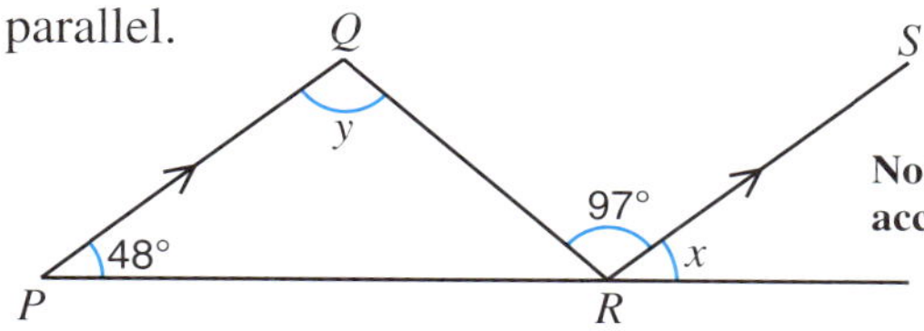

Not drawn accurately

AQA

4 Find the size of the angles marked with letters.

(a)

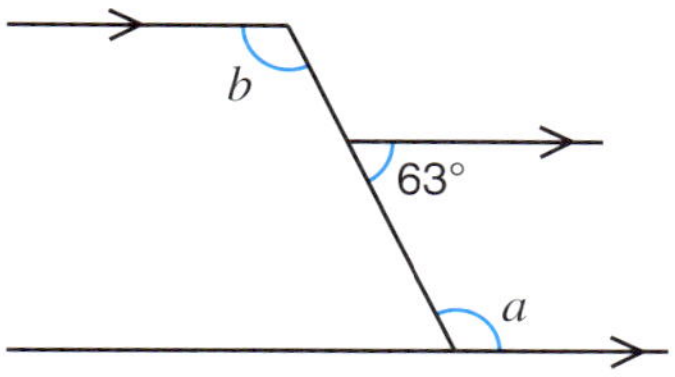

(b)

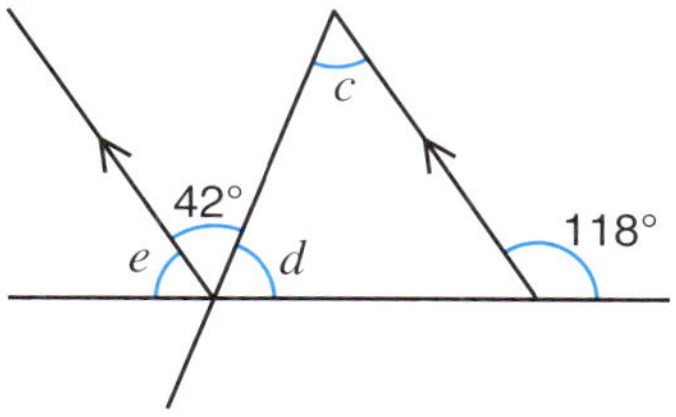

(c)

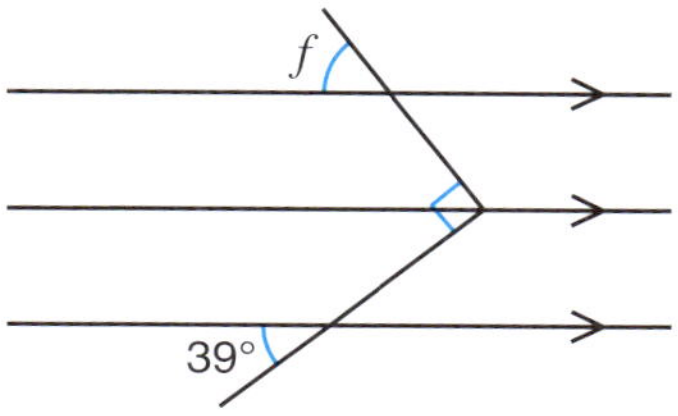

5

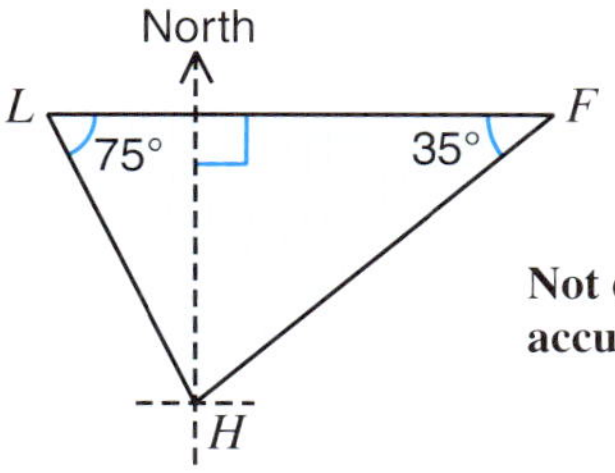

Not drawn accurately

A fishing boat sails from a harbour, H, to a point, F.
F is due east of a lighthouse, L.
Angle FLH is 75° and angle LFH is 35°.

(a) Calculate the bearing of F from H.

(b) Calculate the bearing of L from H.

(c) Calculate the bearing of H from F.

AQA

6 The map shows the positions of a windmill, W, and a pylon, P.

(a) What is the bearing of (i) the pylon from the windmill,
(ii) the windmill from the pylon?

The map has been drawn to a scale of 2 cm to 5 km.

(b) Use the map to find the distance WP in kilometres.

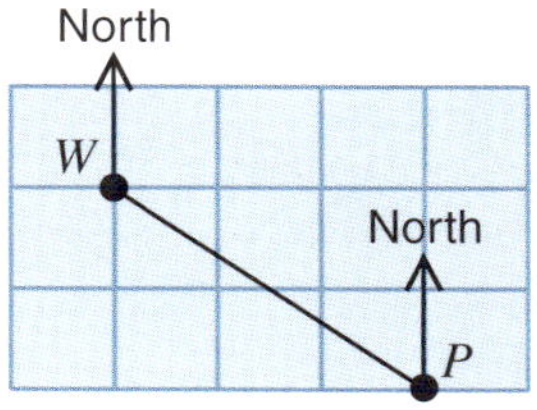

7 The diagram shows a sketch of the course to be used for a running event.

(a) Draw an accurate plan of the course, using a scale of 1 cm to represent 100 m.

(b) Use your plan to find
(i) the bearing of X from Y,
(ii) the distance XY in metres.

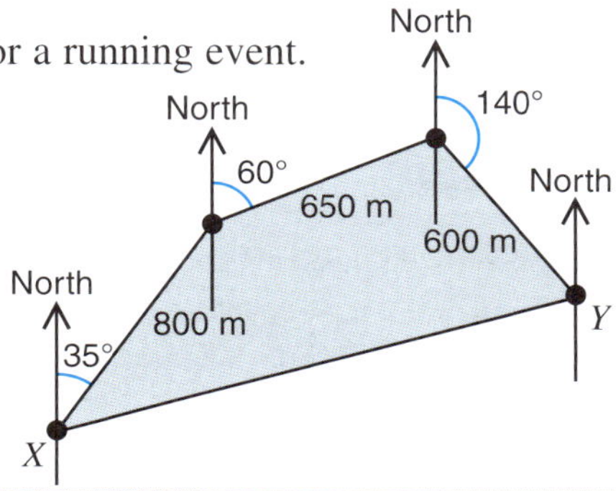

Triangles

What you need to know

- A **triangle** is a shape made by three straight sides.
- Triangles can be: **acute-angled** (all angles less than 90°),
  obtuse-angled (one angle greater than 90°),
  right-angled (one angle equal to 90°).
- The sum of the angles in a triangle is 180°.
  $a + b + c = 180°$
- The exterior angle is equal to the sum of the two opposite interior angles. $a + b = d$

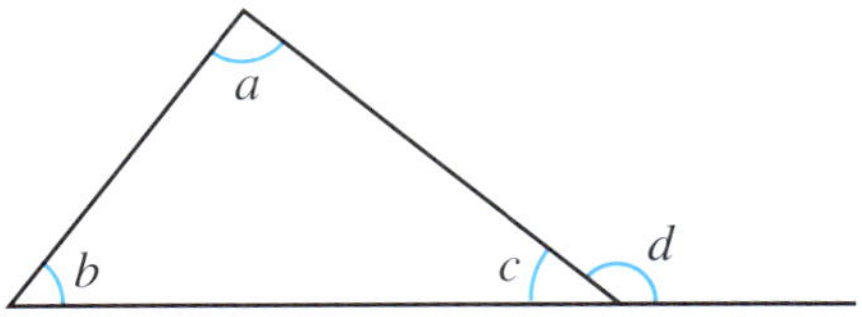

- Types of triangle:

Scalene **Isosceles** **Equilateral**

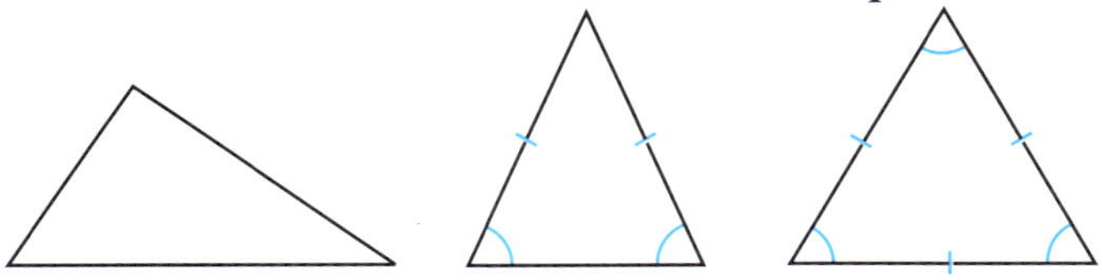

A **sketch** is used when an accurate drawing is not required. Dashes across lines show sides that are equal in length. Equal angles are marked using arcs.

- You should be able to use properties of triangles to solve problems.

Eg 1 Find the size of the angles marked a and b.

$a = 86° + 51°$ (ext. ∠ of a Δ)

$a = 137°$

$b + 137° = 180°$ (supp. ∠'s)

$b = 43°$

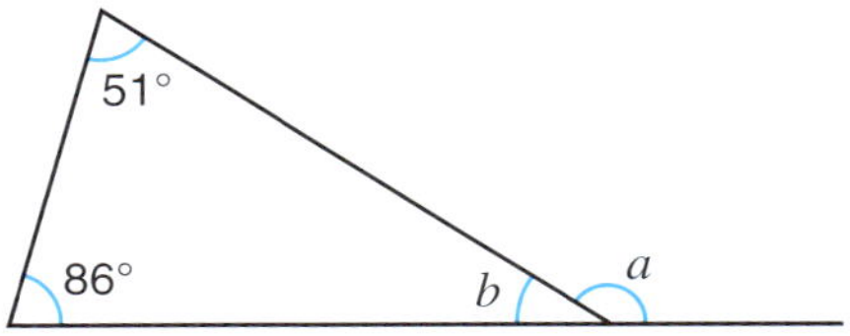

- Perimeter of a triangle is the sum of its three sides.
- Area of a triangle $= \dfrac{\text{base} \times \text{perpendicular height}}{2}$

$$A = \tfrac{1}{2} \times b \times h$$

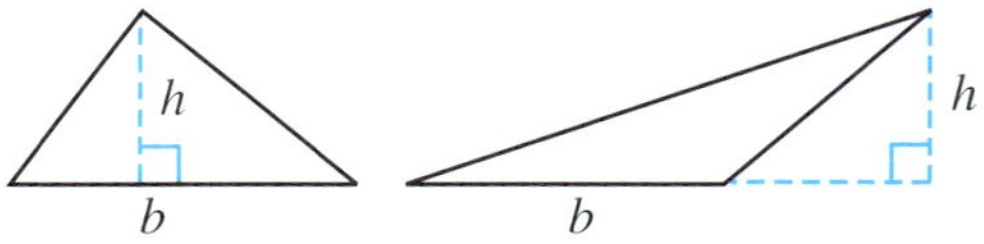

Eg 2 Calculate the area of this triangle.

$A = \frac{1}{2} \times b \times h$

$= \frac{1}{2} \times 9 \times 6\,\text{cm}^2$

$= 27\,\text{cm}^2$

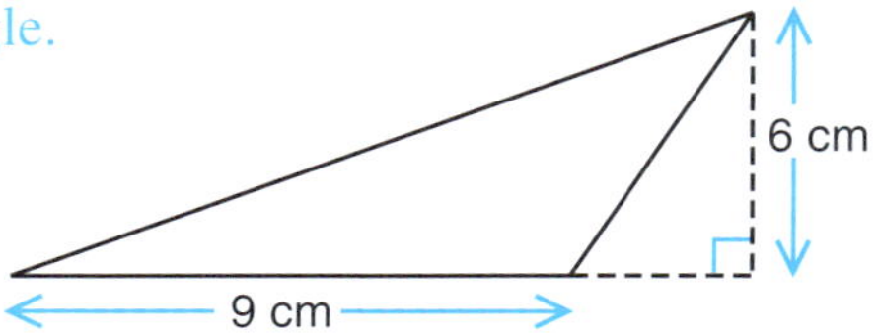

- You should be able to draw triangles accurately, using ruler, compasses and protractor.

Exercise 28

1 Without measuring, work out the size of the angles marked with letters.

(a)

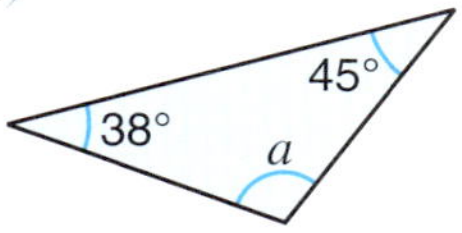

(b)

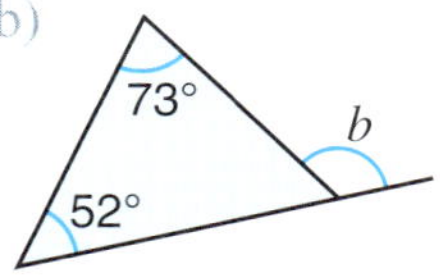

(c)

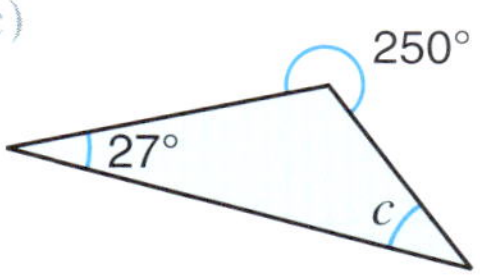

2 In the diagram, *ABX* is a straight line.
Work out the size of angle *ACB*.

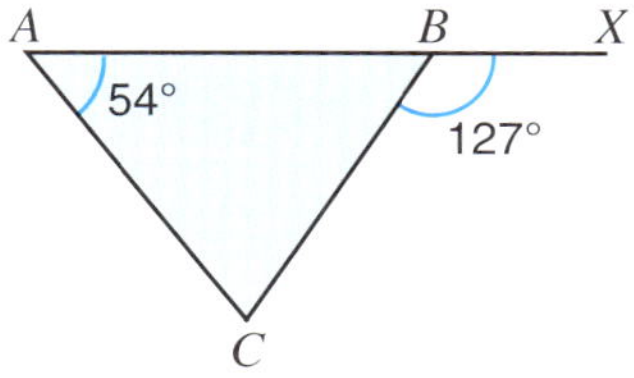

AQA

3 The diagram shows triangle *PQR*, with *PQ* = *PR*.
Work out the value of *x*.
Give a reason for your answer.

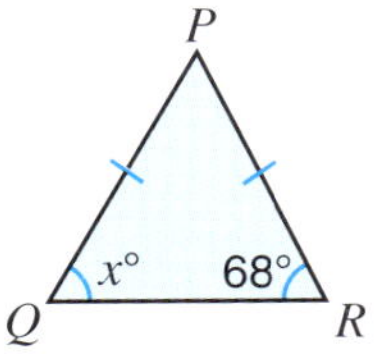

AQA

4 The diagram shows an isosceles triangle with two sides extended.
(a) Work out the size of angle *x*.
(b) Work out the size of angle *y*.

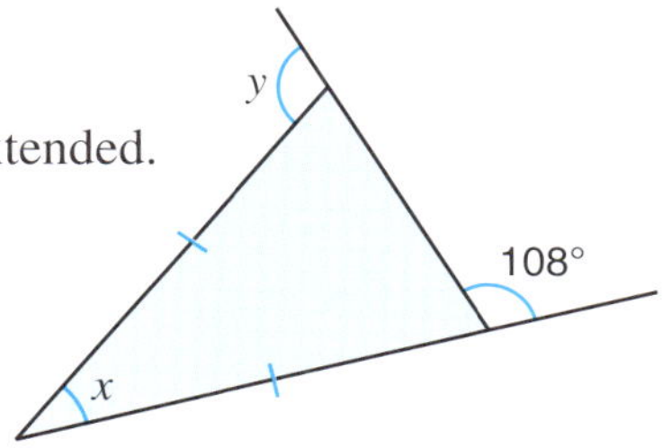

AQA

5 In the diagram *AB* = *BC* = *CA* = *CD*.
Work out the size of angle *CDA*.
Explain how you found your answer.

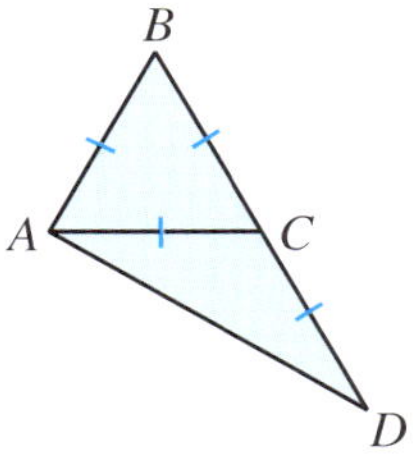

AQA

6 Make accurate drawings of these triangles using the information given.

(a)

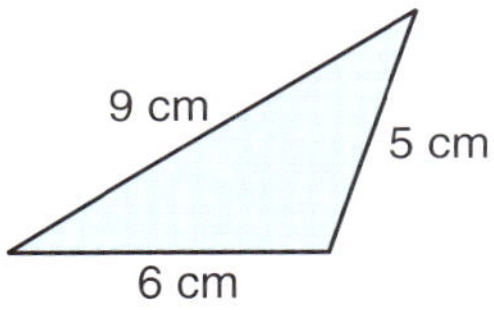

(b)

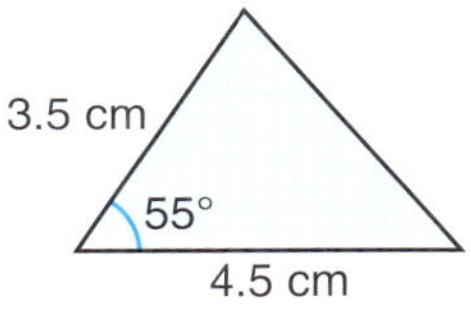

(c)

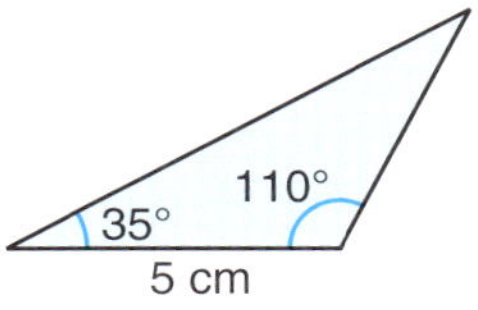

7 Find the areas of these triangles.

(a)

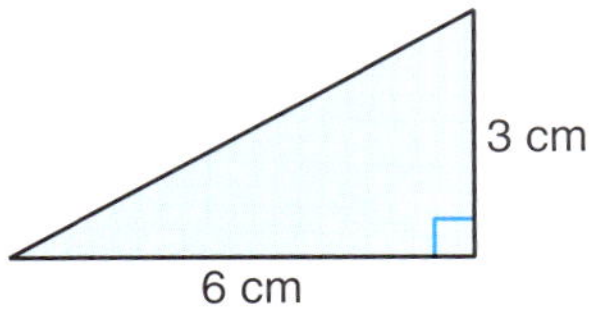

(b)

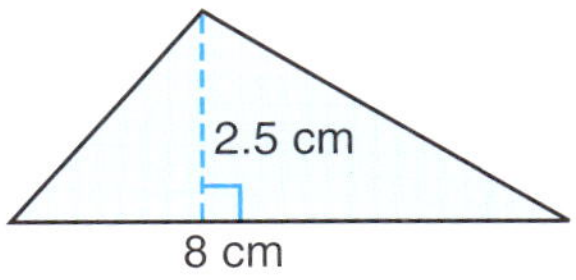

(c)

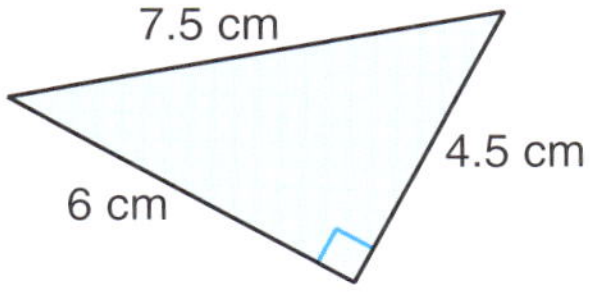

8 (a) Construct accurately a triangle with sides of 8 cm, 6 cm and 5 cm.
(b) By measuring the base and height, calculate the area of the triangle.

9 The diagram shows triangle *PQR*.
Calculate the area of triangle *PQR*.

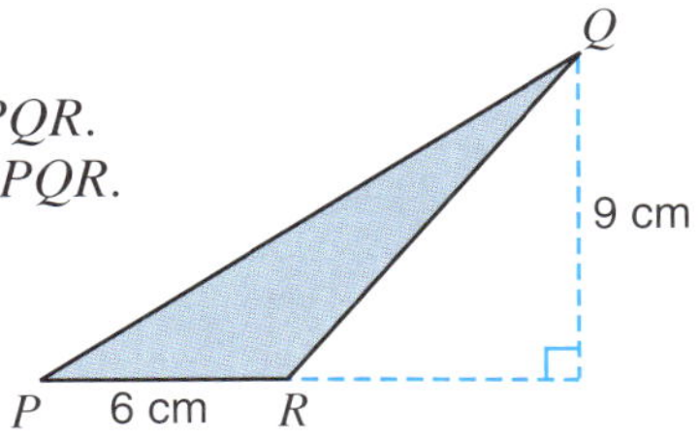

AQA

10 Triangle *XYZ* has an area of $12\,\text{cm}^2$.
XZ = 5 cm.
Calculate *YP*.

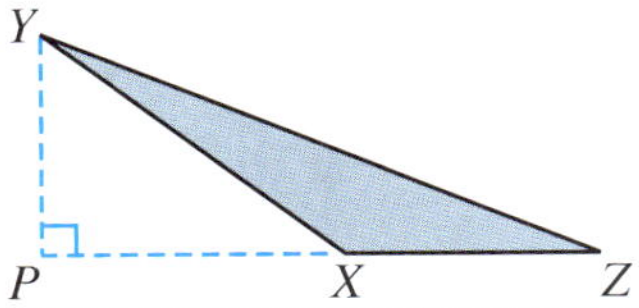

SECTION 29 Symmetry and Congruence

What you need to know

- A two-dimensional shape has **line symmetry** if the line divides the shape so that one side fits exactly over the other.

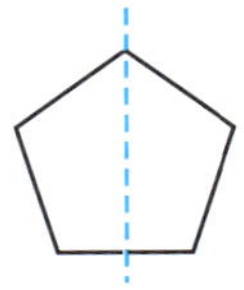

- A two-dimensional shape has **rotational symmetry** if it fits into a copy of its outline as it is rotated through 360°.
- A shape is only described as having rotational symmetry if the order of rotational symmetry is 2 or more.
- The number of times a shape fits into its outline in a single turn is the **order of rotational symmetry**.

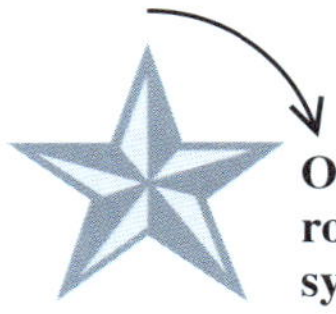

Eg 1 For each of these shapes (a) draw and state the number of lines of symmetry,
(b) state the order of rotational symmetry.

(i)

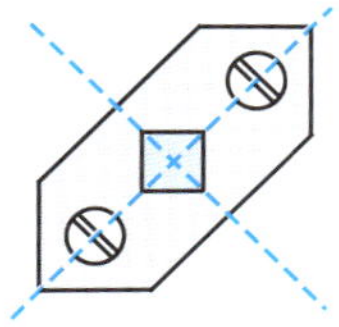

Two lines of symmetry.
Rotational symmetry of order 2.

(ii)

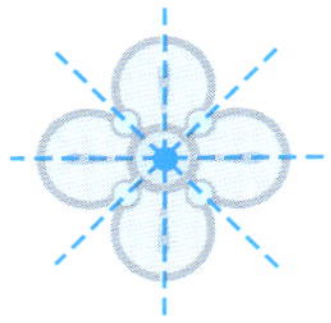

4 lines of symmetry.
Order of rotational symmetry 4.

(iii)

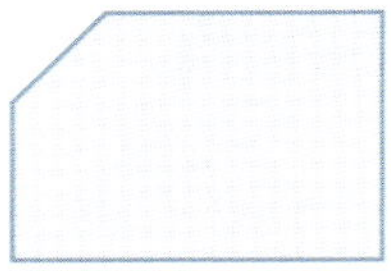

No lines of symmetry.
Order of rotational symmetry 1.
The shape is **not** described as having rotational symmetry.

- A **plane of symmetry** slices through a three-dimensional object so that one half is the mirror image of the other half.

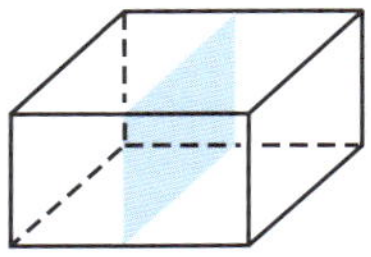

- Three-dimensional objects can have **axes of symmetry**.

Eg 2 Sketch a cuboid and show its axes of symmetry.

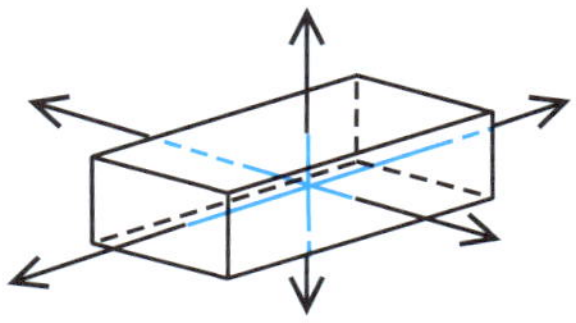

A cuboid has three axes of symmetry.
The order of rotational symmetry about each axis is 2.

- When two shapes are the same shape and size they are said to be **congruent**.
- There are four ways to show that a pair of triangles are congruent.

SSS	3 corresponding sides.	**ASA**	2 angles and a corresponding side.
SAS	2 sides and the included angle.	**RHS**	Right angle, hypotenuse and one other side.

Eg 3 Which of these triangles are congruent to each other? Give a reason for your answer.

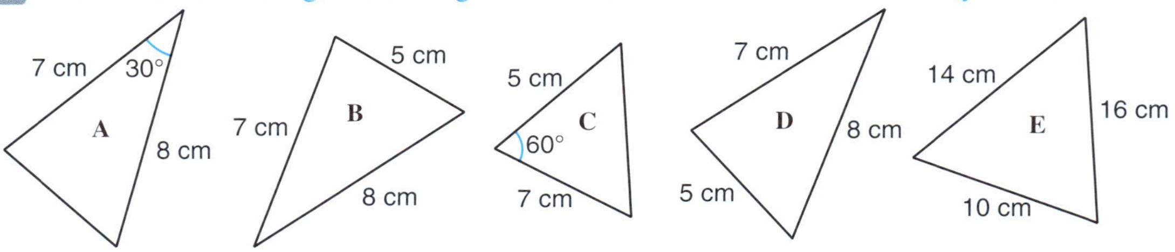

B and D. Reason: 3 corresponding sides (SSS)

Exercise 29

1 Half of a shape is drawn on squared paper, as shown.
AB is a line of symmetry for the complete shape.
Copy the diagram and complete the shape.

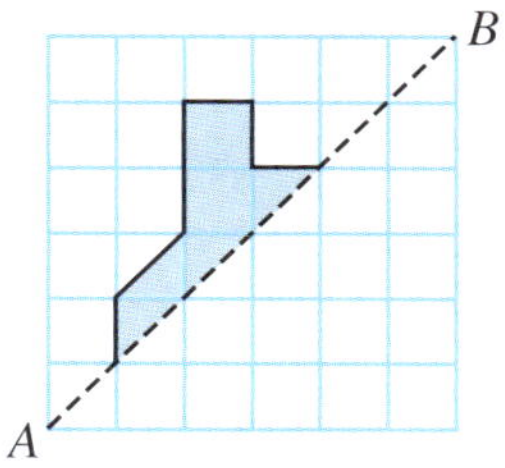

2 Consider the letters of the word **O R A N G E**

Which letters have
(a) line symmetry only,
(b) rotational symmetry only,
(c) line symmetry and rotational symmetry?

3 For each of these shapes state
(i) the number of lines of symmetry,
(ii) the order of rotational symmetry.

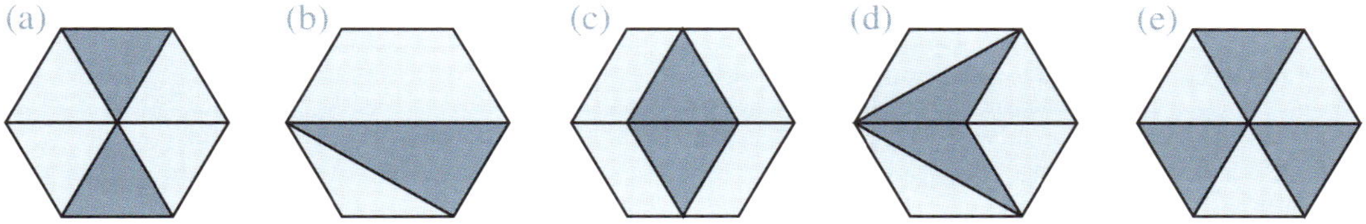

4 The diagram shows part of a shape.
Complete the shape so that it has rotational symmetry of order 2.

AQA

5 The diagram shows a square-based pyramid.
(a) How many planes of symmetry has the pyramid?
(b) How many axes of symmetry has the pyramid?

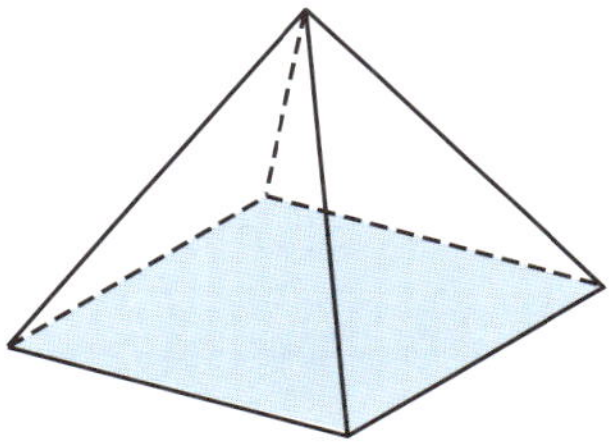

6

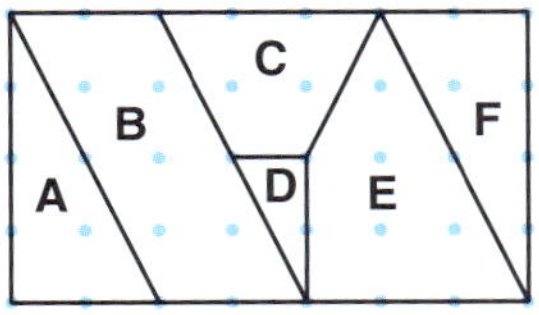

The diagram shows a rectangle which has been cut into 6 pieces.
Which two pieces are congruent to each other?

7 (a) Complete this shape so that it has both line symmetry and rotational symmetry.

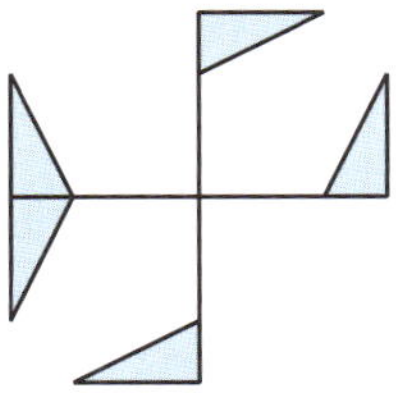

(b) Which of these triangles are congruent to each other?
Give a reason for your answer.

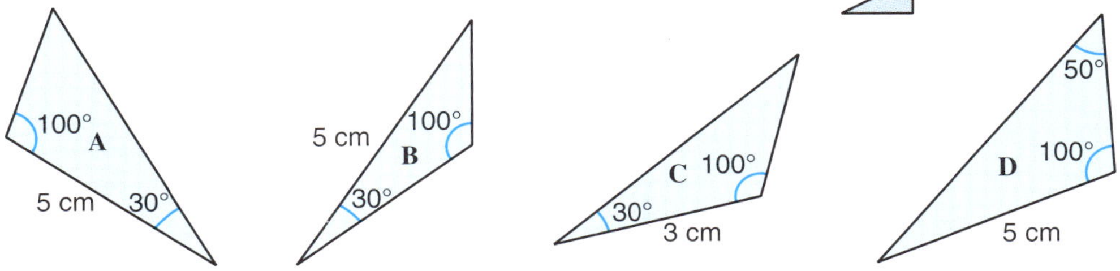

AQA

Quadrilaterals

What you need to know

- A **quadrilateral** is a shape made by four straight lines.
- The sum of the angles in a quadrilateral is 360°.
- The **perimeter** of a quadrilateral is the sum of the lengths of its four sides.

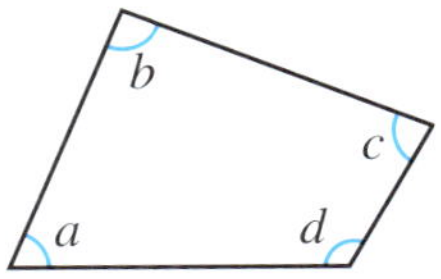

$a + b + c + d = 360°$

- Facts about these special quadrilaterals:

Quadrilateral	Sides	Angles	Diagonals	Line symmetry	Order of rotational symmetry	Area formula
Parallelogram	Opposite sides equal and parallel	Opposite angles equal	Bisect each other	0	2	$A = bh$
Rectangle	Opposite sides equal and parallel	All 90°	Bisect each other	2	2	$A = bh$
Rhombus	4 equal sides, opposite sides parallel	Opposite angles equal	Bisect each other at 90°	2	2	$A = bh$
Square	4 equal sides, opposite sides parallel	All 90°	Bisect each other at 90°	4	4	$A = l^2$
Trapezium	1 pair of parallel sides					$A = \frac{1}{2}(a + b)h$
Isosceles trapezium	1 pair of parallel sides, non-parallel sides equal	2 pairs of equal angles	Equal in length	1	1*	$A = \frac{1}{2}(a + b)h$
Kite	2 pairs of adjacent sides equal	1 pair of opposite angles equal	One bisects the other at 90°	1	1*	

*A shape is only described as having rotational symmetry if the order of rotational symmetry is 2 or more.

- You should be able to use properties of quadrilaterals to solve problems.

Eg 1 Work out the size of the angle marked x.

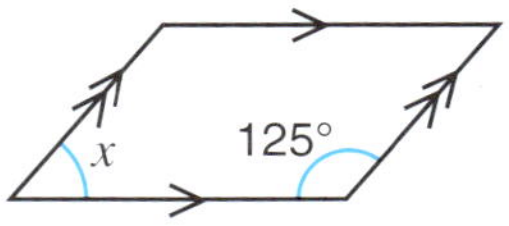

Opposite angles are equal.
So, $125° + 125° + x + x = 360°$
$x = 55°$

Eg 2 Find the area of this trapezium.

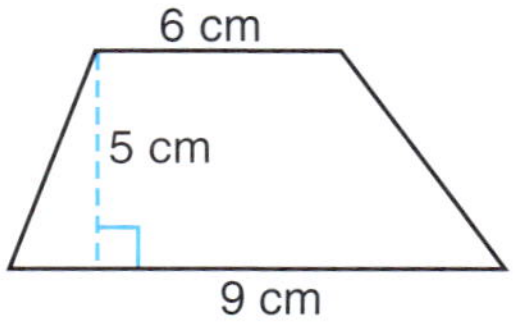

$A = \frac{1}{2}(a + b)h$
$= \frac{1}{2}(6 + 9)5$
$= \frac{1}{2} \times 15 \times 5$
$= 37.5 \text{ cm}^2$

- You should be able to construct a quadrilateral from given information using ruler, protractor, compasses.

Exercise 30

1 A quadrilateral with 4 equal sides and 4 right angles is called a square.
What is the mathematical name given to:
(a) A quadrilateral with 4 equal sides but no right angles?
(b) A quadrilateral with 2 pairs of opposite sides equal but diagonals of different lengths?
(c) A quadrilateral with only 1 pair of parallel sides of unequal lengths? AQA

2 Find the size of the lettered angles.

(a)
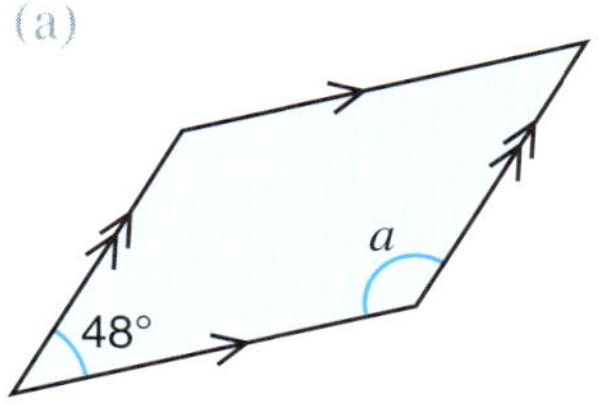

(b)
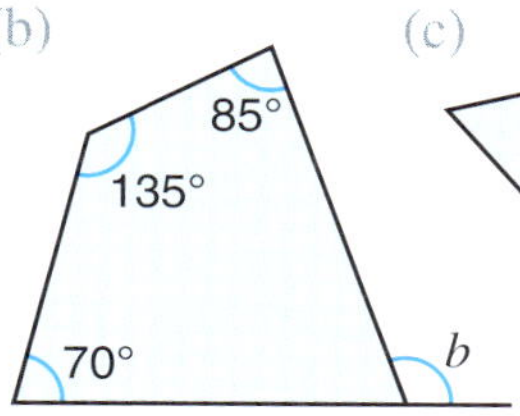

(c)
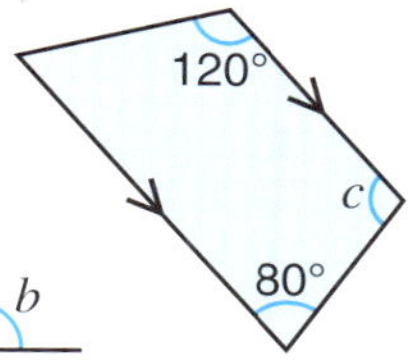

(d)
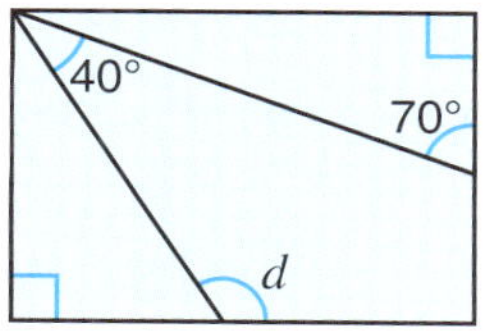

3 The diagram shows a quadrilateral $ABCD$.
$AB = BC$ and $CD = DA$.
(a) Which of the following correctly describes the quadrilateral $ABCD$?
rhombus **parallelogram** **kite** **trapezium**
(b) Angle $ADC = 36°$ and angle $BCD = 108°$.
Work out the size of angle ABC.

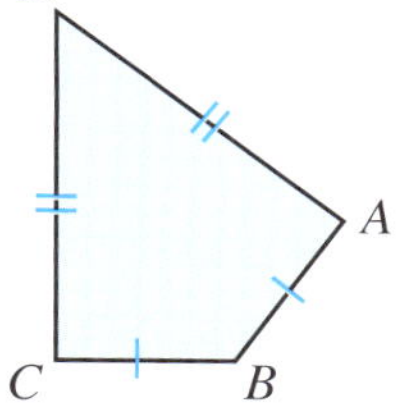

4 In the figure, $AB = AD$ and $BD = BC$.
AB is parallel to DC and angle $DBC = 62°$.
(a) Copy the diagram and calculate the sizes of the other angles.
Write the answers on your diagram.
Hence decide whether each of the following statements is true or false.
(i) BD bisects angle ABC.
(ii) BD bisects angle ADC.
(iii) Angle DAB is equal to angle DBC.
(b) Explain why BC is not parallel to AD.

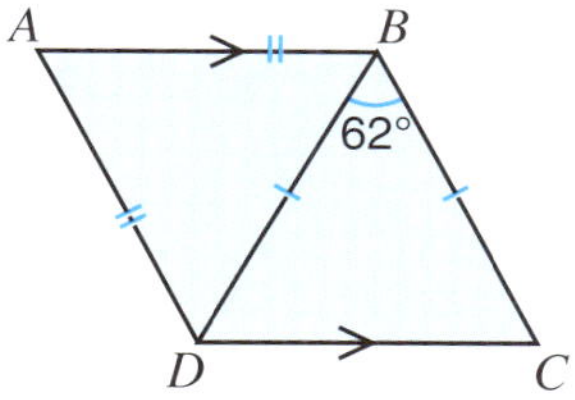

AQA

5 A rectangle measures 8.6 cm by 6.4 cm.
(a) Find the perimeter of the rectangle.
(b) Find the area of the rectangle.

6 Two triangles are joined together to form a rhombus as shown.
The perimeter of the rhombus is 36 cm.
The perimeter of each triangle is 24 cm.
Find the value of b.

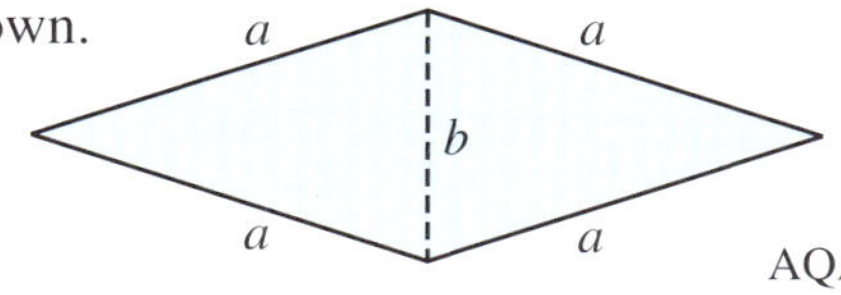

AQA

7
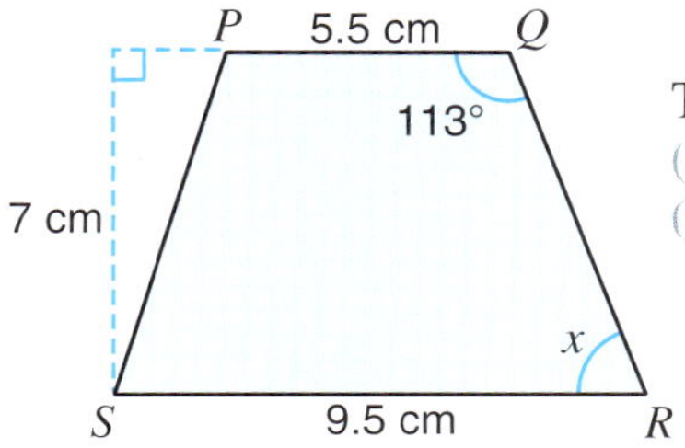

The diagram shows a trapezium $PQRS$.
(a) Work out the size of the angle marked x.
(b) Calculate the area of the trapezium.

8 A rectangular carpet is twice as long as it is wide.
The carpet covers an area of 24.5 m².
Calculate the length of the carpet.

SECTION 31

Polygons

What you need to know

- A **polygon** is a many-sided shape made by straight lines.
- A polygon with all sides equal and all angles equal is called a **regular polygon**.
- Shapes you need to know: A 5-sided polygon is called a **pentagon**.
  A 6-sided polygon is called a **hexagon**.
  An 8-sided polygon is called an **octagon**.
- The sum of the exterior angles of any polygon is 360°.
- At each vertex of a polygon: interior angle + exterior angle = 180°
- The sum of the interior angles of an n-sided polygon is given by:
  $(n - 2) \times 180°$
- For a regular n-sided polygon: exterior angle $= \dfrac{360°}{n}$
- You should be able to use the properties of polygons to solve problems.

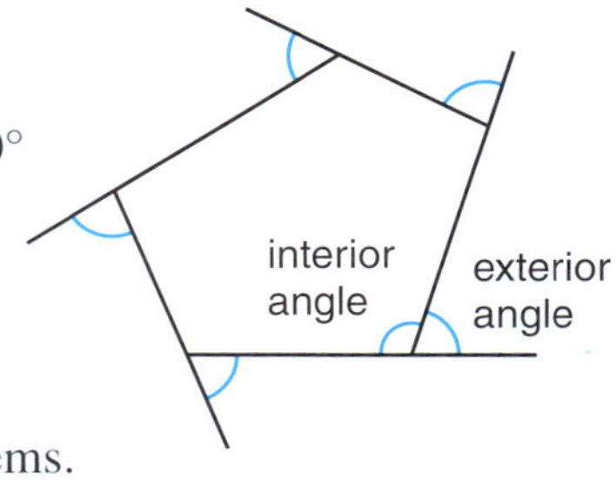

Eg 1 Find the sum of the interior angles of a pentagon.
$(5 - 2) \times 180° = 3 \times 180° = 540°$

> A pentagon has 5 sides, so substitute $n = 5$ into $(n - 2) \times 180°$.

Eg 2 A regular polygon has an exterior angle of 30°.
(a) How many sides has the polygon?
(b) What is the size of an interior angle of the polygon?

(a) $n = \dfrac{360°}{\text{exterior angle}}$

$n = \dfrac{360°}{30°}$

$n = 12$

(b) int. ∠ + ext. ∠ = 180°
int. ∠ + 30° = 180°
interior angle = 150°

- A shape will **tessellate** if it covers a surface without overlapping and leaves no gaps.
- All triangles tessellate.
- All quadrilaterals tessellate.
- Equilateral triangles, squares and hexagons can be used to make **regular tessellations**.
- A regular pentagon cannot be used to make a regular tessellation.

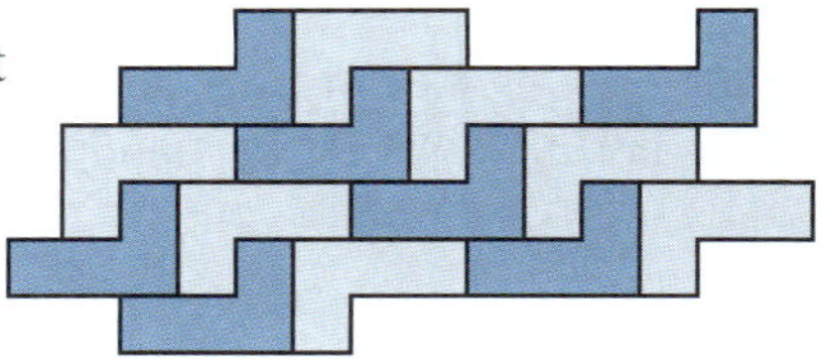

Exercise 31

1 Work out the size of the angles marked with letters.

(a)

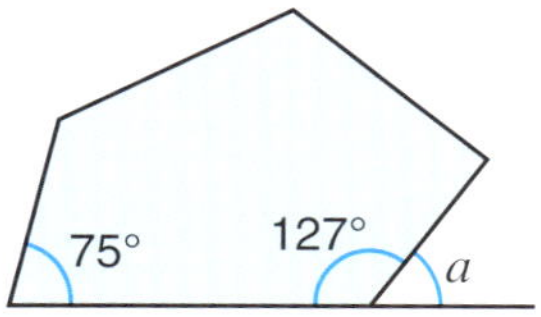

(b)

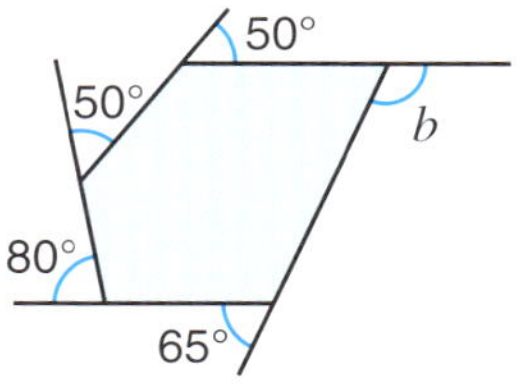

(c)

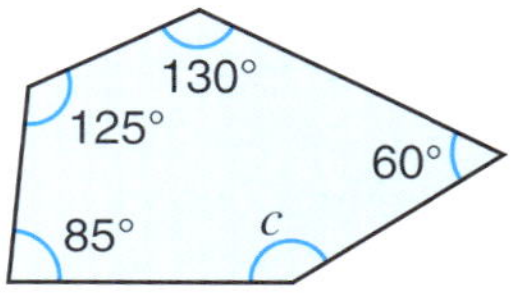

2 These shapes are regular polygons.
Work out the size of the lettered angles.

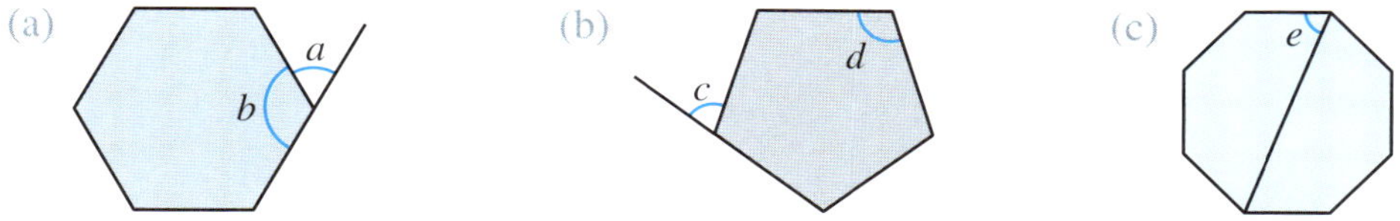

3 Each diagram shows part of a regular polygon.
How many sides has each polygon?

4 (a) Here is a tessellation of regular hexagons and equilateral triangles.
Explain why these shapes fit together exactly at point P.

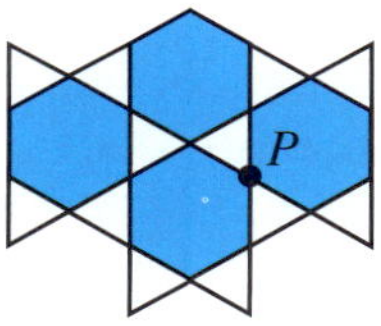

(b) Draw a tessellation which uses squares and regular octagons.

(c) Explain clearly why regular octagons will **not** tessellate with equilateral triangles.
(You may wish to use sketches to illustrate your answer.)

(d) A different regular polygon will tessellate with equilateral triangles.
Here is a sketch of part of the tessellation.
How many sides must the regular polygon have?
Show your working.

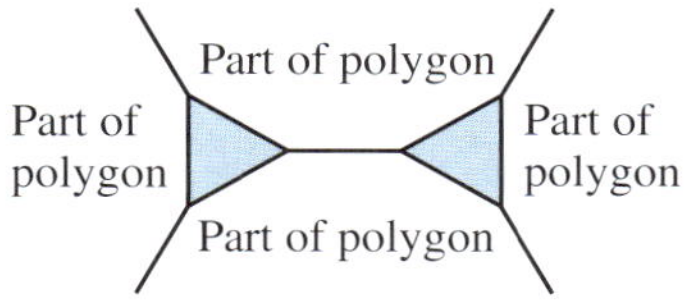

AQA

5 $ABCDEFGHI$ is a regular nonagon with centre O.

(a) Calculate the size of angle x.
(b) Calculate the size of angle y.

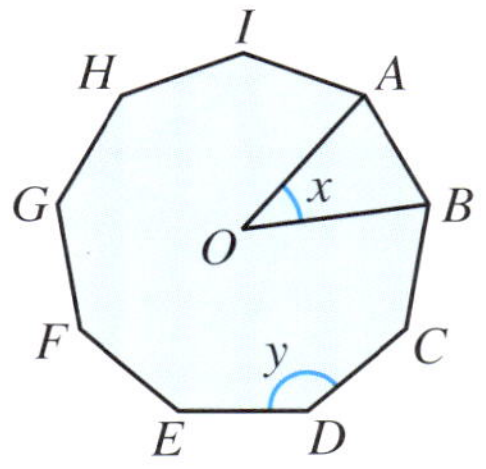

AQA

6 Four regular pentagons are placed together, as shown, to form a rhombus, $ABCD$.

Calculate the size of
(a) angle ABC,
(b) angle XCY.

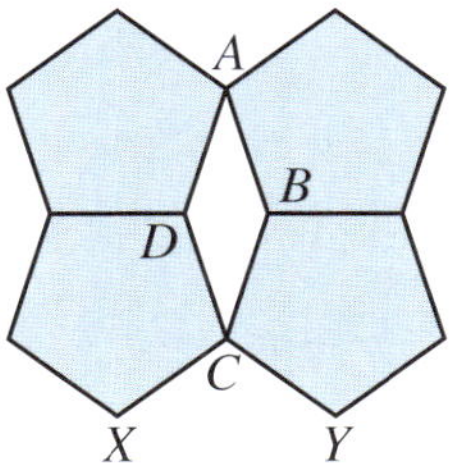

7 (a) A regular polygon has 9 sides.
Find the size of an interior angle.
(b) A regular polygon has an exterior angle of 20°.
Show that the sum of the interior angles is 2880°.

8 LM and MN are two sides of a regular 10-sided polygon.
MNX is an isosceles triangle with $MX = XN$.
Angle $MXN = 30°$.

Work out the size of the obtuse angle LMX.

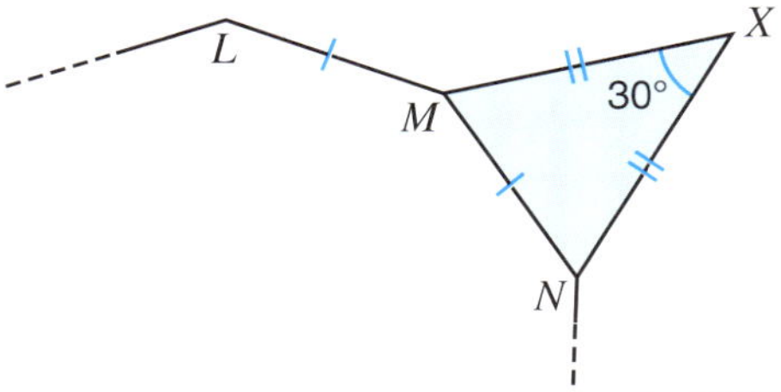

AQA

Circle Properties

What you need to know

- A **circle** is the shape drawn by keeping a pencil the same distance from a fixed point on a piece of paper.
- The meaning of the following words:
  Circumference – special name used for the perimeter of a circle.
  Radius – distance from the centre of the circle to any point on the circumference.
  The plural of radius is **radii**.
  Diameter – distance right across the circle, passing through the centre point. The diameter is twice as long as the radius.
  Chord – a line joining two points on the circumference.
  The longest chord is the diameter.
  Tangent – a line which touches the circumference of a circle at one point only.
  Arc – part of the circumference of a circle.
  Segment – a chord divides a circle into two segments.
  Sector – two radii divide a circle into two sectors.

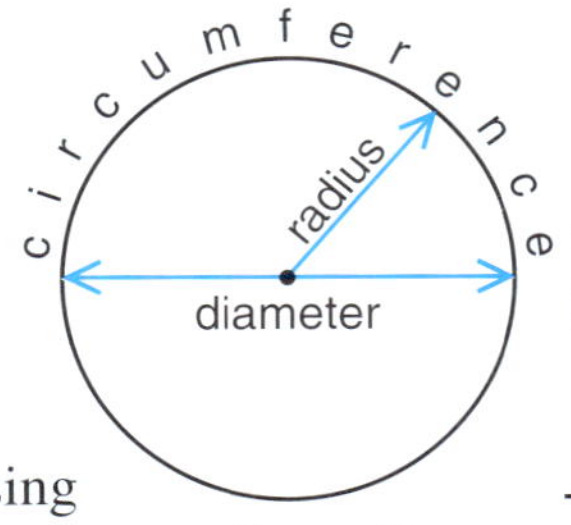

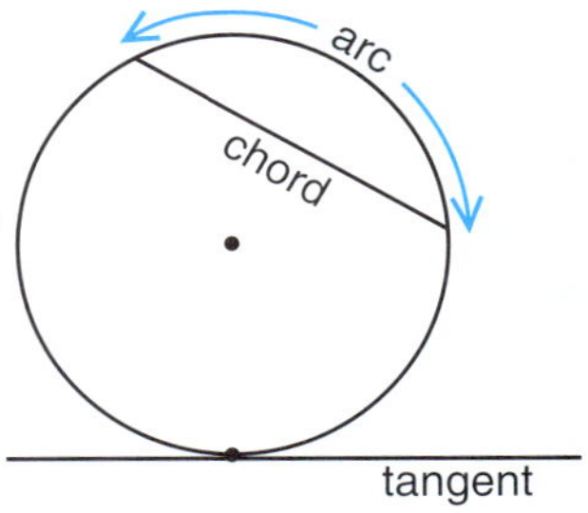

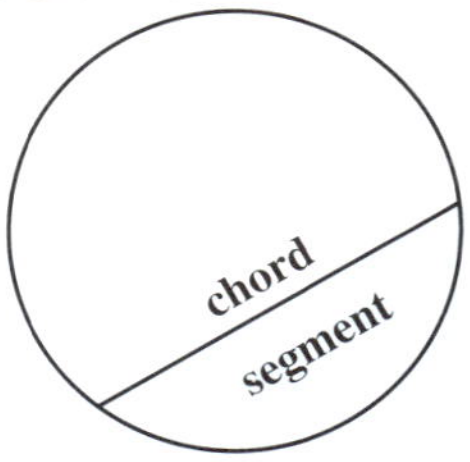

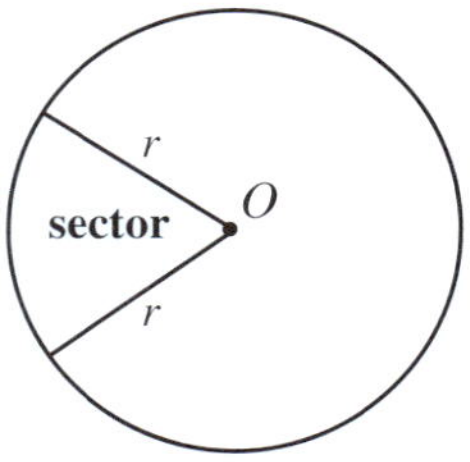

- The vertices of a **cyclic quadrilateral** lie on the circumference of a circle.
- **Circle properties**

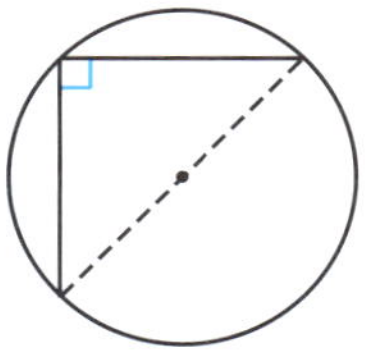

The angle in a semi-circle is a right angle.

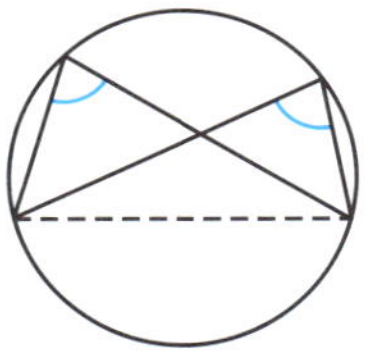

Angles in the same segment are equal.

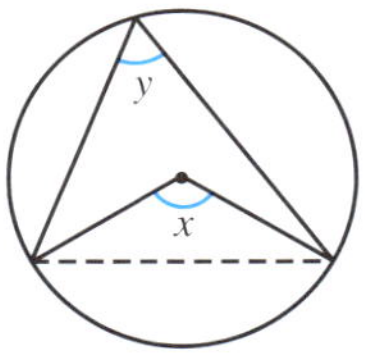

$x = 2y$
The angle at the centre is twice the angle at the circumference.

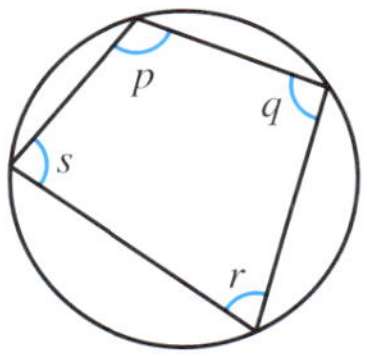

$p + r = 180°$ and $q + s = 180°$
Opposite angles of a cyclic quadrilateral are supplementary.

- A tangent is perpendicular to the radius at the point of contact.

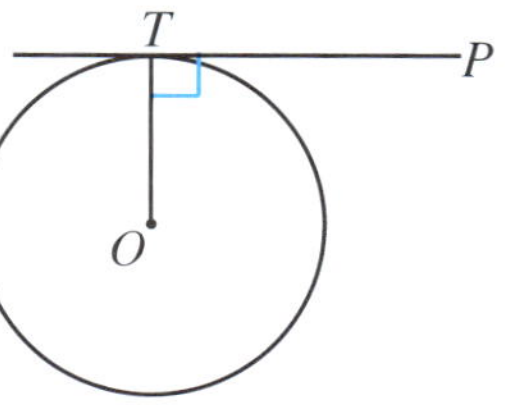

- Tangents drawn to a circle from the same point are equal in length.

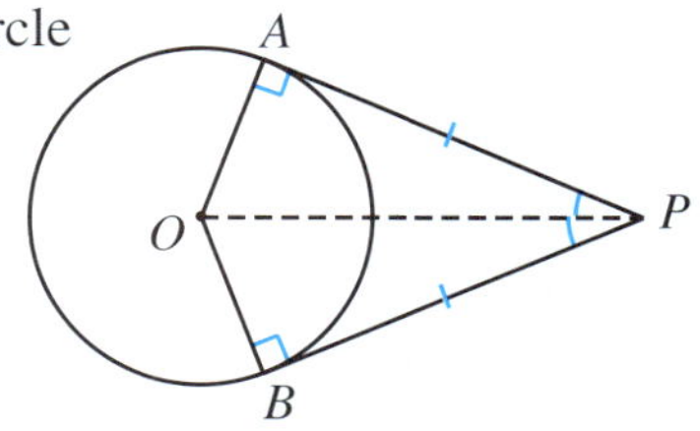

- You should be able to use circle properties to solve problems.

Eg 1 O is the centre of the circle. Find the marked angles.
$a = 43°$ (angles in the same segment)
$b = 2 \times 43°$ ($\angle$ at centre = twice $\angle$ at circum.)
$b = 86°$
$c = 180° - 43°$ (opp. $\angle$s of a cyclic quad)
$c = 137°$

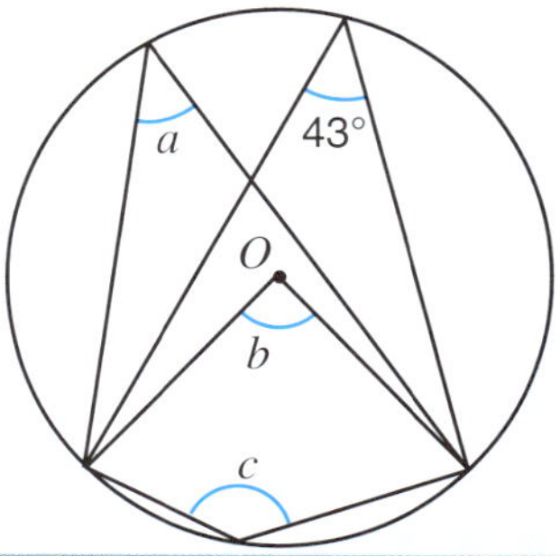

Exercise 32

The diagrams in this exercise have not been drawn accurately.

1 O is the centre of the circle.
Work out the size of the lettered angles. Give a reason for each of your answers.

(a)
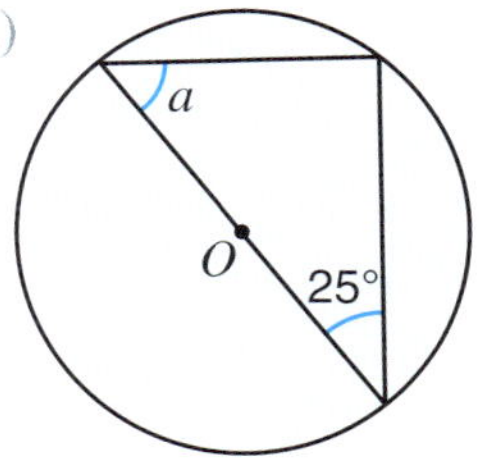

(b)
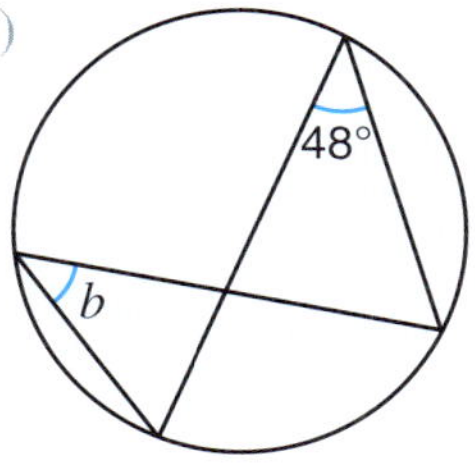

(c)
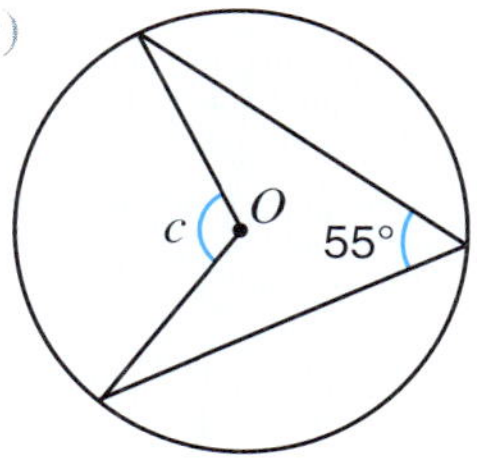

(d)
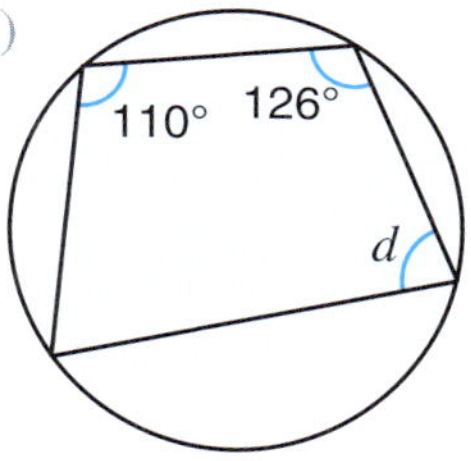

2 Look at the diagram.
Find angles a and d, when $b = 48°$ and $c = 32°$.

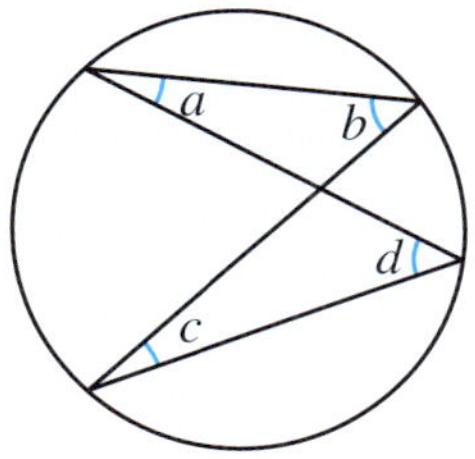

3
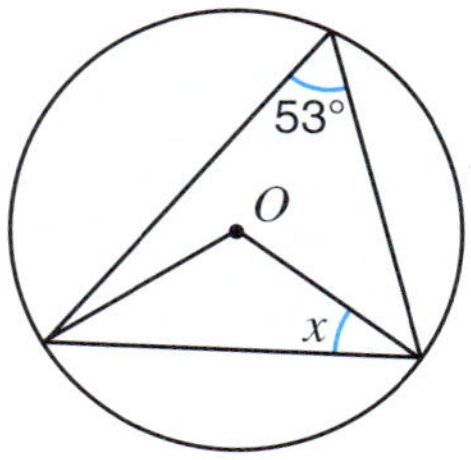

O is the centre of the circle.
Work out the size of angle x.

4 AB is a tangent to the circle centre O.
Angle $OAB = 28°$.
Find the size of angle BCO.

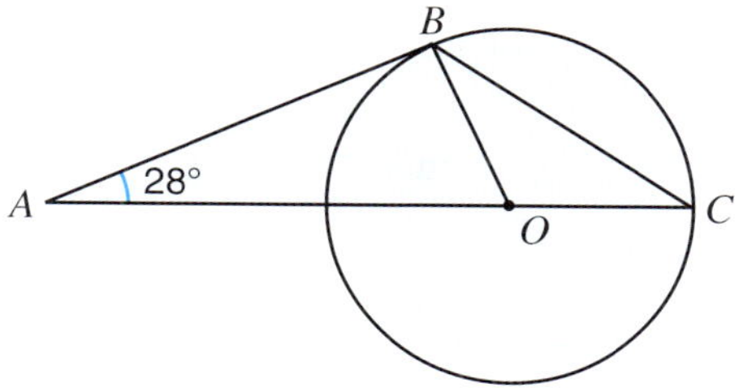

5
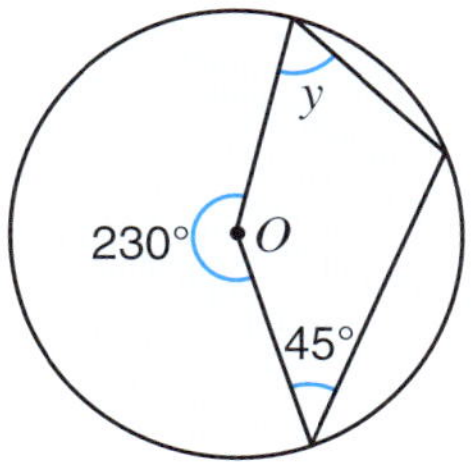

O is the centre of the circle.
Work out the size of angle y.

6 AXB is a tangent to the circle, centre O.
Find the size of the angles marked a, b and c.

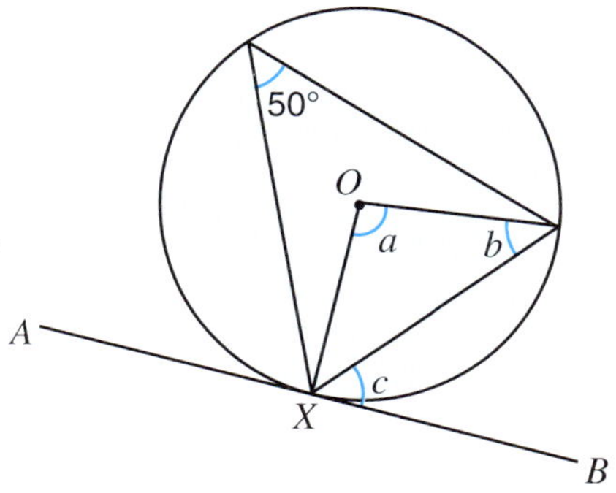

7
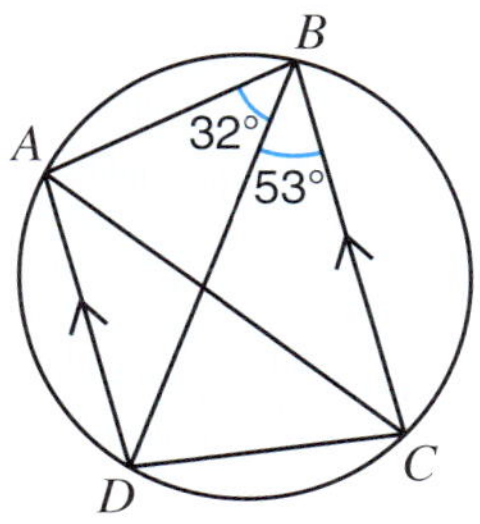

$ABCD$ is a cyclic quadrilateral.
AD is parallel to BC. $\angle ABD = 32°$ and $\angle CBD = 53°$.
Find (a) angle ADB, (b) angle ACD,
(c) angle ADC, (d) angle BAD.

8 The diagram shows a semi-circle, centre O.
Angle $CAD = x°$ and BC is parallel to AD.
Find, in terms of x, angle ABC.

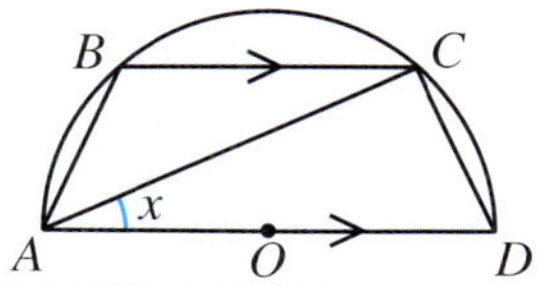

SECTION 33

Circles and Other Shapes

What you need to know

- The meaning of the words radius, diameter, circumference.
- The **circumference** of a circle is given by:

$C = \pi \times d$ or $C = 2 \times \pi \times r$

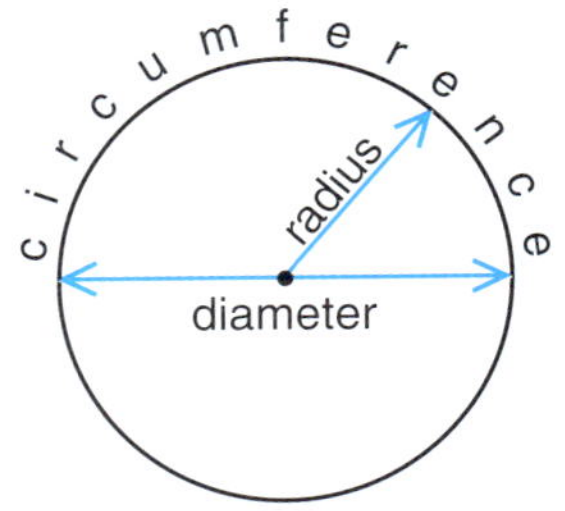

diameter = 2 × radius

- The **area** of a circle is given by:

$A = \pi \times r^2$

- You should be able to solve problems which involve finding the circumference or the area of a circle.

In all calculations take π to be 3.14 or use the π key on your calculator.

Eg 1 Find the circumference of a circle with radius 9 cm. Give your answer to 1 d.p.

$C = 2 \times \pi \times r$
$C = 2 \times \pi \times 9$
$C = 56.548\ldots$
$C = 56.5$ cm, correct to 1 d.p.

Eg 2 Find the area of a circle with radius 6 cm. Give your answer to 3 sig. figs.

$A = \pi \times r^2$
$A = \pi \times 6 \times 6$
$A = 113.097\ldots$
$A = 113\text{ cm}^2$, correct to 3 sig. figs.

Eg 3 A circle has a circumference of 25.2 cm. Find the diameter of the circle.

$C = \pi d$ so $d = \frac{C}{\pi}$
$d = \frac{25.2}{\pi}$
$d = 8.021\ldots$
$d = 8.0$ cm, correct to 1 d.p.

Eg 4 A circle has an area of 154 cm^2. Find the radius of the circle.

$A = \pi r^2$ so $r^2 = \frac{A}{\pi}$
$r^2 = \frac{154}{\pi} = 49.019\ldots$
$r = \sqrt{49.019\ldots} = 7.001\ldots$
$r = 7$ cm, to the nearest cm.

- Shapes formed by joining different shapes together are called **compound shapes**. To find the area of a compound shape we must first divide the shape up into rectangles, triangles, circles, etc, and find the area of each part.

Eg 5 Find the area of this metal plate.

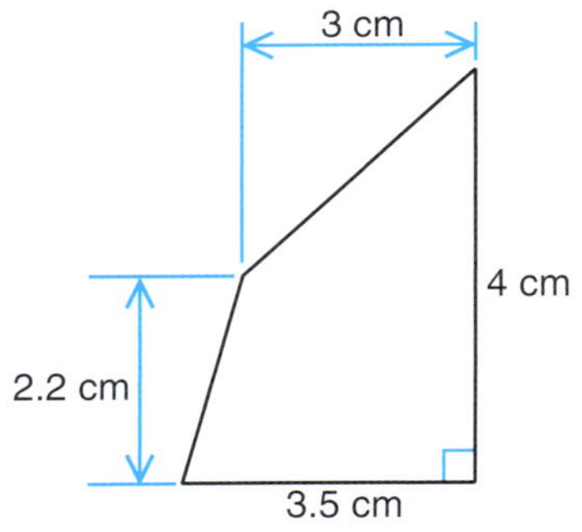

The plate can be split into a rectangle, A, and two triangles, B and C.

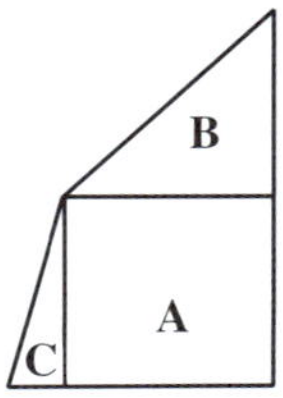

Area $A = 3 \times 2.2 = 6.6\text{ cm}^2$

Area $B = \frac{3 \times 1.8}{2} = 2.7\text{ cm}^2$

Area $C = \frac{0.5 \times 2.2}{2} = 0.55\text{ cm}^2$

Total area $= 6.6 + 2.7 + 0.55 = 9.85\text{ cm}^2$

Exercise 33

Take π to be 3.14 or use the π key on your calculator.
Do not use a calculator for question 1.

1 A coin has a diameter of 1.96 cm.
Estimate the circumference of the coin.

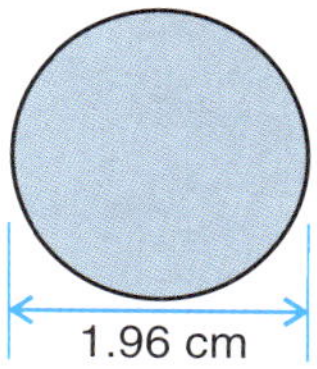

AQA

2 A circular pond has a radius of 3 metres.
(a) Calculate the circumference of the pond.
(b) Calculate the area of the pond.

AQA

3 (a) Calculate the circumference of a circle of diameter 26 cm.
(b) Calculate the area of a circle of radius 2.5 cm.

AQA

4 In the rectangle a triangular region has been shaded.
What percentage of the rectangle is shaded?
Give your answer to an appropriate degree of accuracy.

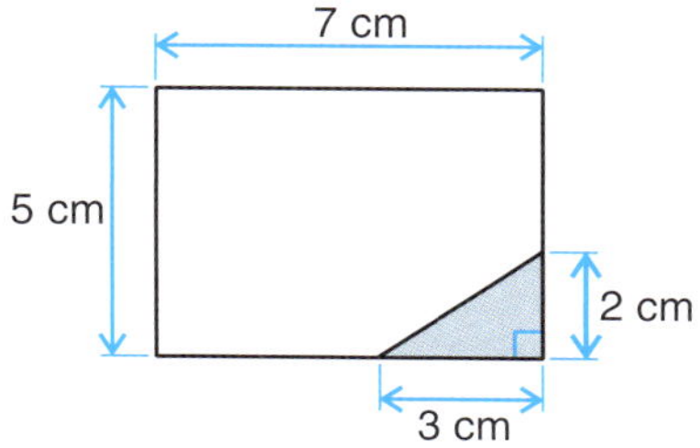

AQA

5 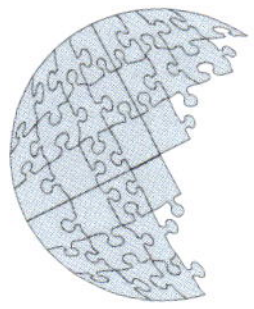

Tranter has completed three-fifths of a circular jigsaw puzzle.
The puzzle has a radius of 20 cm.
What area of the puzzle is complete?

6 The diagram shows the plan of a swimming pool.
The arc QR is a semi-circle.
$PS = 12\text{ m}$ and $PQ = RS = 20\text{ m}$.
Calculate the area of the pool.

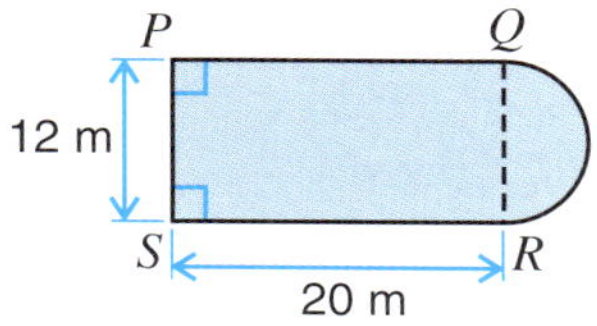

7 Louise does a sponsored bicycle ride.
Each wheel of her bicycle is of radius 25 cm.
(a) Calculate the circumference of one of the wheels.
(b) She cycles 50 km.
How many complete revolutions does a wheel make during the sponsored ride?

AQA

8 (a) Jayne has a circular hoop of radius 35 cm.
Calculate the circumference of her hoop.
(b) Rashida has a hoop with a circumference of 300 cm.
Calculate the radius of Rashida's hoop.

AQA

9 Three circles overlap, as shown.
The largest circle has a diameter of 12 cm.
The ratio of the diameters $x : y$ is $1 : 2$.
Calculate the shaded area.
Give your answer in terms of π.

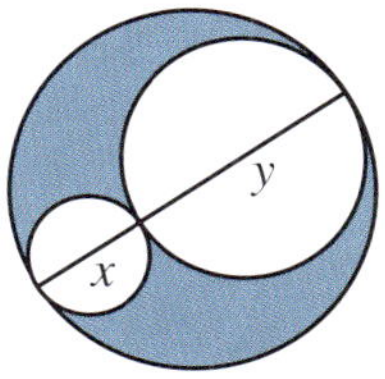

10 A circle has an area of 100 cm^2.
Calculate the circumference of the circle.
Give your answer correct to three significant figures.

11 Alfie says, "A semi-circle with a radius of 10 cm has a larger area than a whole circle with half the radius." Is he correct?
You **must** show working to justify your answer.

SECTION 34

Loci and Constructions

What you need to know

- The path of a point which moves according to a rule is called a **locus**.
- The word **loci** is used when we talk about more than one locus.
- You should be able to draw the locus of a point which moves according to a given rule.

Eg 1 A ball is rolled along this zig-zag. Draw the locus of P, the centre of the ball, as it is rolled along.

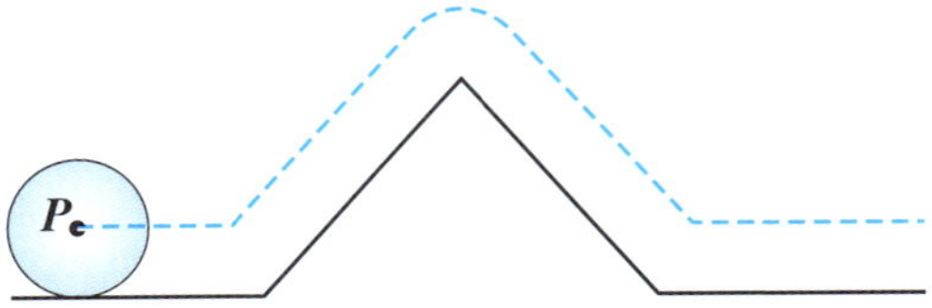

- Using a ruler and compasses you should be able to carry out the **constructions** below.

1 The perpendicular bisector of a line.

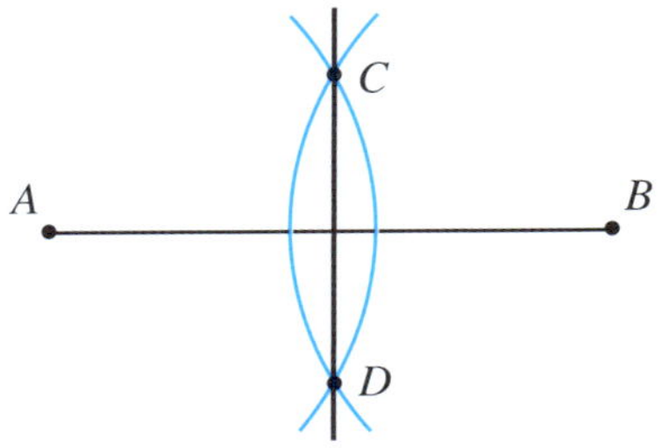

Points on the line CD are **equidistant** from the points A and B.

2 The bisector of an angle.

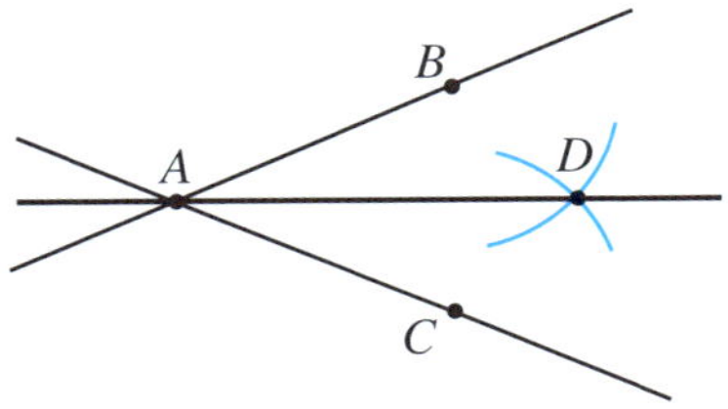

Points on the line AD are **equidistant** from the lines AB and AC.

3 The perpendicular from a point to a line.

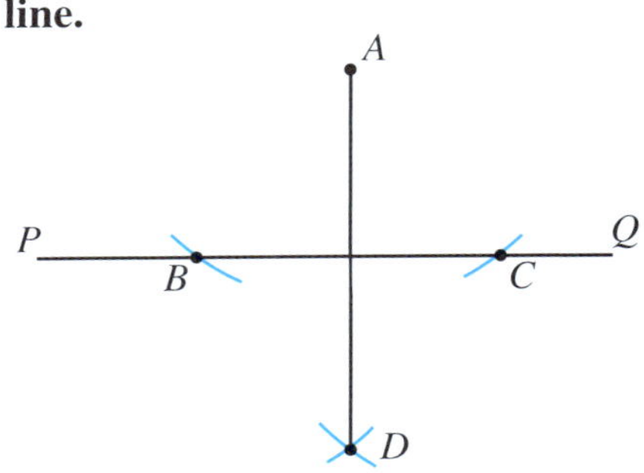

4 The perpendicular from a point on a line.

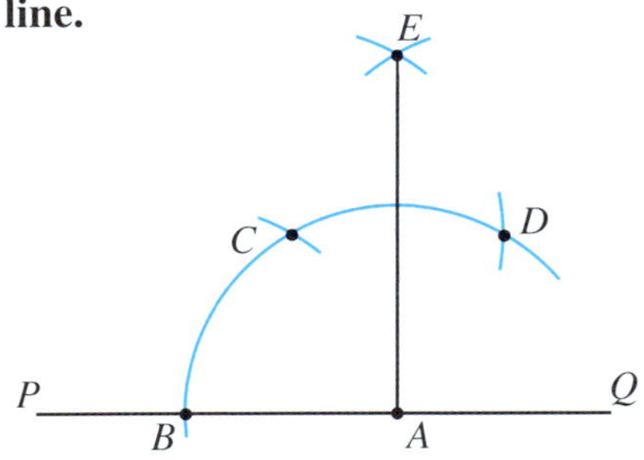

- You should be able to solve loci problems which involve using these constructions.

Eg 2 P is a point inside triangle ABC such that:
(i) P is equidistant from points A and B,
(ii) P is equidistant from lines AB and BC.
Find the position of P.

To find point P:
(i) construct the perpendicular bisector of line AB,
(ii) construct the bisector of angle ABC.

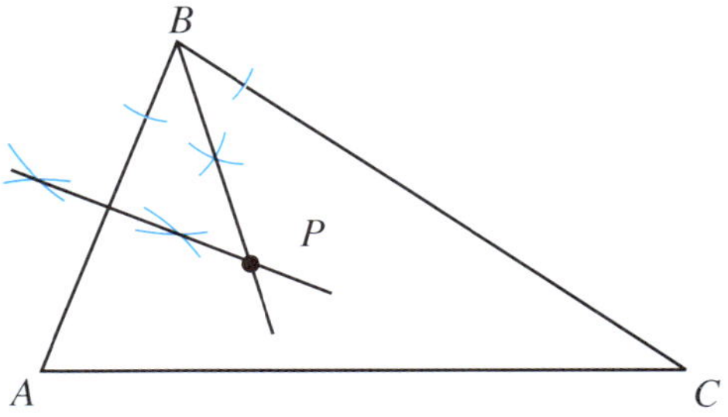

P is at the point where these lines intersect.

Exercise 34

1. The ball is rolled along the zig-zag.
Copy the diagram and draw the locus of the centre of the ball as it is rolled from X to Y.

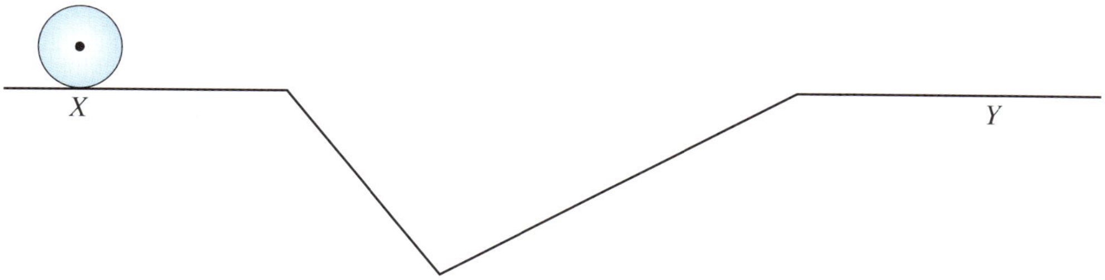

2. The diagram shows a plan of Paul's garden.
Draw the diagram using a scale of 1 cm to 1 m.

Paul has an electric lawnmower.
The lawnmower is plugged in at point P.

It can reach a maximum distance of 12 metres from P.
Using the same scale, show on your diagram the area of the garden which the lawnmower can reach.

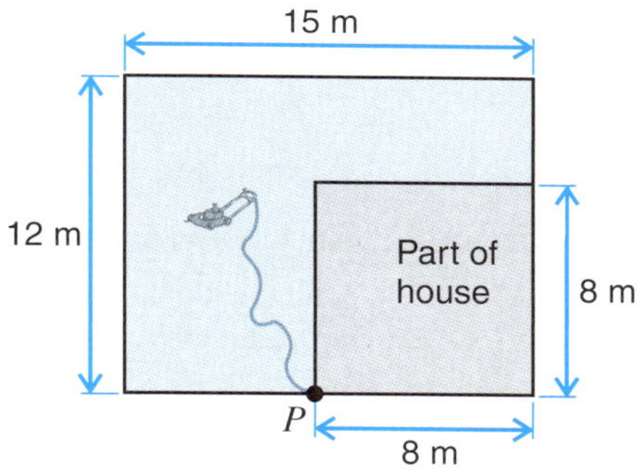

AQA

3. The map shows the positions of three villages A, B and C.
The map has been drawn to a scale of 1 cm to 2 km.

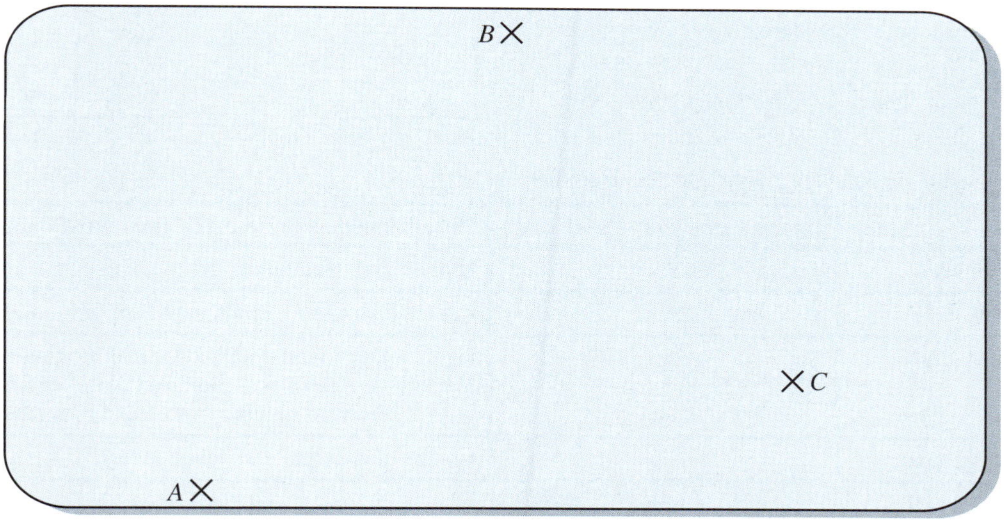

A supermarket is equidistant from villages A, B and C.
(a) Copy the map and find the position of the supermarket on your diagram.
(b) How many kilometres is the supermarket from village A?

4. (a) Construct a kite $PQRS$ in which $PQ = PS = 7$ cm, $QR = RS = 5$ cm and the diagonal $QS = 6$ cm.
X is a point inside the kite such that:
(i) X is equidistant from P and Q,
(ii) X is equidistant from sides PQ and PS.
(b) By constructing the loci for (i) and (ii) find the position of X.
(c) Measure the distance PX.

Transformations

What you need to know

- The movement of a shape from one position to another is called a **transformation**.
- **Single transformations** can be described in terms of a reflection, a rotation, a translation or an enlargement.
- **Reflection**: The image of the shape is the same distance from the mirror line as the original.
- **Rotation**: All points are turned through the same angle about the same point, called a centre of rotation.
- **Translation**: All points are moved the same distance in the same direction without turning.
- **Enlargement**: All lengths are multiplied by a scale factor.

  Scale factor $= \dfrac{\text{new length}}{\text{original length}}$ New length $=$ scale factor $\times$ original length

  The size of the original shape is:
  increased by using a scale factor greater than 1,
  reduced by using a scale factor which is a fraction, i.e. between 0 and 1.

- You should be able to draw the transformation of a shape.

Eg 1 Draw the image of triangle P after it has been translated with vector $\begin{pmatrix} -3 \\ 2 \end{pmatrix}$.

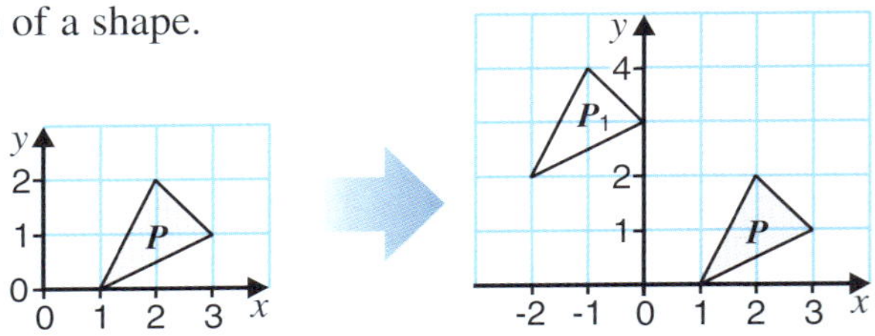

- You should be able to fully describe transformations.

Transformation	Image same shape and size?	Details needed to describe the transformation
Reflection	Yes	Mirror line, sometimes given as an equation.
Rotation	Yes	Centre of rotation, amount of turn, direction of turn.
Translation	Yes	Horizontal movement and vertical movement. Vector: top number = horizontal movement, bottom number = vertical movement.
Enlargement	No	Centre of enlargement, scale factor.

Eg 2 Describe the single transformation which maps
(a) A onto B,
(b) A onto C,
(c) A onto D,
(d) D onto E.

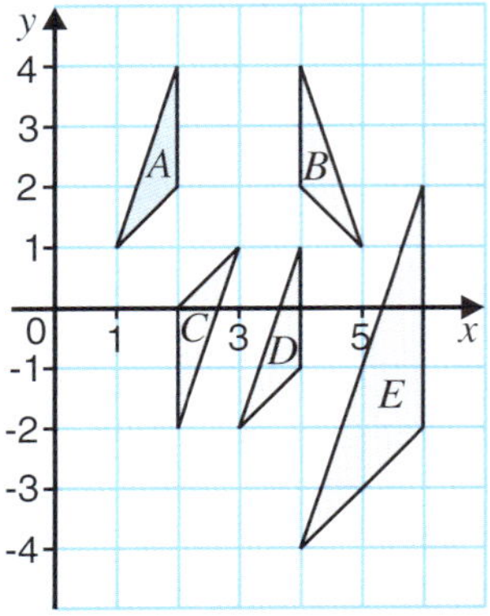

(a) **Reflection** in the line $x = 3$.

(b) **Rotation** of 180° about (2, 1).

(c) **Translation** with vector $\begin{pmatrix} 2 \\ -3 \end{pmatrix}$.

(d) **Enlargement** scale factor 2, centre (2, 0).

Exercise 35

1 Copy each diagram and draw the transformation given.

(a) Reflect the shape in the x axis.

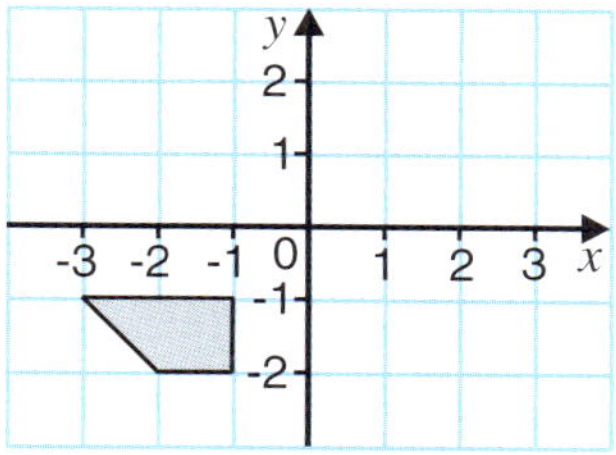

(b) Translate the shape, 2 units left and 3 units up.

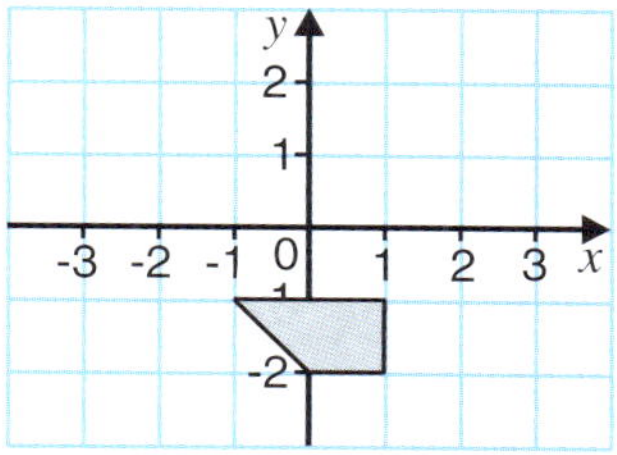

(c) Rotate the shape, 90° clockwise about the origin.

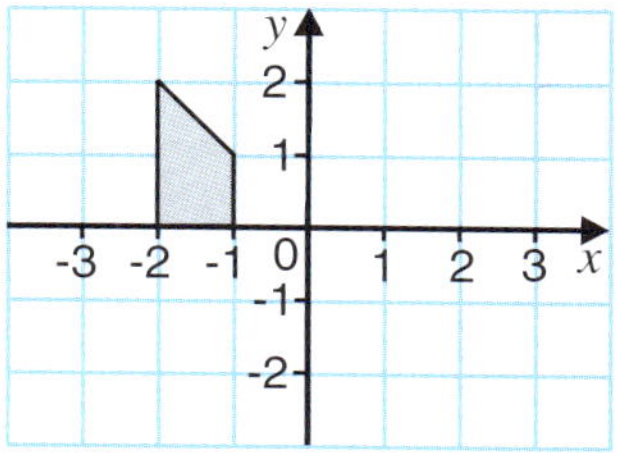

2 In each diagram A is mapped onto B by a single transformation. Describe each transformation.

(a)

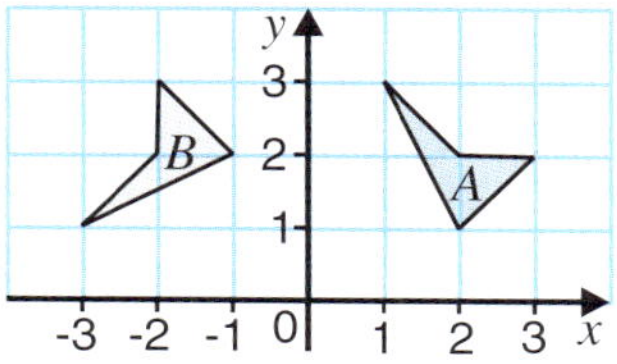

(b)

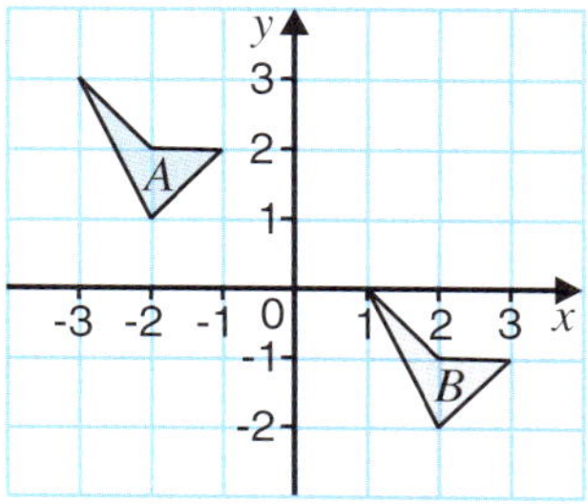

(c)

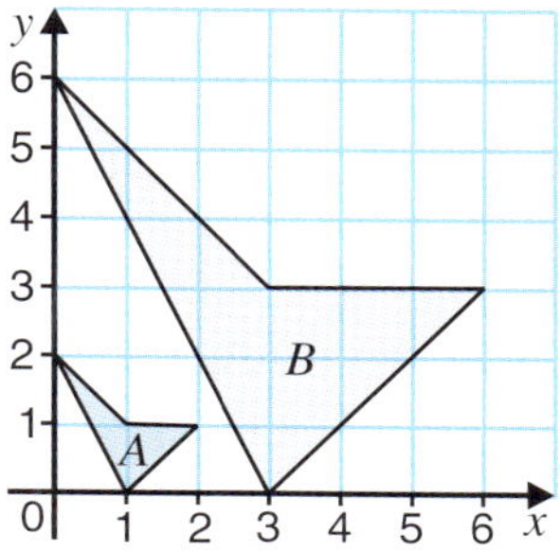

3 The diagram shows the positions of kites P, Q, R and S.

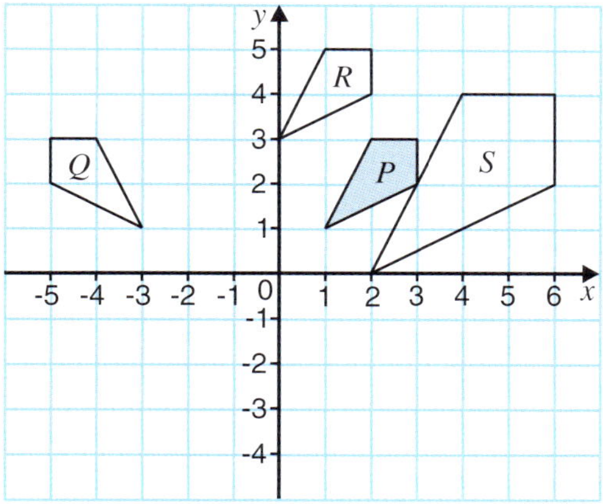

(a) (i) P is mapped onto Q by a reflection. What is the equation of the line of reflection?

(ii) P is mapped onto R by a translation. What is the vector of the translation?

(iii) P is mapped onto S by an enlargement. What is the centre and scale factor of the enlargement?

(b) P is mapped onto T by a rotation through 90° clockwise about $(1, -2)$. On squared paper, copy P and draw the position of T.

4 (a) Triangle PQR is mapped onto triangle $P_1Q_1R_1$, by an enlargement, centre O, scale factor 3. Copy the diagram and draw $P_1Q_1R_1$.

(b) Describe fully the single transformation which maps $P_1Q_1R_1$ onto PQR.

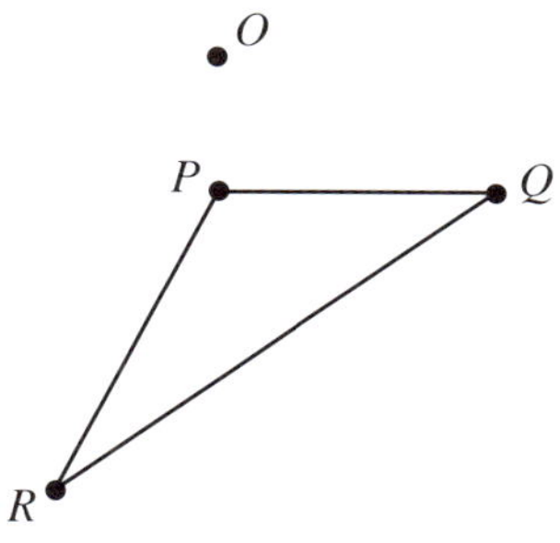

AQA

5 The diagram shows shapes Q and R which are transformations of shape P.

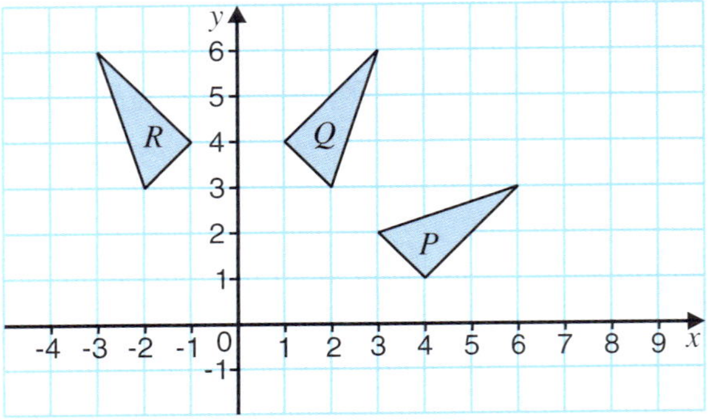

(a) Describe fully the **single** transformation which takes P onto R.
(b) Describe fully the **single** transformation which takes P onto Q.
(c) Copy shape P onto squared paper.
Draw an enlargement of shape P with scale factor 2, centre (3, 2). AQA

6 Find the coordinates of the reflection of the point (1, 4) in the line $y = -x$.
(You may find it useful to draw a diagram.) AQA

7 Describe fully the single transformation which maps $ABCD$ onto $PQRS$.

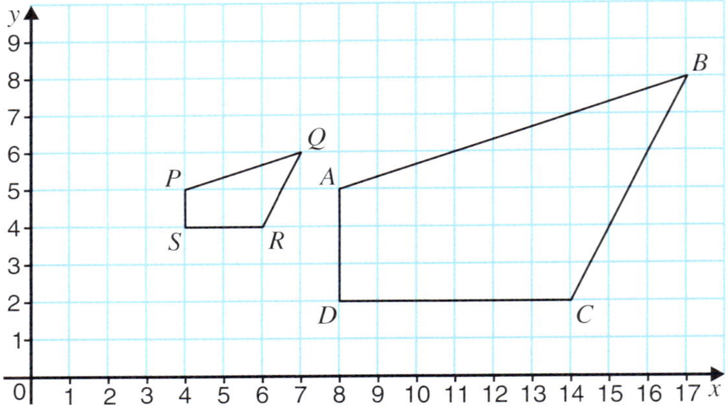

8 The diagram shows the position of P.
P has coordinates (3, 1).

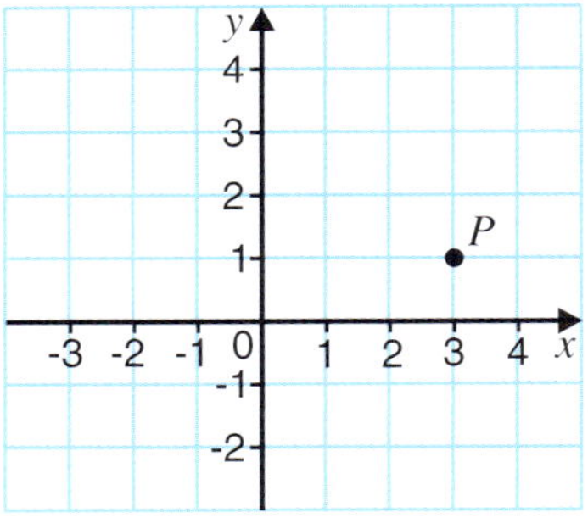

(a) P is mapped onto Q by a reflection in the line $y = x$.
What are the coordinates of Q?

The translation $\begin{pmatrix} -2 \\ 1 \end{pmatrix}$ maps P onto R.

The translation $\begin{pmatrix} 3 \\ -4 \end{pmatrix}$ maps R onto S.

(b) (i) What are the coordinates of S?
(ii) What is the translation which maps S onto P?

(c) T has coordinates $(-1, 1)$.
P is mapped onto T by a rotation through 90° anticlockwise about centre X.
What are the coordinates of X? AQA

SECTION 36

Volumes and Surface Areas

What you need to know

- **Faces**, **vertices** (corners) and **edges**.

  A cube has 6 faces, 8 vertices and 12 edges.

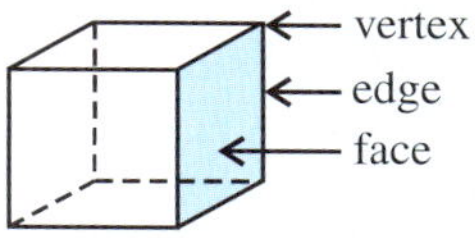

- A **net** can be used to make a solid shape.

  Eg 1 Draw a net of a cube.

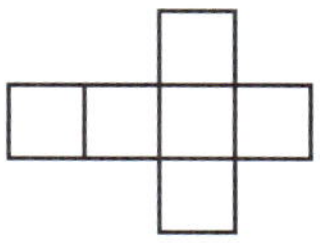

- **Isometric paper** is used to make 2-dimensional drawings of 3-dimensional shapes.

  Eg 2 Draw a cube of edge 2 cm on isometric paper.

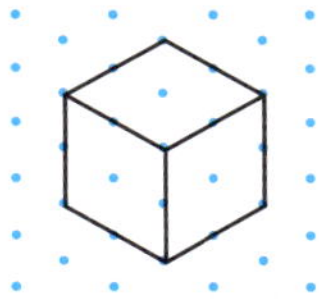

- **Plans and Elevations**
  The view of a 3-dimensional shape looking from above is called a **plan**.
  The view of a 3-dimensional shape from the front or sides is called an **elevation**.

  Eg 3 Draw diagrams to show the plan and elevation from **X**, for this 3-dimensional shape.

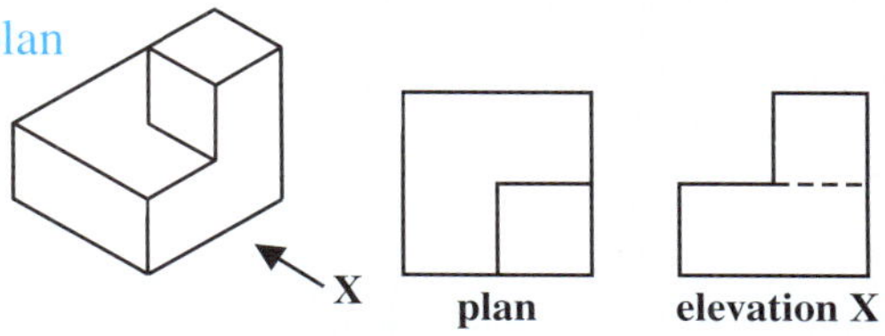

Dotted lines are used to show hidden edges.

- **Volume** is the amount of space occupied by a 3-dimensional shape.

- The formula for the volume of a **cuboid** is:
  Volume = length × breadth × height
  $V = l \times b \times h$

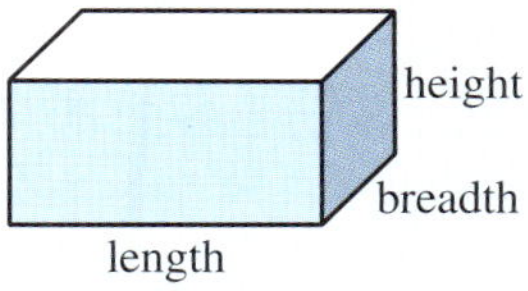

- Volume of a **cube** is: $V = l^3$

- To find the **surface area** of a cuboid, find the areas of the 6 rectangular faces and add the answers together.

  Eg 4 Find the volume and surface area of a cuboid measuring 7 cm by 5 cm by 3 cm.

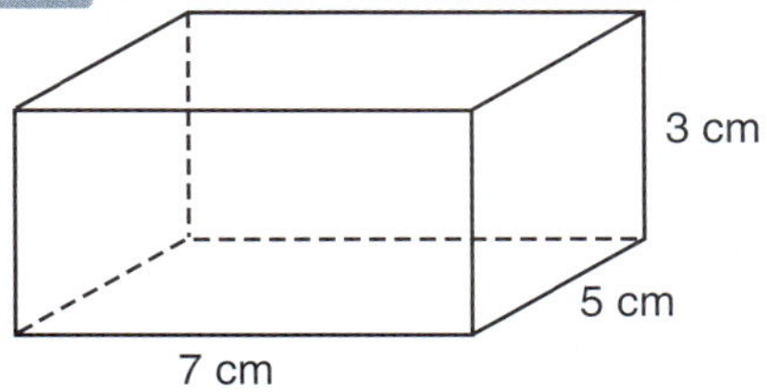

Volume $= lbh$
$= 7\text{ cm} \times 5\text{ cm} \times 3\text{ cm}$
$= 105\text{ cm}^3$

Surface area $= (2 \times 7 \times 5) + (2 \times 5 \times 3) + (2 \times 3 \times 7)$
$= 70 + 30 + 42$
$= 142\text{ cm}^2$

Eg 5 This cuboid has a volume of 75 cm^3.
Calculate the height, h, of the cuboid.

Volume $= lbh$
$75 = 6 \times 5 \times h$
$h = \frac{75}{30}$
$= 2.5\text{ cm}$

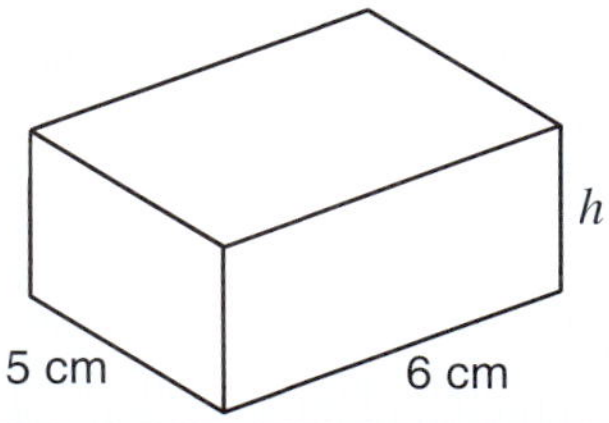

- **Prisms**
  If you make a cut at right angles to the length of a prism you will always get the same cross-section.
- Volume of a prism = area of cross-section × length

Triangular prism

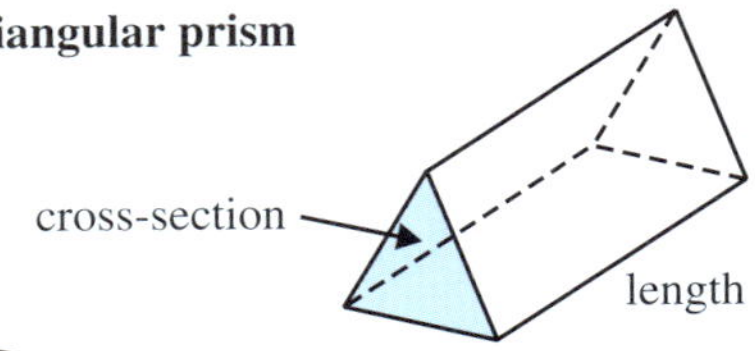

- A **cylinder** is a prism.
  Volume of a cylinder is: $V = \pi \times r^2 \times h$

  Surface area of a cylinder is:
  Surface area $= 2\pi r^2 + 2\pi rh$

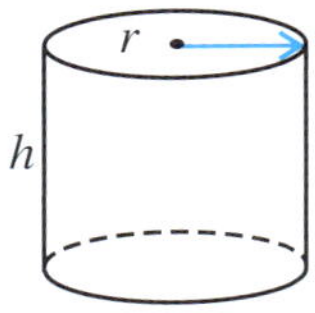

Eg 6 Calculate the volume of this cylinder.

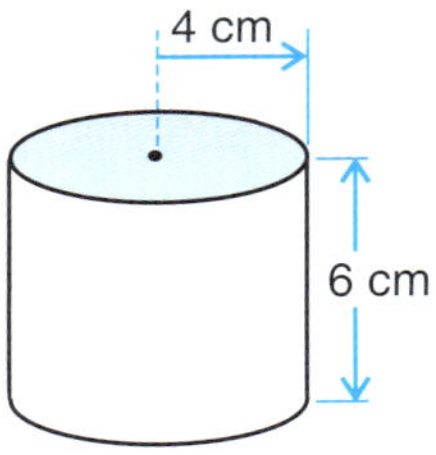

Volume $= \pi r^2 h$
$= \pi \times 4 \times 4 \times 6$
$= 301.592\ldots$
$= 302\text{ cm}^3$, correct to 3 s.f.

Eg 7 This cylinder has a volume of 550 cm^3. Calculate the radius, r, of the cylinder.

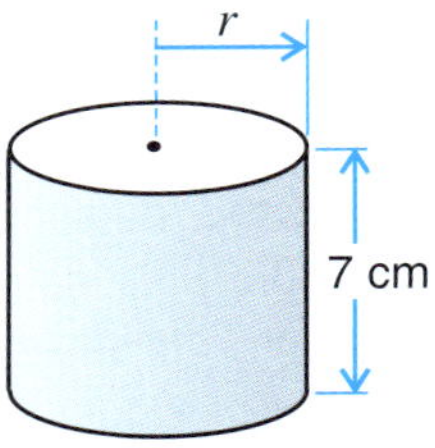

Volume $= \pi r^2 h$
$550 = \pi \times r^2 \times 7$
$r^2 = \frac{550}{7\pi} = 25.01\ldots$
$r = \sqrt{25.01\ldots} = 5\text{ cm}$

Exercise 36

Do not use a calculator for question 1.

1 (a) Which of these cuboids has the largest volume?
Show all your working.

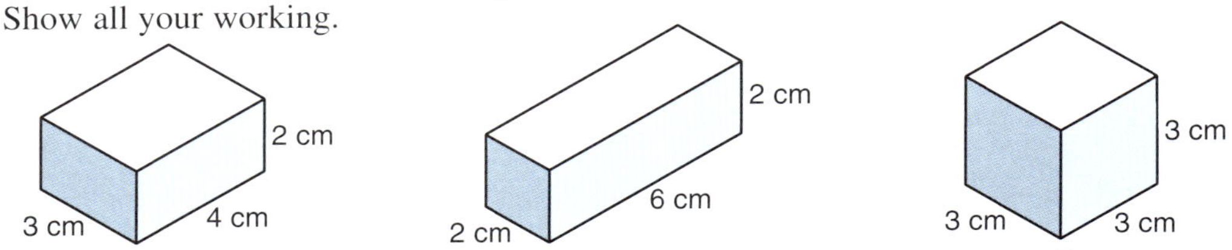

A B C

(b) (i) Draw an accurate net of cuboid **A**. (ii) Find the total surface area of cuboid **A**.
(c) Which cuboid has the largest surface area?

2 Which of these nets is the net of a pyramid?

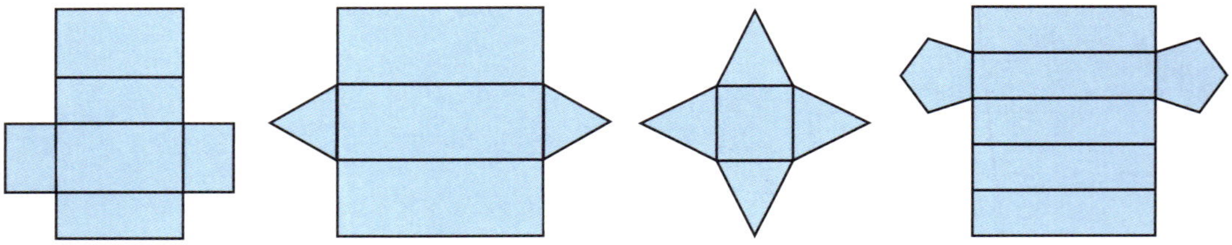

P Q R S

3 My cats eat two types of food.
Whiskat comes in a square-based tin of side 8.5 cm.
Yummy comes in a round-based tin of radius 5 cm.
(a) (i) Calculate the area of the base of the Whiskat tin.
(ii) Calculate the area of the base of the Yummy tin.
Give your answer correct to two decimal places.
(b) The heights of the two tins are the same.
Which tin holds more food when full? Give a reason for your answer. AQA

4 A girder is 5 metres long.
Its cross-section is L-shaped, as shown.
Find the volume of the girder.

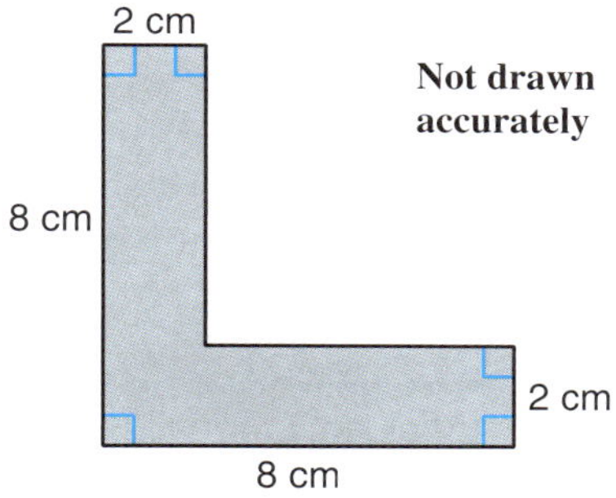

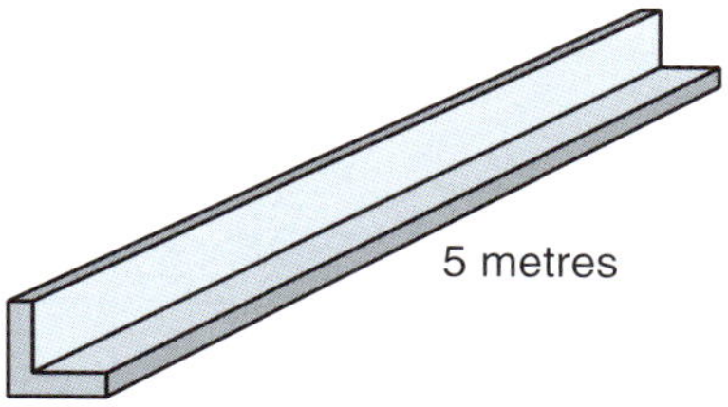

AQA

5 A triangular prism has dimensions, as shown.
(a) Calculate the total surface area of the prism.
(b) Calculate the volume of the prism.

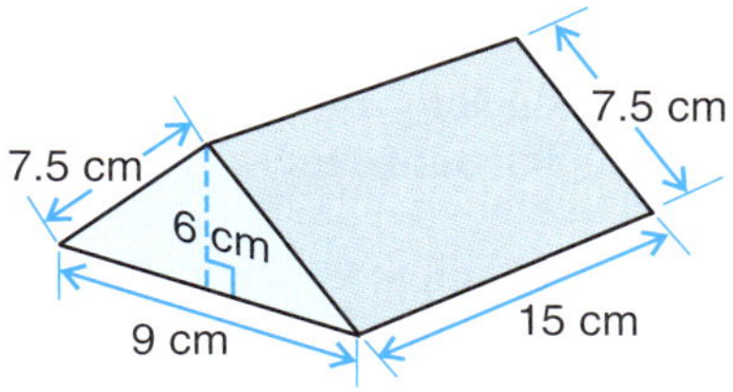

6

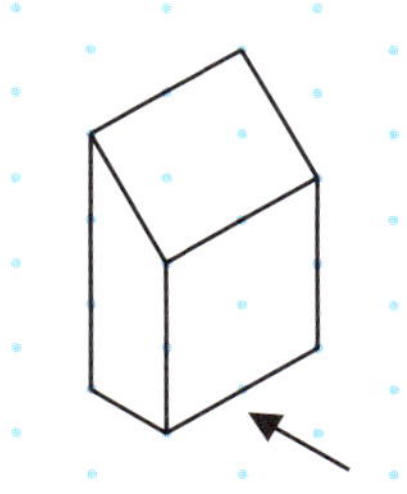

The diagram shows a solid.
Draw the elevation of this solid, from the direction shown by the arrow.

AQA

7 Ellie is cutting out circles of pastry to make jam tarts.
The radius of each circle is 3.5 cm.
She cuts 6 of these circles from a rectangular piece of pastry 28 cm by 15 cm.
The pastry is 0.8 cm thick.
Calculate the volume of the pastry that is left.

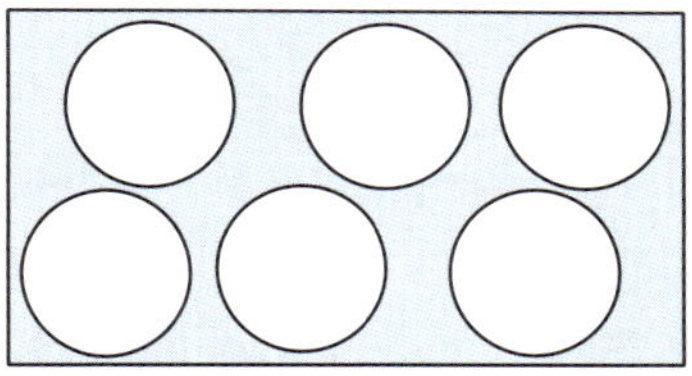

AQA

8 A cuboid has a volume of 100 cm^3.
The cuboid is 8 cm long and 5 cm wide.
Calculate the height of the cuboid.

9 A cylinder of radius 7 cm and height 18 cm is half full of water.
One litre of water is added.
Will the water overflow?
You must show all your working.

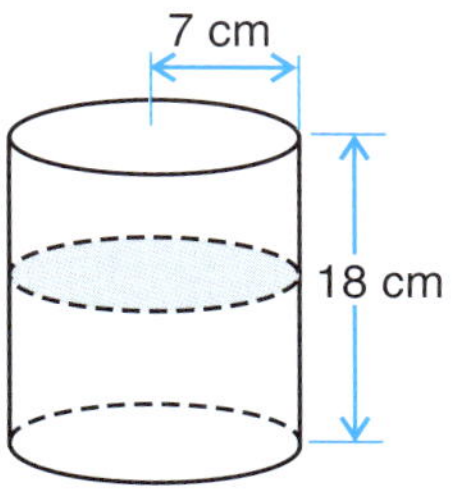

AQA

10 A cylindrical water tank has radius 40 cm and height 90 cm.
(a) Calculate the total surface area of the tank.

A full tank of water is used to fill a paddling pool.
(b) The paddling pool is a cylinder with diameter 2.4 metres.
Calculate the depth of water in the pool.

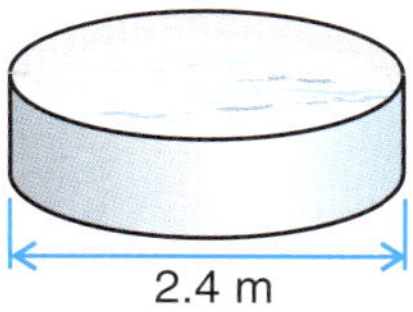

SECTION 37

Enlargements and Similar Figures

What you need to know

- When a shape is **enlarged**: all **lengths** are multiplied by a **scale factor**, **angles** remain unchanged.

- When two figures are **similar**:
  their **shapes** are the same,
  their **angles** are the same,
  corresponding **lengths** are in the same ratio,
  this ratio is the **scale factor** of the enlargement.

> All circles are similar to each other.
> All squares are similar to each other.

> $\text{Scale factor} = \dfrac{\text{new length}}{\text{original length}}$

- For **similar triangles**:
  corresponding lengths are opposite equal angles,
  the scale factor is the ratio of the corresponding sides.

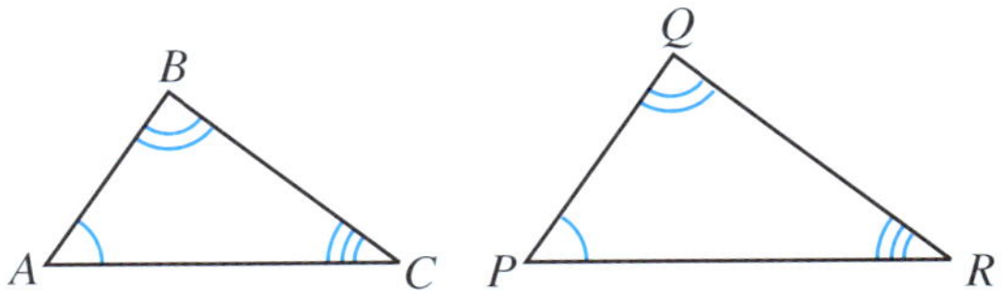

$$\frac{AB}{PQ} = \frac{BC}{QR} = \frac{CA}{RP} = \text{scale factor}$$

- You should be able to find corresponding lengths in similar triangles.

Eg 1 These two triangles are similar.
Find the lengths of the sides marked x and y.

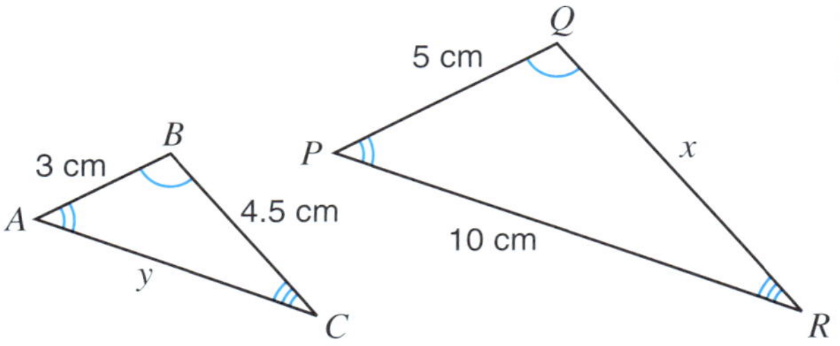

> AB and PQ are corresponding sides.
> $\text{Scale factor} = \dfrac{PQ}{AB} = \dfrac{5}{3}$

$x = 4.5 \times \frac{5}{3} = 7.5\,\text{cm}$

$y = 10 \div \frac{5}{3} = 6\,\text{cm}$

Exercise 37

The diagrams in this exercise have not been drawn accurately.

1 These triangles are similar.

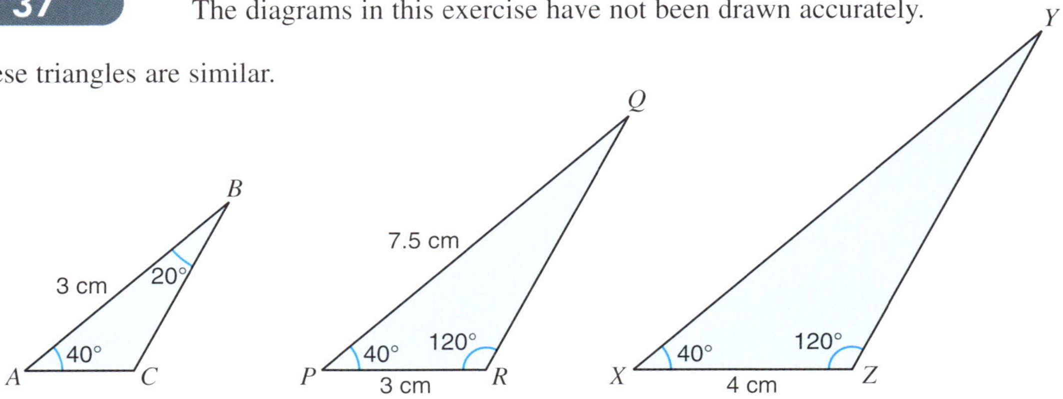

(a) Work out the length of the side XY.
(b) Work out the length of the side AC.

2 The diagram shows rectangles **A**, **B** and **C**.

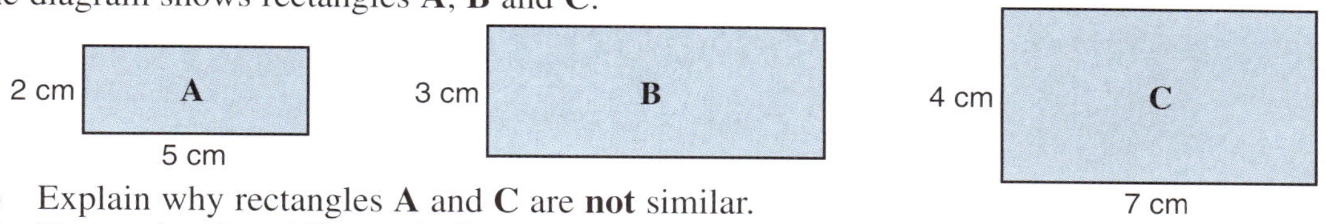

(a) Explain why rectangles **A** and **C** are **not** similar.
(b) Rectangles **A** and **B** are similar.
Work out the length of rectangle **B**.

3 One of the earliest cameras was the pinhole camera.
Rays of light pass from the object through a small pinhole and form an upside down image on the photographic film at the back of the camera, as shown in the diagram.

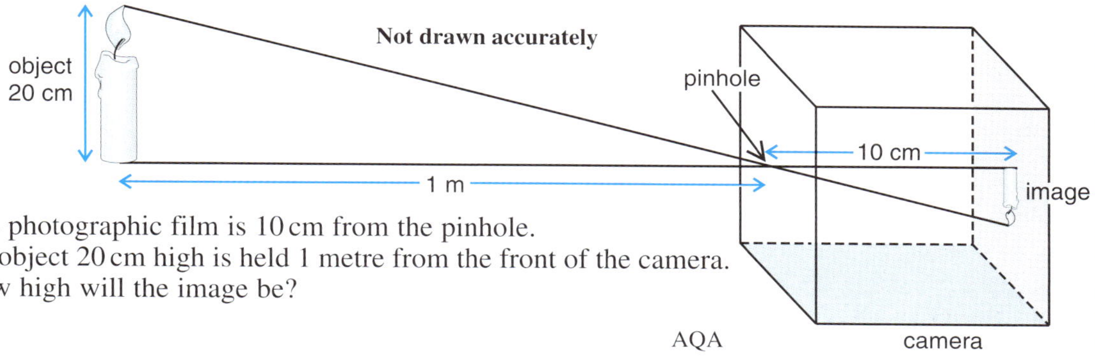

The photographic film is 10 cm from the pinhole.
An object 20 cm high is held 1 metre from the front of the camera.
How high will the image be?

AQA

4 Noel (N) can just see the top of the church tower (C) appearing over the tree (T).

Noel is 20 metres from the tree.
The tree is 30 metres from the tower.
The tower is 44 metres high.
Calculate the height of the tree.

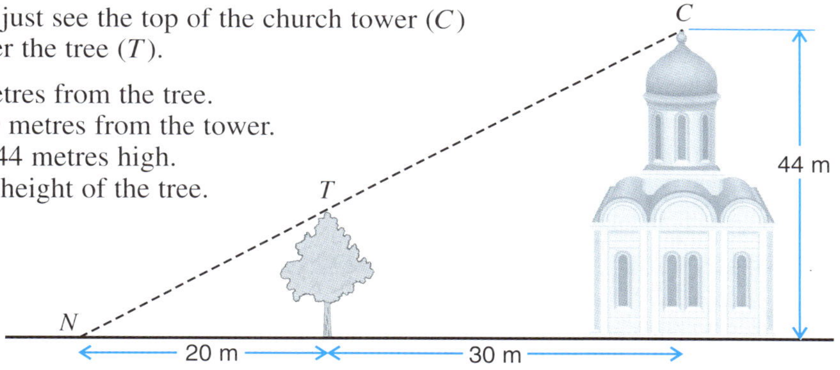

AQA

5 The diagram shows two regular hexagons.
(a) Name a triangle which is similar but **not** congruent to triangle BCD.

(b) $AB : PQ$ is $2 : 3$.
(i) Angle $AEF = 30°$.
What is the size of angle PTU?
(ii) $AF = 2.4$ cm.
Calculate the perimeter of the hexagon $PQRSTU$.

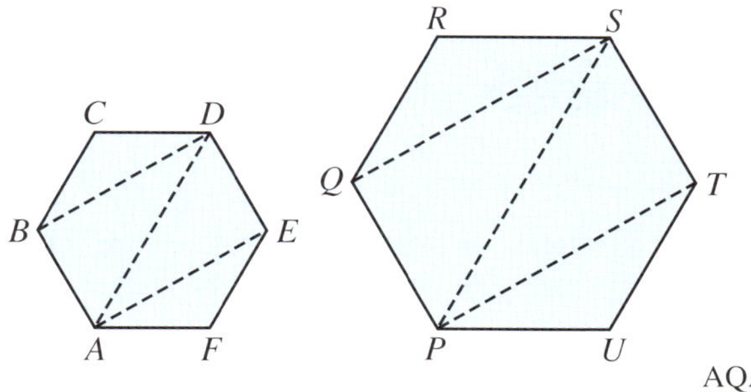

AQA

6 In the diagram, AB is parallel to DE.
$AB = 4.5$ cm, $AC = 2.7$ cm and $CE = 2.4$ cm.

(a) Explain why triangle ABC is similar to triangle EDC.
(b) Calculate the length of DE.

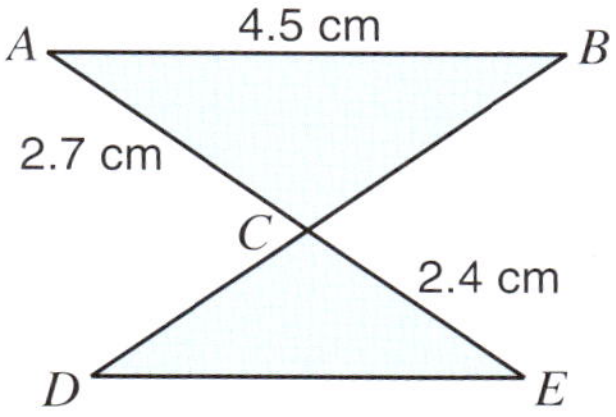

SECTION 38 Pythagoras' Theorem

What you need to know

- The longest side in a right-angled triangle is called the **hypotenuse**.
- The **Theorem of Pythagoras** states:
  "In any right-angled triangle the square on the hypotenuse is equal to the sum of the squares on the other two sides."
  $$a^2 = b^2 + c^2$$

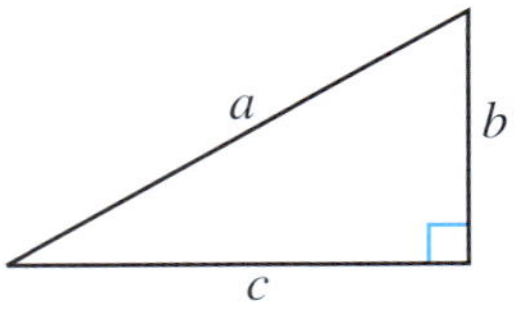

- When we know the lengths of two sides of a right-angled triangle, we can use the Theorem of Pythagoras to find the length of the third side.

> $a^2 = b^2 + c^2$
> Rearranging gives: $b^2 = a^2 - c^2$
> $c^2 = a^2 - b^2$

Eg 1 Calculate the length of side a, correct to 1 d.p.

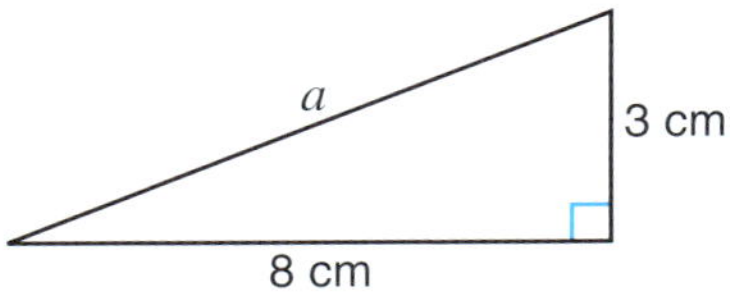

$a^2 = b^2 + c^2$
$a^2 = 8^2 + 3^2$
$a^2 = 64 + 9 = 73$
$a = \sqrt{73} = 8.544\ldots$
$a = 8.5$ cm, correct to 1 d.p.

Eg 2 Calculate the length of side b, correct to 1 d.p.

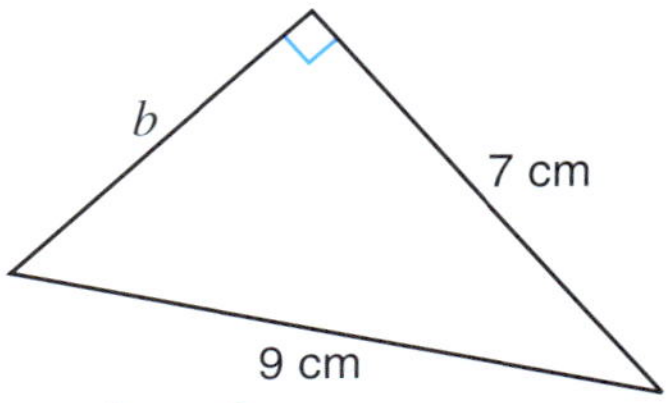

$b^2 = a^2 - c^2$
$b^2 = 9^2 - 7^2$
$b^2 = 81 - 49 = 32$
$b = \sqrt{32} = 5.656\ldots$
$b = 5.7$ cm, correct to 1 d.p.

Exercise 38

The diagrams in this exercise have not been drawn accurately.
Do not use a calculator for questions 1 and 2.

1 ABC is a right-angled triangle.
$AB = 5$ cm and $AC = 12$ cm.
Calculate the length of BC.

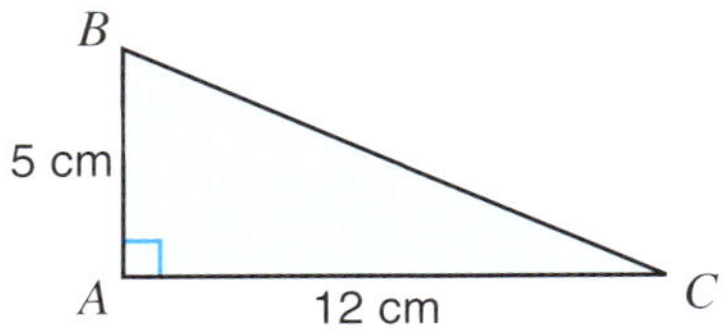

2 The positions of three villages, Oldacre (O), Adchester (A) and Byetoft (B), are shown on the diagram.
Angle $OAB = 90°$.
The distance from Oldacre to Adchester is 8 km.
The distance from Oldacre to Byetoft is 10 km.
Calculate the distance from Adchester to Byetoft.

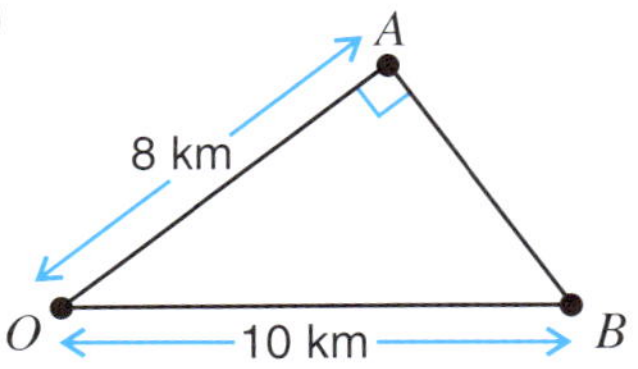

AQA

3

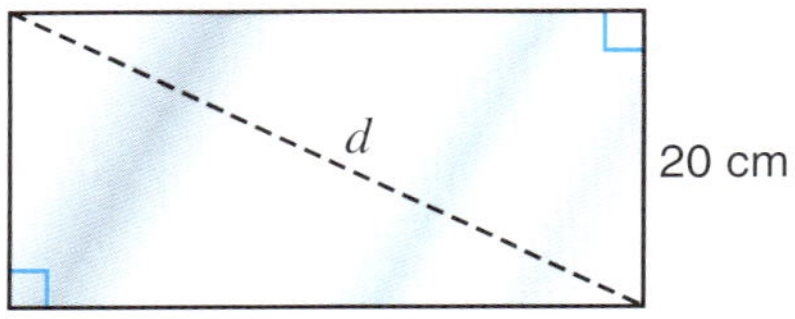

The diagram shows a rectangular sheet of paper.
The paper is 20 cm wide and the diagonal, d, is 35 cm.
Calculate the length of the sheet of paper.

4. Calculate the length of the line joining the points $A(-3, 2)$ and $B(6, -2)$.

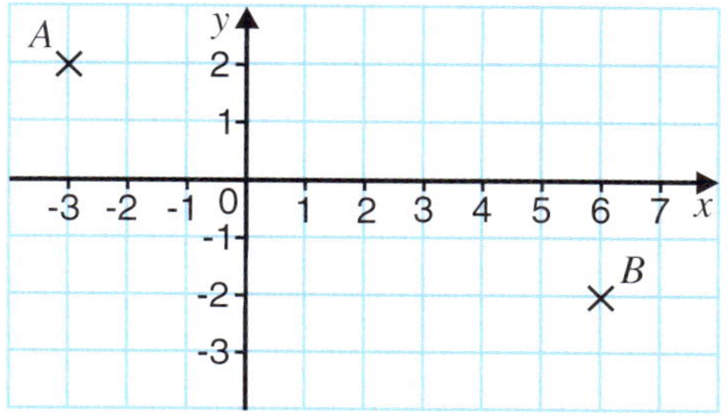

AQA

5. Three similar triangles, OPQ, OQR and ORS, are connected as shown.
$OP = 1$ cm and $OQ = 2$ cm.

Calculate the exact length of RS.

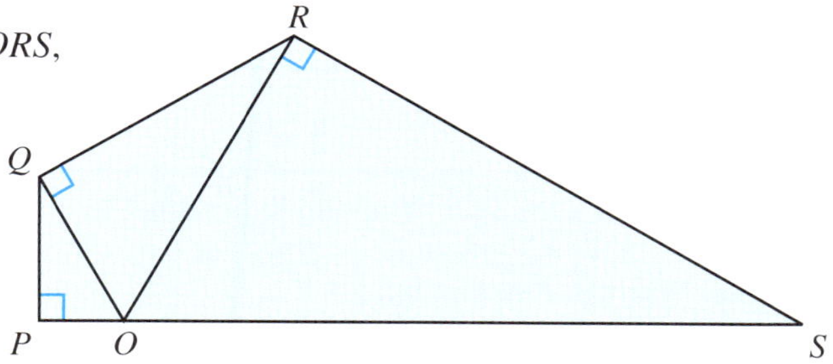

6. An oil rig is 15 km East and 12 km North from Kirrin.

(a) Calculate the direct distance from Kirrin to the oil rig.
(b) An engineer flew 14 km from Faxtown to the oil rig.
The oil rig is 10 km West of Faxtown.
Calculate how far South the oil rig is from Faxtown.

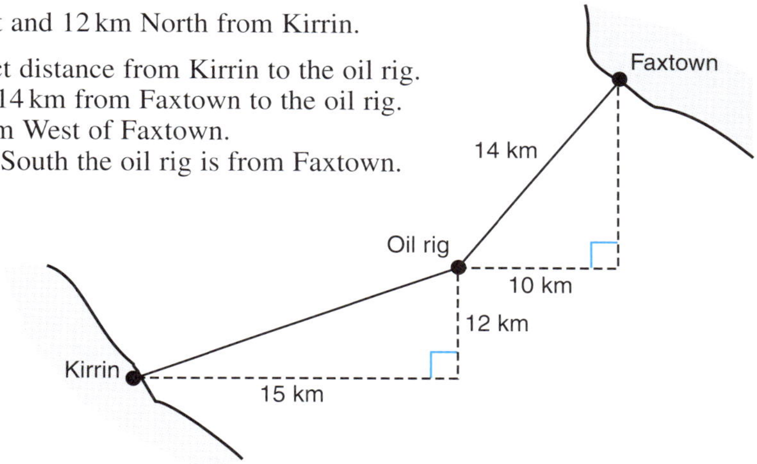

AQA

7. In the diagram, $BCDX$ is a square.
AXE is a straight line with $AX = 6.5$ cm and $XE = 3$ cm. $DE = 2$ cm.

(a) Calculate the area of $BCDX$.
(b) Calculate the length of AB, correct to one decimal place.

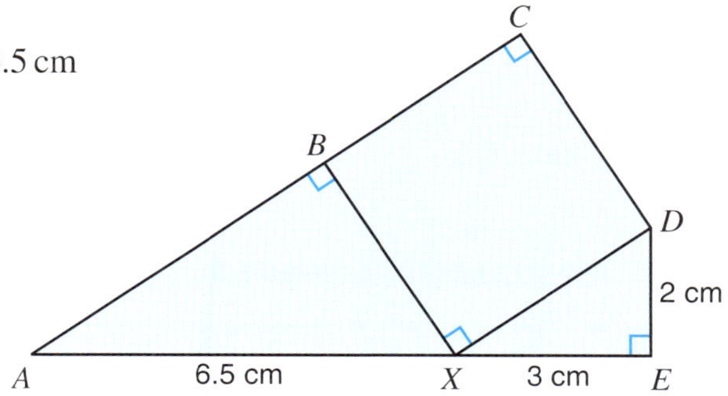

8. 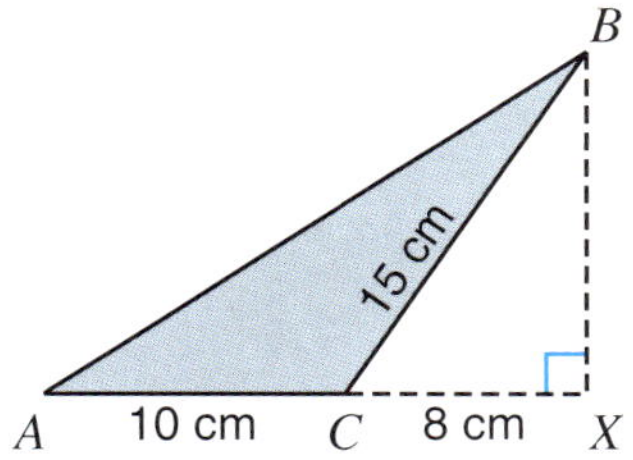

The diagram shows a triangle ABC.
Angle $BXA = 90°$, $BC = 15$ cm, $CX = 8$ cm and $AC = 10$ cm.

Calculate the area of triangle ABC.
Give your answer correct to 3 significant figures.

AQA

SECTION 39

Trigonometry

What you need to know

- **Trigonometry** is used to find the lengths of sides and the sizes of angles in right-angled triangles.
- You must learn the **sine**, **cosine** and **tangent** ratios.

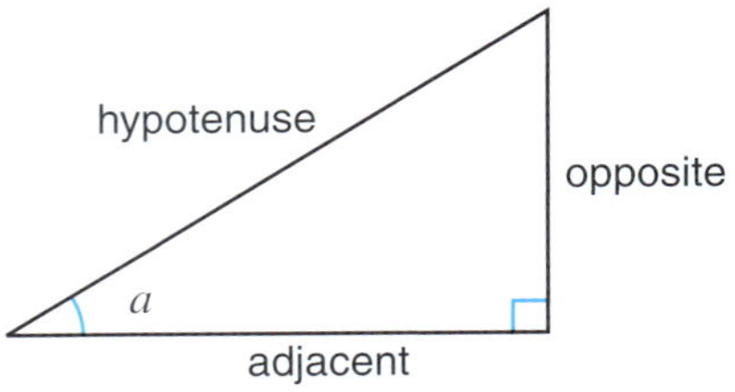

$\sin a = \dfrac{\text{opposite}}{\text{hypotenuse}}$ $\quad \cos a = \dfrac{\text{adjacent}}{\text{hypotenuse}}$ $\quad \tan a = \dfrac{\text{opposite}}{\text{adjacent}}$

- Each ratio links the size of an angle with the lengths of two sides. If we are given the values for two of these we can find the value of the third.
- When we look **up** from the horizontal the angle we turn through is called the **angle of elevation**.
- When we look **down** from the horizontal the angle we turn through is called the **angle of depression**.

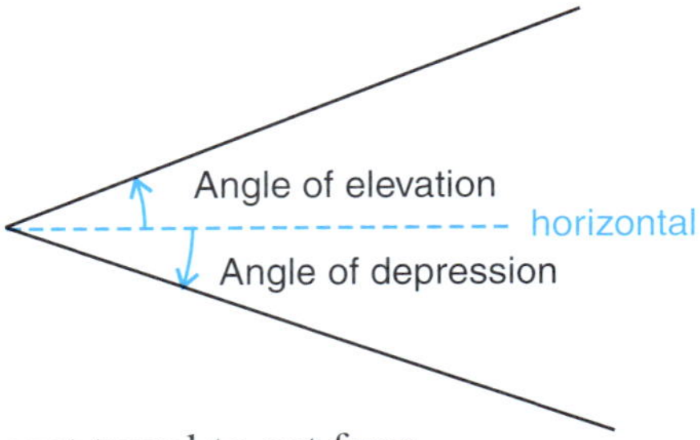

- **Three-figure bearings**
  Bearings are used to describe the direction in which you must travel to get from one place to another. They are measured from the North line in a clockwise direction. A bearing can be any angle from 0° to 360° and is written as a three-figure number.
- You should be able to use trigonometry to find the lengths of sides and the sizes of angles when solving problems involving right-angled triangles.

Eg 1 Find the length, d, giving the answer to 3 significant figures.

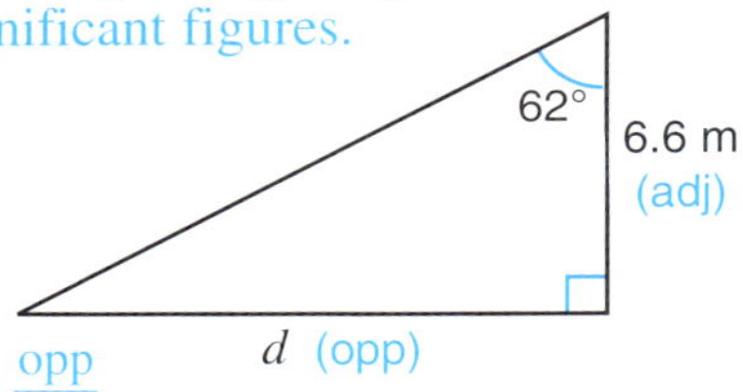

$\tan a = \dfrac{\text{opp}}{\text{adj}}$

$\tan 62° = \dfrac{d}{6.6}$

$d = 6.6 \times \tan 62°$

$d = 12.412\ldots$

$d = 12.4$ m, correct to 3 s.f.

Eg 2 Find the size of angle a, correct to one decimal place.

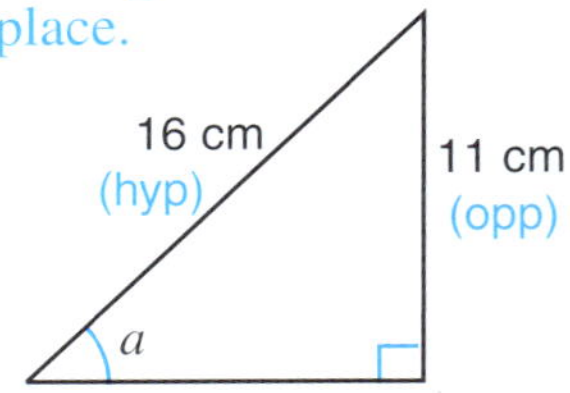

$\sin a = \dfrac{\text{opp}}{\text{hyp}}$

$\sin a° = \dfrac{11}{16}$

$a = \sin^{-1} \dfrac{11}{16}$

$a = 43.432\ldots$

$a = 43.4°$, correct to 1 d.p.

Exercise 39

The diagrams in this exercise have not been drawn accurately.
Do not use a calculator for question 1.

1 LMN is a right-angled triangle.
$LN = 8$ cm.
$\sin x = 0.6$, $\quad \cos x = 0.8$ $\quad$ and $\quad \tan x = 0.75$.

Calculate the length of MN.

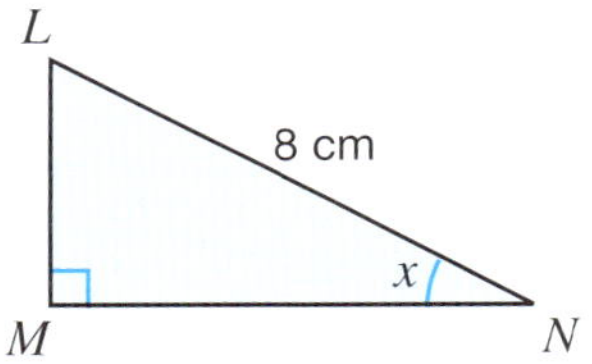

AQA

2 Calculate the length of the side AB in each of these triangles.

(a)

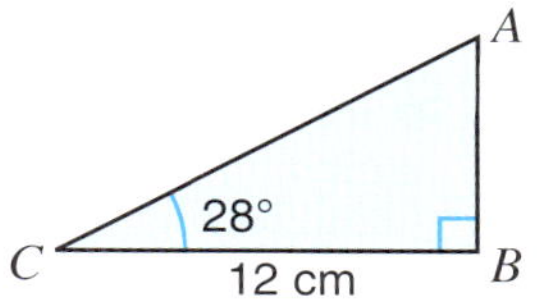

(b)

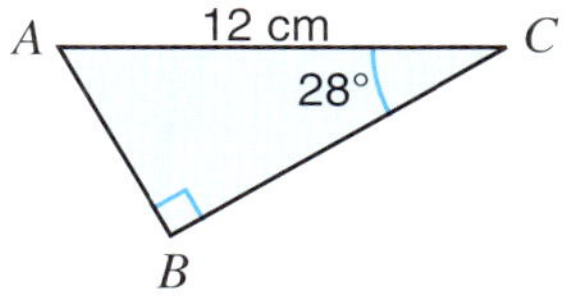

3 (a) Calculate angle x in triangle ABC.

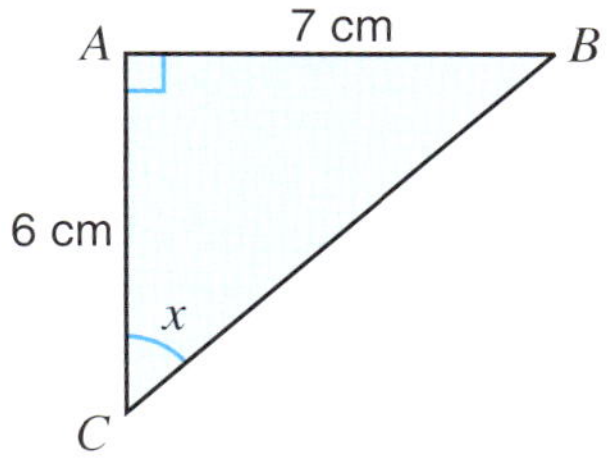

(b) Calculate length QR in triangle PQR.

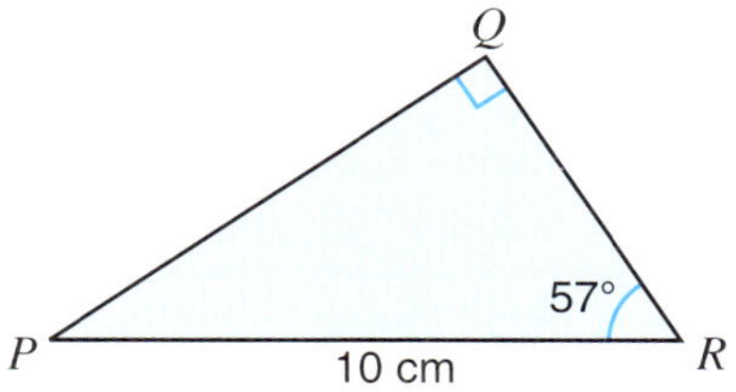

AQA

4 Points P and Q are on level ground.
The diagram shows P and Q and the position of a hot air balloon at R, which is vertically above Q.
$PQ = 500$ m and $QR = 200$ m.

Calculate angle RPQ.

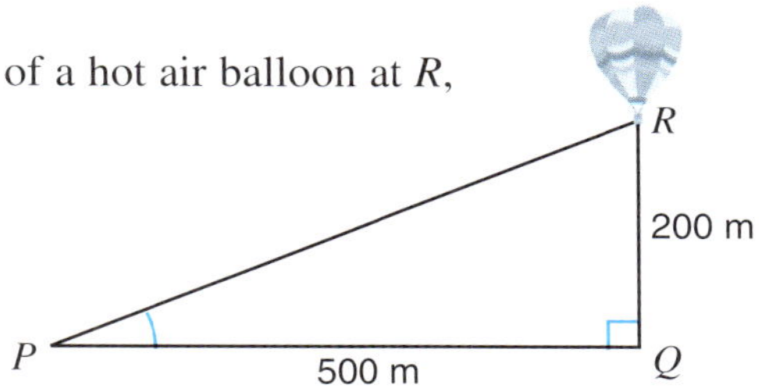

AQA

5 The diagram shows the side view of a wheelchair ramp.
The ramp makes an angle of 4° with the horizontal.
Calculate the length, marked x, of the ramp.
Give your answer in metres to a sensible degree of accuracy.

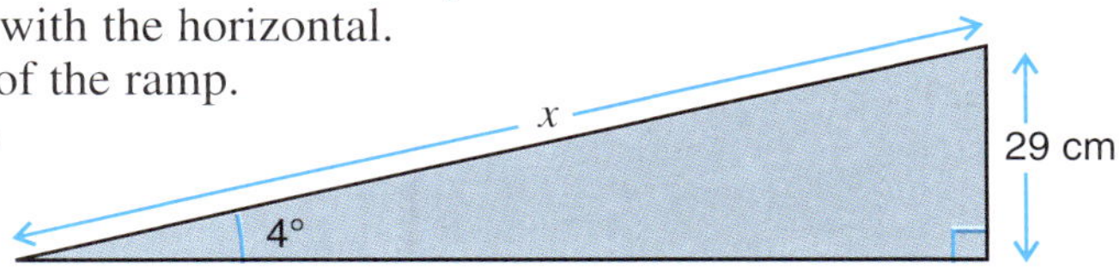

AQA

6 The diagram shows the path of a jet-ski from P to Q to R.

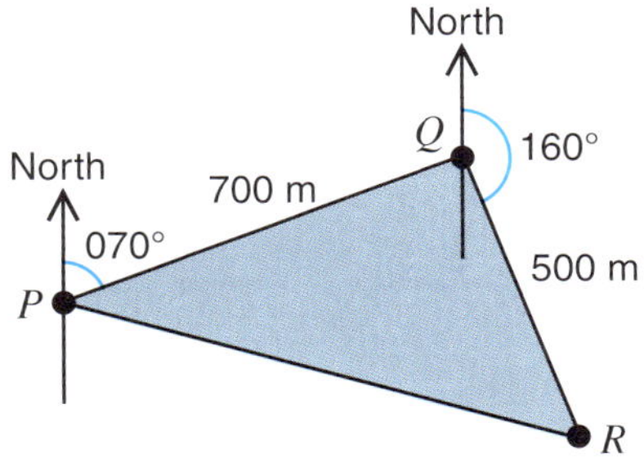

Q is 700 m from P on a bearing of 070°.
R is 500 m from Q on a bearing of 160°.

Calculate the bearing of P from R.

7 A helicopter is 200 m from a lighthouse which stands on a vertical cliff.

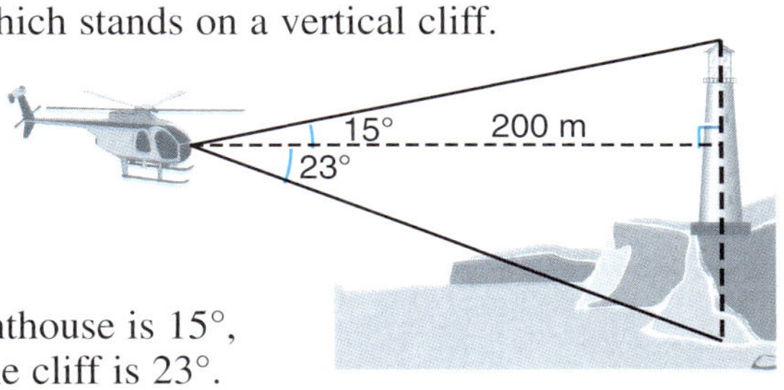

From the helicopter:
the angle of elevation to the top of the lighthouse is 15°,
the angle of depression to the bottom of the cliff is 23°.

Calculate the distance from the top of the lighthouse to the bottom of the cliff.

SECTION 40

Understanding and Using Measures

What you need to know

- The common units – both **metric** and **imperial** – used to measure **length**, **mass** and **capacity**.
- How to estimate measurements using sensible units and a suitable degree of accuracy.
- How to convert from one unit to another. This includes knowing the connection between one metric unit and another and the approximate equivalents between metric and imperial units.

Metric Units

Length
1 kilometre (km) = 1000 metres (m)
1 m = 100 centimetres (cm)
1 cm = 10 millimetres (mm)

Mass
1 tonne (t) = 1000 kilograms (kg)
1 kg = 1000 grams (g)

Capacity and volume
1 litre = 1000 millilitres (ml)
1 cm^3 = 1 ml

Imperial Units

Length
1 foot = 12 inches
1 yard = 3 feet

Mass
1 pound = 16 ounces
14 pounds = 1 stone

Capacity and volume
1 gallon = 8 pints

Conversions

Length
5 miles is about 8 km
1 inch is about 2.5 cm
1 foot is about 30 cm

Mass
1 kg is about 2.2 pounds

Capacity and volume
1 litre is about 1.75 pints
1 gallon is about 4.5 litres

- How to change between units of area. For example 1 m^2 = 10 000 cm^2.
- How to change between units of volume. For example 1 m^3 = 1 000 000 cm^3.
- You should be able to solve problems involving different units.

Eg 1 A tank holds 6 gallons of water.
How many litres is this? $6 \times 4.5 = 27$ litres

Eg 2 A cuboid measures 1.5 m by 90 cm by 80 cm.
Calculate the volume of the cuboid, in m^3. $1.5 \times 0.9 \times 0.8 = 1.08\ m^3$

- Be able to recognise limitations on the accuracy of measurements.

A **discrete measure** can only take a particular value and a **continuous measure** lies within a range of possible values which depends upon the degree of accuracy of the measurement.

Eg 3 A log is 12 m in length. The length is correct to the nearest metre.
What is the minimum length of the log? Minimum length = $12 - 0.5 = 11.5$ m

Eg 4 A road is 400 m long, to the nearest 10 m.
Between what lengths is the actual length of the road?
Actual length = 400 m $\pm$ 5 m 395 m $\leq$ actual length $<$ 405 m

- By analysing the **dimensions** of a formula it is possible to decide whether a given formula represents a **length** (dimension 1), an **area** (dimension 2) or a **volume** (dimension 3).

Eg 5 p, q, r and s represent lengths.
By using dimensions, decide whether the expression $pq + qr + rs$ could represent a perimeter, an area or a volume.
Writing $pq + qr + rs$ using dimensions:

$$L \times L + L \times L + L \times L = L^2 + L^2 + L^2 = 3L^2$$

So, $pq + qr + rs$ has dimension 2 and could represent an area.

Exercise 40

1 Write each of the following using a more suitable unit.
(a) The distance between two towns is 6000 metres.
(b) A mouse weighs 0.06 kilograms.
(c) A piece of paper has an area of $0.006\,\text{m}^2$.
(d) A room has a volume of $60\,000\,000\,\text{cm}^3$.

2 On a map the distance between two hospitals is 14.5 cm.
The map has been drawn to a scale of 1 to 250 000.
Calculate the actual distance between the hospitals in kilometres.

3 Jemma has 3 litres of milk and 20 glasses. Each glass holds one third of a pint.
How many glasses can Jemma fill?

4 Serena measures the height of door A as 2 metres.
Tom measures the height of door B as 70 inches.
Which door is the higher, A or B? You must show all your working. AQA

5 Mum's Traditional Jam is sold in two sizes.
A 1 lb pot of jam costs 71 pence. A 1 kg pot of jam costs £1.50.
Which pot of jam is better value for money? You must show all your working.

6 Debbie is 5 feet 4 inches tall and weighs 9 stone 2 lb. Joyce is 155 cm tall and weighs 60 kg.
Who is taller? Who is heavier? You must show your working.

7 Last year Felicity drove 2760 miles on business.
Her car does 38 miles per gallon. Petrol costs 69 pence per litre.
She is given a car allowance of 25 pence per kilometre.
How much of her car allowance is left after paying for her petrol?
Give your answer to the nearest £.

8 Mr Jones weighs his case on his bathroom scales which weigh to the nearest kilogram.
He finds that his case weighs 20 kg.
What are the greatest and least weights of the case? AQA

9 Bags of potatoes each weigh 25 kg correct to the nearest kg.
What is the minimum weight of 9 bags of potatoes? AQA

10 Vicky measures her handspan and writes down the result as:

18 cm, correct to the nearest centimetre.

(a) Write down the greatest length her handspan could be.

Chris has measured his handspan as 17.5 cm, correct to the nearest half centimetre.
(b) Write down the smallest length his handspan could be.

Paul says that Chris should write his answer down as 17.50 cm.
(c) Give a reason why this is not appropriate. AQA

11 The dimensions of a triangular prism are shown.
The following formulae represent certain quantities connected with the prism.

$d(a + b + c)$ $\quad \frac{abd}{2}$ $\quad \sqrt{(a^2 + b^2)}$ $\quad cd$ $\quad \frac{1}{2}ab$

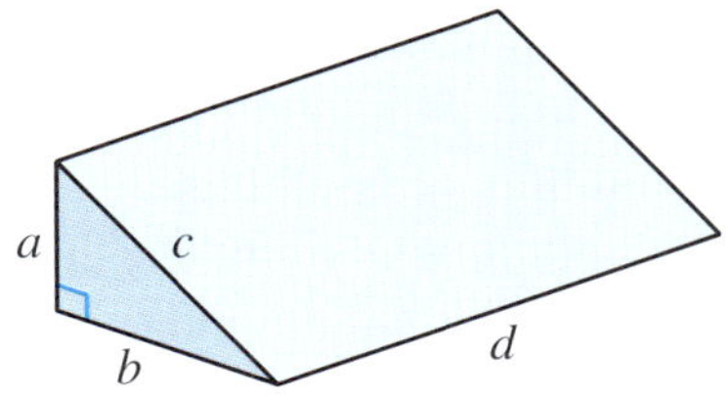

(a) Which of these formulae represents a length?
(b) Which of these formulae represents a volume?

AQA

Section Review - Shape, Space and Measures

The diagrams in this exercise have not been drawn accurately.
Do not use a calculator for questions 1 to 15.

1 Find the size of the angles a, b and c. Give a reason for each of your answers.

(a)

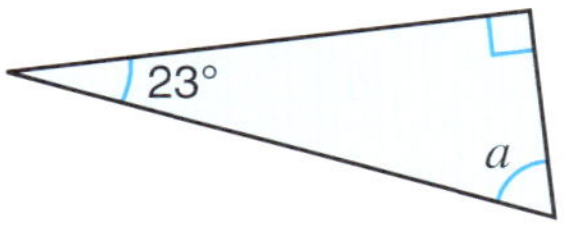

(b)

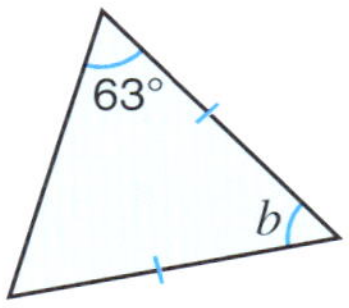

(c)

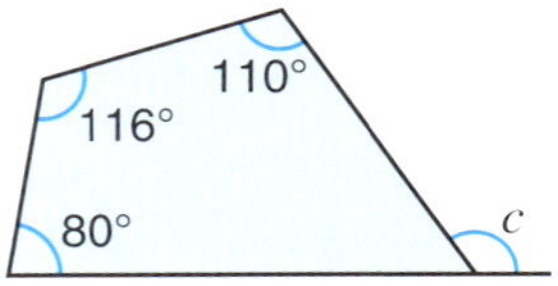

2 The descriptions of two different quadrilaterals are given in the boxes below.
Choose the correct names from this list.

kite **rectangle** **rhombus** **square** **trapezium**

(a) One pair of sides are parallel but they are not equal in length.

(b) The diagonals are of different lengths and cross at 90°.
Each diagonal is a line of symmetry of the quadrilateral.

AQA

3

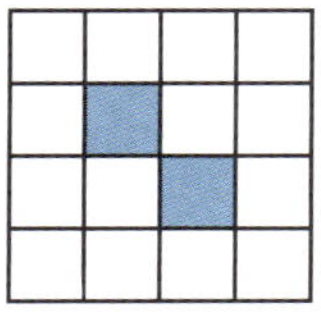

(a) Copy the diagram.
Shade two more squares so that the final diagram has line symmetry only.

(b) Make another copy of the diagram.
Shade two more squares so that the final diagram has rotational symmetry only.

4 (a) Part of a tessellation of triangles is shown.
Copy the diagram.
Continue the tessellation by drawing four more triangles.

(b) Do all regular polygons tessellate?
Give a reason for your answer.

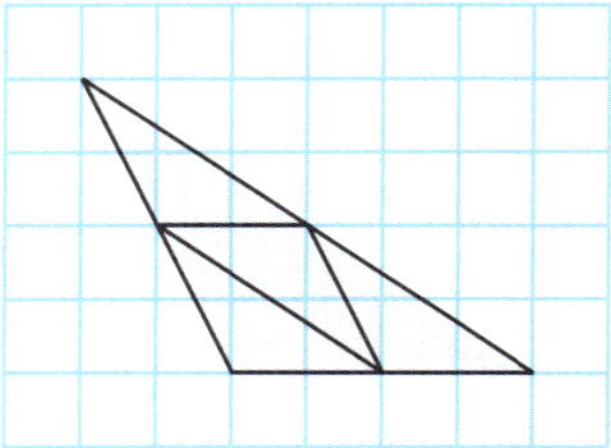

5 (a) A cuboid measures 2 cm by 2.5 cm by 4 cm.

(i) Draw an accurate net of the cuboid.

(ii) Calculate the total surface area of the cuboid.

(b) Another cuboid has a volume of 50 cm^3. The base of the cuboid measures 4 cm by 5 cm.
Calculate the height of the cuboid.

6 The diagram shows a sketch of a triangle.
By making an accurate drawing of the triangle,
find the size of angle PQR.

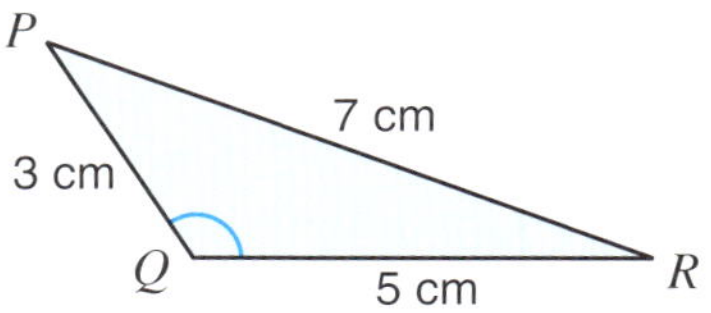

7 Use only the information given to find two triangles which are congruent to each other.
Give a reason for your answer.

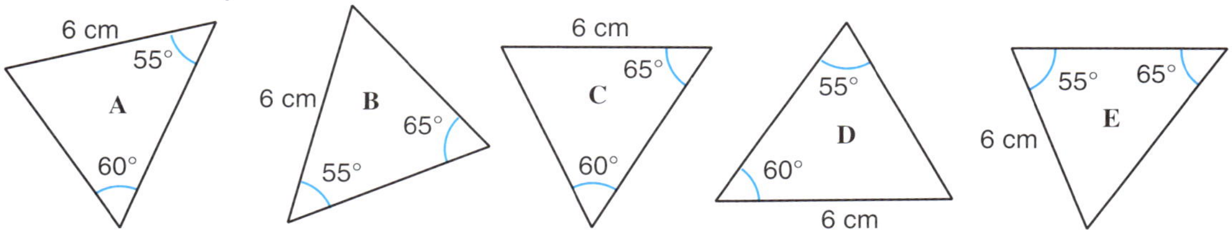

8 Colin is 5 feet 10 inches tall and weighs 11 stones.
On a medical form he is asked to give his height in centimetres and his weight in kilograms.
What values should he give?

9 The diagram shows the positions of shapes P, Q and R.

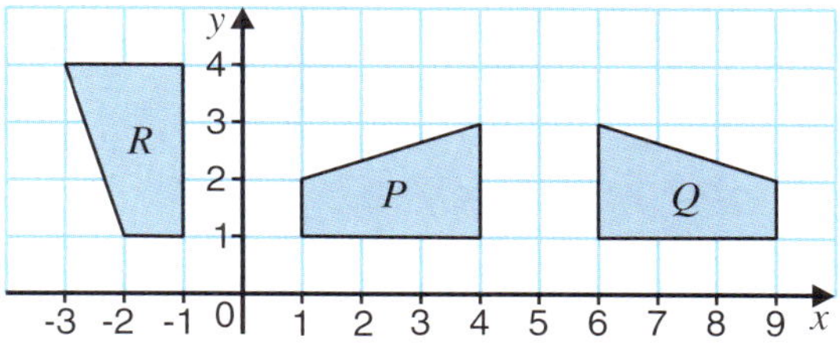

(a) Describe the single transformation which takes P onto Q.
(b) Describe the single transformation which takes P onto R.

Copy shape P onto squared paper.
(c) P is translated 3 units to the left and 2 units up.
(i) Draw the new position of P on your diagram. Label it S.
(ii) Describe the translation which takes S back onto P.

10 Find the size of the angles a, b, c and d.

(a)

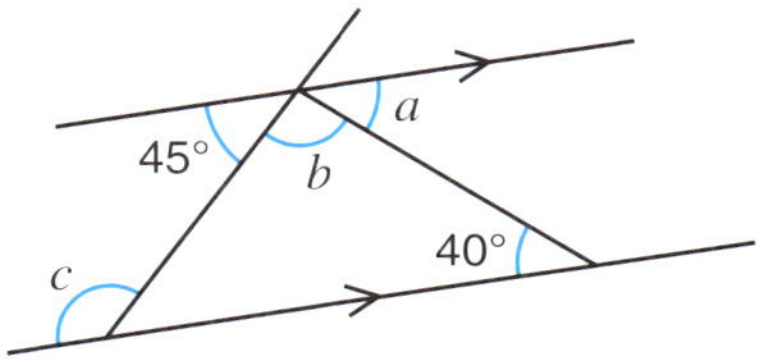

(b)

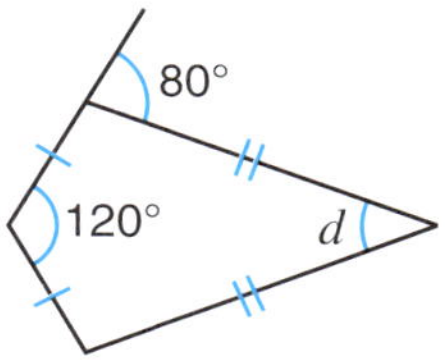

11

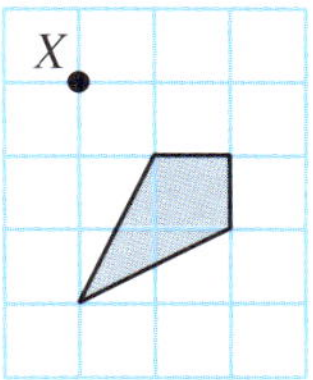

Copy the diagram onto squared paper.
Draw an enlargement of the kite, scale factor 2, centre X.

AQA

12 The diagram shows the angle formed when three regular polygons are placed together, as shown.

(a) Explain why angle a is 120°.
(b) Work out the size of the angle marked b.

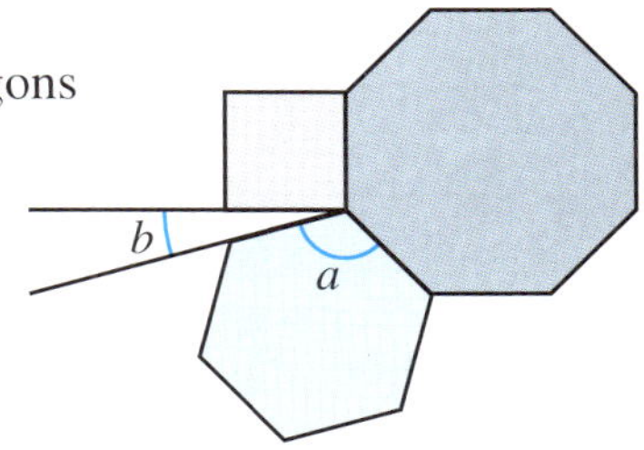

13

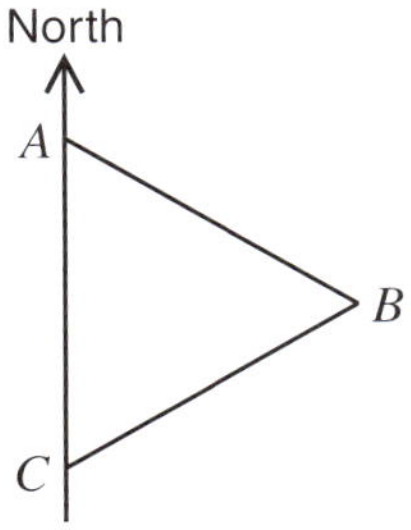

The sketch shows the positions of three footpaths which meet at A, B and C.
A is due north of C.
Triangle ABC is equilateral.

(a) Write down the three-figure bearing of B from C.
(b) Write down the three-figure bearing of A from B.

AQA

14 The area of the trapezium is $20\,\text{m}^2$.
The parallel sides a and b are different lengths.
The perpendicular height, h, is 4 m.
Find a possible pair of values for a and b.

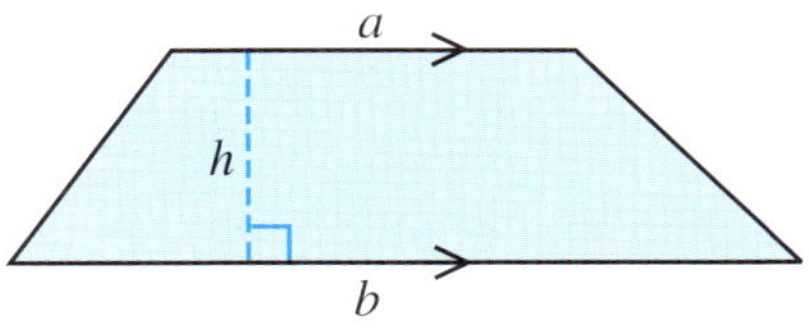

AQA

15 A circle of radius 5 cm is cut into quarters.
The quarters are put together to make shape S, as shown.

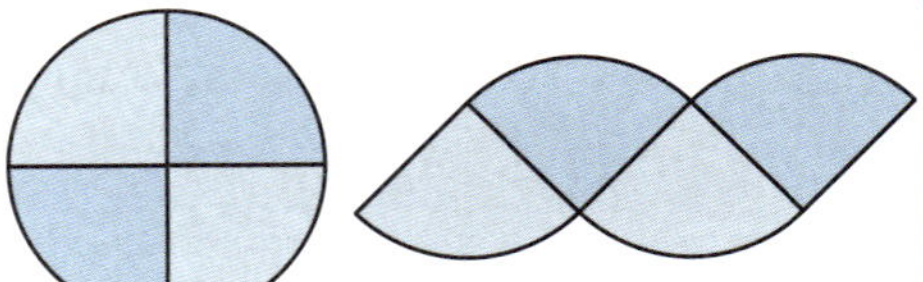

Shape S

(a) Calculate the area of the shape S.
Give your answer in terms of π.

(b) Calculate the perimeter of shape S.
Give your answer in terms of π.

(c) A different shape, T, is made from two of the quarter circles, of radius 5 cm, as shown.

(i) Calculate the width of shape T (marked w on the diagram).
Leave your answer as a square root.

(ii) State the height of shape T (marked h on the diagram).

Shape T

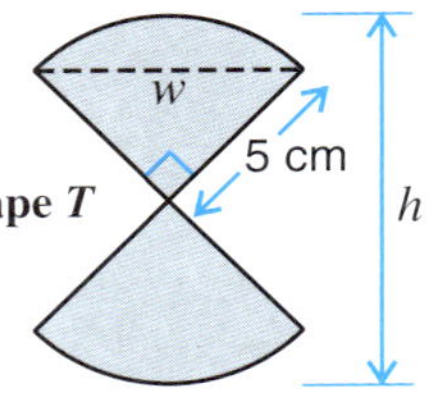

AQA

16

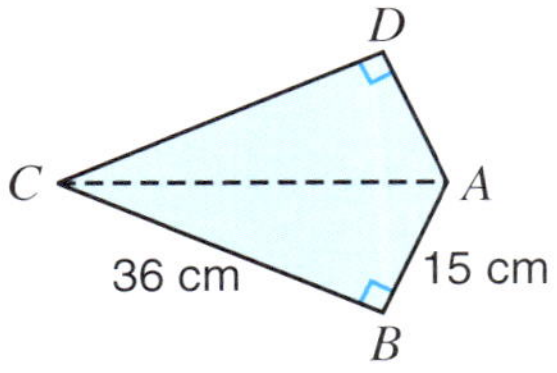

The diagram shows a kite $ABCD$.

(a) Calculate the area of the kite $ABCD$.

(b) Calculate the length of AC.

AQA

17 The diagram shows a bale of straw.
The bale is a cylinder with radius 70 cm and height 50 cm.
Calculate the volume of the bale.

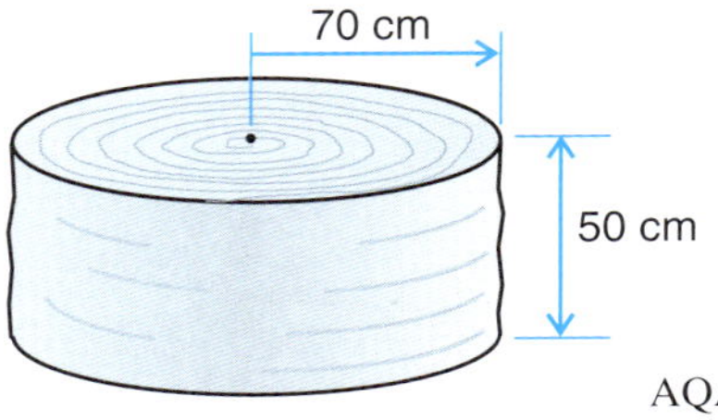

AQA

18 Three oil rigs, X, Y and Z, are supplied by boats from port P.
X is 15 km from P on a bearing of 050°.
Y is 20 km from P on a bearing of 110°.
Z is equidistant from X and Y and 30 km from P.

(a) By using a scale of 1 cm to represent 5 km, draw an accurate diagram to show the positions of P, X, Y and Z.

(b) Use your diagram to find

(i) the bearing of Y from Z, (ii) the distance, in kilometres, of Y from Z.

19 The diagram shows Fay's house, H, and her school, S.
To get to school Fay has a choice of two routes.
She can either walk along Waverly Crescent or along the footpaths HX and XS.
Waverly Crescent is a semi-circle with diameter 650 m.
The footpath HX is 250 m and meets the footpath XS at right-angles.
Which of these routes is shorter? By how much?

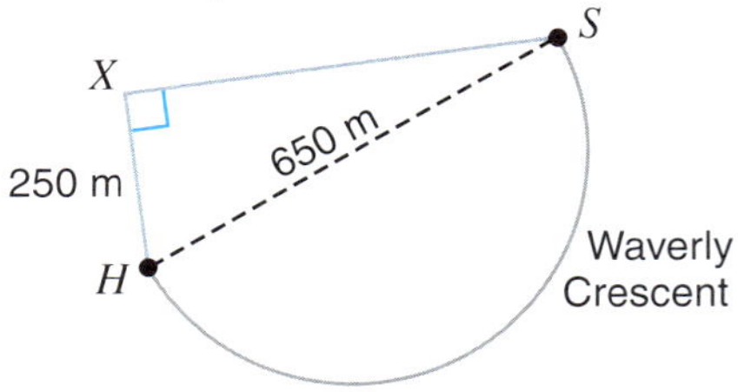

20 (a)

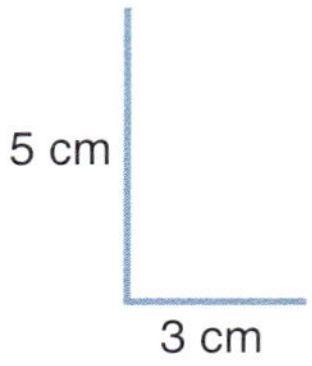

A letter L is drawn, as shown.
Draw the letter L accurately.
A point P is 2 cm from the letter L.
Draw the locus of all the possible positions of P.

(b) A letter Z is drawn in a rectangle measuring 7 cm by 9 cm, as shown.
Calculate the size of the angle marked x.

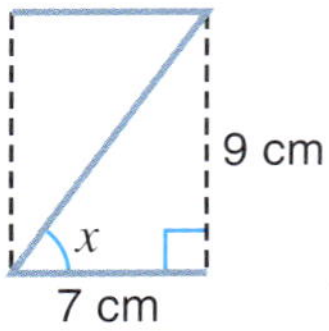

AQA

21 A circle has an area of $49\pi\,\text{cm}^2$.
Calculate the circumference of the circle, in terms of π.

22 Copy the diagram onto squared paper.

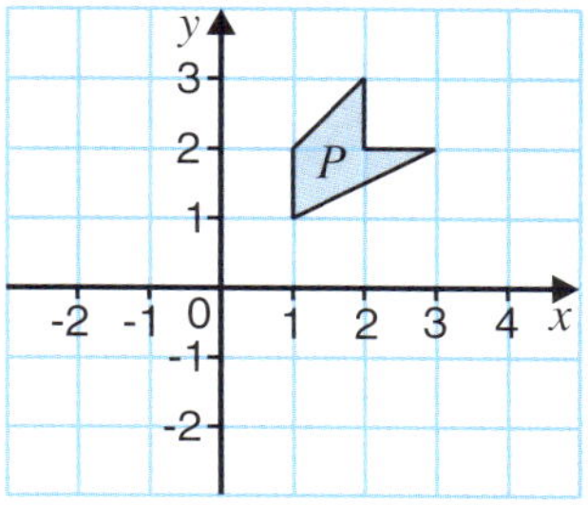

(a) P is mapped onto Q by an enlargement, scale factor 2, centre $(-1, 3)$. Draw and label Q.

(b) P is mapped onto R by a translation with vector $\begin{pmatrix} -3 \\ 2 \end{pmatrix}$. Draw and label R.

(c) Describe the single transformation which maps Q onto R.

23 The following formulae represent certain quantities connected with containers, where a, b and c are dimensions.

$$\pi a \qquad abc \qquad \sqrt{a^2 - c^2} \qquad \pi a^2 b \qquad 2(a + b + c)$$

(a) Explain why abc represents a volume.

(b) Which of these formulae represent lengths?

24 (a) The diagram shows a right-angled triangle, ABC. Angle $C = 90°$ and $AB = 10$ cm. Given that $\cos B = 0.8$, $\sin B = 0.6$ and $\tan B = 0.75$, calculate the length of AC.

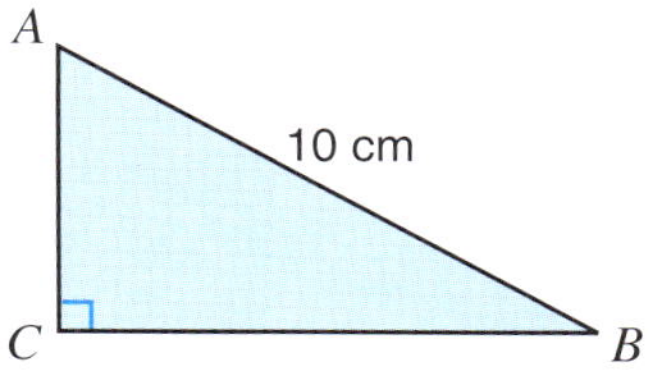

(b)

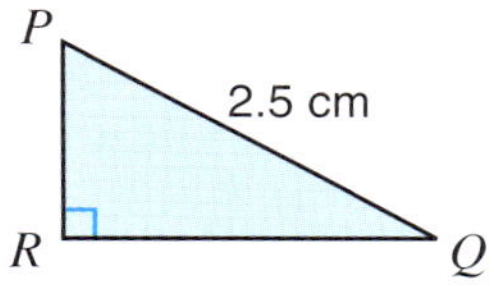

Triangle PQR is similar to triangle ABC. Given that angle P = angle A, angle Q = angle B and $PQ = 2.5$ cm, calculate the length of PR.

AQA

25 Triangle ABC is similar to triangle APQ.

$AB = 4.5$ cm, $BC = 3$ cm, $PQ = 5$ cm and $CQ = 1.6$ cm.

(a) Calculate the length of AP.
(b) Calculate the length of AC.

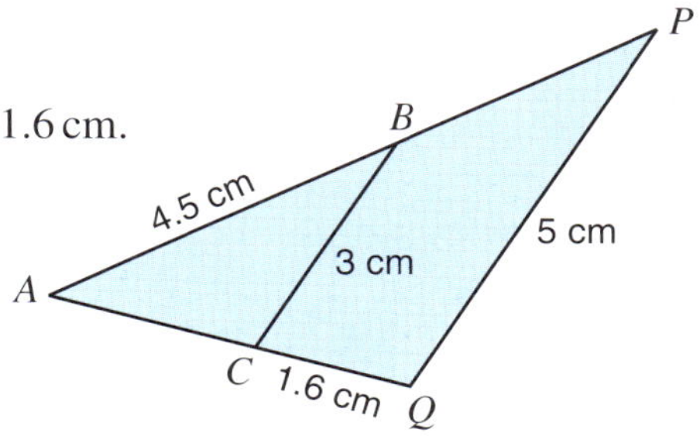

26 In these diagrams O is the centre of the circle.
Find the size of the angles a, b, c and x.
Give a reason for each of your answers.

(a)

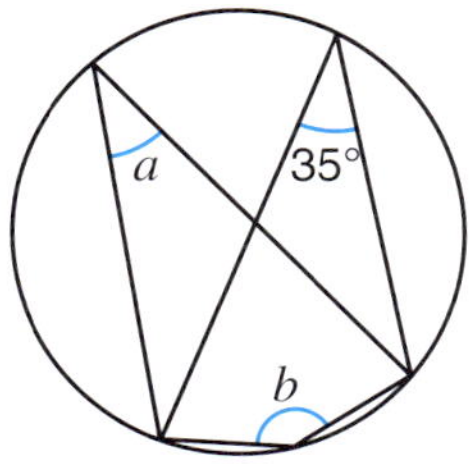

(b)

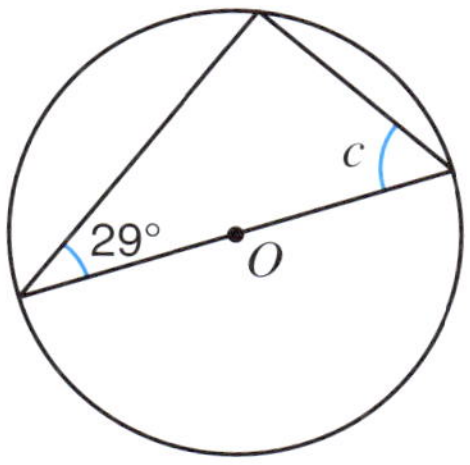

(c)

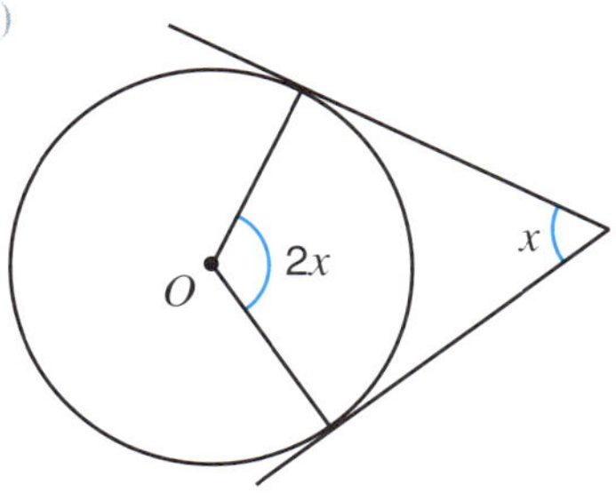

27 A sports field is bounded by three straight roads, PQ, QR and RP, as shown.

Angle $PRQ = 63°$ and angle $PQR = 90°$.
The length of QR is 4.7 km.
Calculate the area of the sports field.

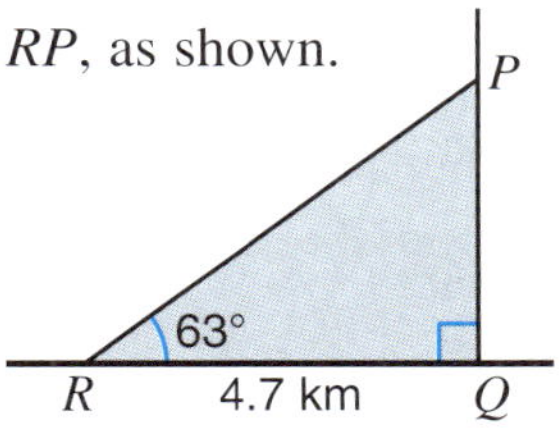

AQA

Module 5 Exam Practice Non-calculator Paper

Do not use a calculator for this exercise.

1 (a) Simplify. (i) $a + 2a - 2$ (ii) $2a \times 2a \times 2a$
(b) Solve. (i) $3x - 2 = 10$ (ii) $2x + 1 = 6$

2 The diagram shows part of a map of Tasmania.

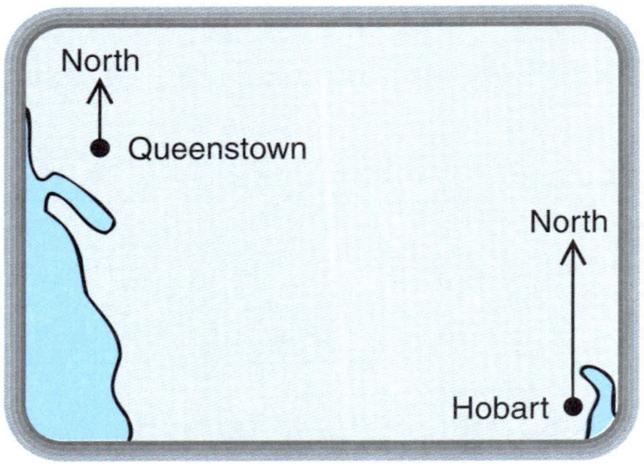

(a) What is the three-figure bearing of Queenstown from Hobart?

The map has been drawn to a scale of 1 cm to 30 km.

(b) (i) What is the actual distance between Queenstown and Hobart in kilometres?
(ii) Calculate the distance between Queenstown and Hobart in miles.

AQA

3 (a) In the diagram, angle $BCD = 76°$, $AC = BC$ and ACD is a straight line.
Work out the size of angle BAC.

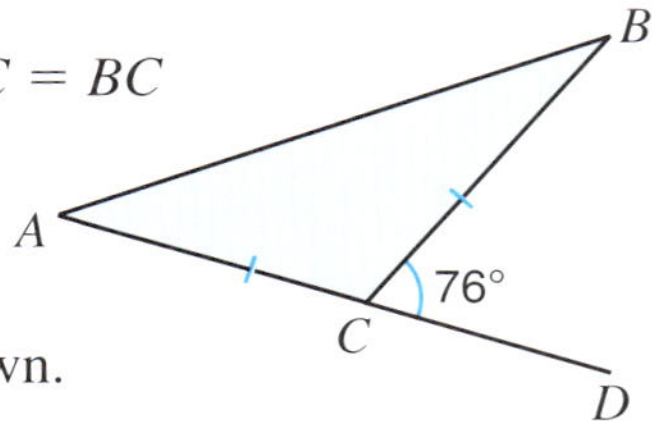

(b) Information about some triangles is shown.

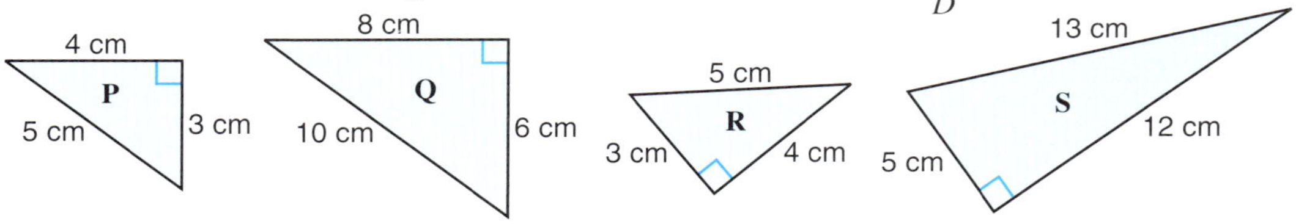

Which two of these triangles are congruent to each other?
Give a reason for your answer.

(c) This shape is made using equilateral triangles.

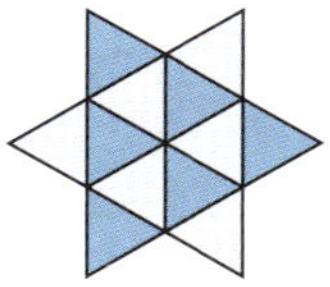

Describe the symmetries of the shape.

4 Triangle PQR is equilateral with sides of length 60 cm.
(a) Use a scale of 1 : 10 to make a scale drawing of triangle PQR.
(b) Use your scale drawing to work out the area of triangle PQR.

5 Each term in a sequence of numbers is obtained by multiplying the previous terms by -2.
The first three terms are: $1, \ -2, \ 4, \ \dots$
(a) Write down the next two terms in the sequence.
(b) Will the 50th term of the sequence be positive or negative?
Explain your reasoning.

AQA

6 A is the point $(-4, -1)$. B is the point $(2, 3)$. What is the midpoint of AB?

7 Solve the equations (a) $3a - 2 = -5$, (b) $5m + 3 = 7 - m$, (c) $3(a - 2) = 6$.

8

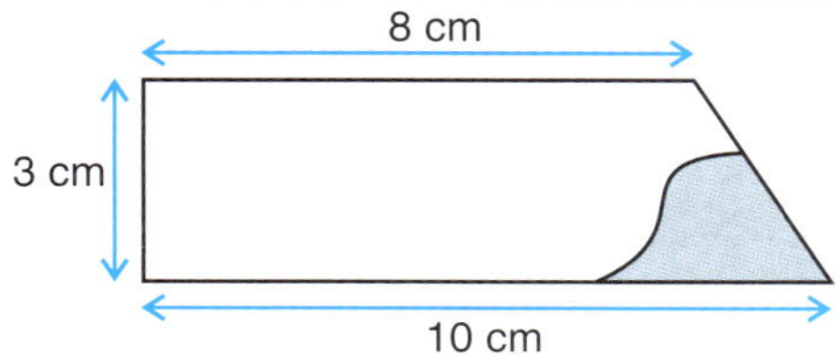

Three-tenths of the area of this shape is shaded.
Calculate the shaded area.

AQA

9 The numbers on these cards are coded. x | $2x - 1$ | $3x$

The sum of the numbers on these 3 cards is 41.

(a) Form an equation in x.

(b) By solving your equation, find the numbers on the cards.

10 A cuboid has a volume of $50\,\text{cm}^3$.
The base of the cuboid measures 4 cm by 5 cm.
Calculate the height of the cuboid.

11 A farmer has two crop circles in his field.
One circle has a radius of 9 m and the other has a diameter of 12 m.

(a) What is the ratio of the diameter of the small circle to the diameter of the large circle?
Give your answer in its simplest form.

(b) Calculate, in terms of π, the circumference of the smaller circle.

12 A concrete block weighs 11 kg, correct to the nearest kilogram.
Write down the greatest and least possible weight of the block.

13 OBC is a straight line.
AOB is an isosceles triangle with $OB = AB$.
Angle $AOB = x°$.

(a) Write down, in terms of x, (i) angle OAB,
(ii) angle ABC.

(b) Angle OBA is $(x - 12)$ degrees.
Find the value of x.

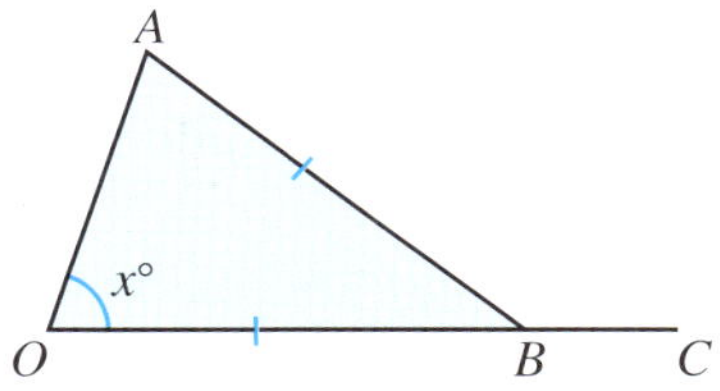

AQA

14 Draw a rectangle 4 cm by 5 cm.
Construct, on the outside of the rectangle, the locus of points that are 2 cm from the edges of the rectangle.

15 A sequence begins: $-1,\ 2,\ 5,\ 8,\ 11,\ \ldots$
Write in terms of n, the nth term of the sequence.

16 Copy shape A onto squared paper.

(a) A is mapped onto B by a translation with vector $\begin{pmatrix} 0 \\ -4 \end{pmatrix}$.
Draw the position of B on your diagram.

(b) A is mapped onto C by a rotation through 180° about (3, 1).
Draw the position of C on your diagram.

(c) Describe the single transformation which maps B onto C.

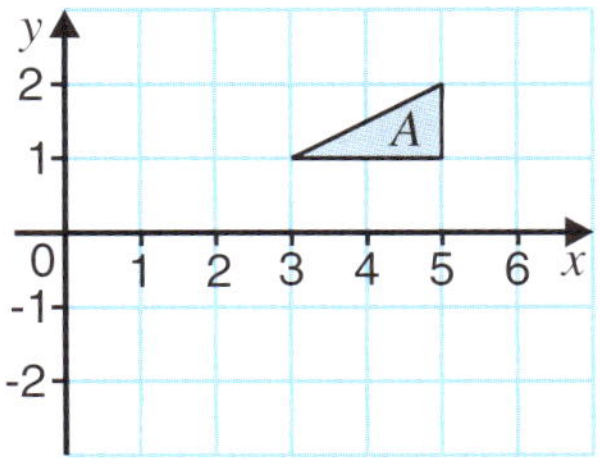

17 (a) Copy and complete the table of values for $y = x^2 - 3x + 1$.

x	-1	0	1	2	3	4
y		1	-1			5

(b) Draw the graph of $y = x^2 - 3x + 1$ for values of x from -1 to 4.

(c) Use your graph to find the value of y when $x = 1.5$.

(d) Use your graph to solve the equation $x^2 - 3x + 1 = 0$.

18 Cocoa is sold in cylindrical tins. The height of a tin is 7.9 cm. The radius of a tin is 4.1 cm.
Use approximations to estimate the volume of a tin. Show all your working.

19 Solve the equation $\frac{1}{3}(2x - 1) = \frac{1}{5}(3x + 2)$.

20 The diagram shows the positions of shapes P, Q and R.

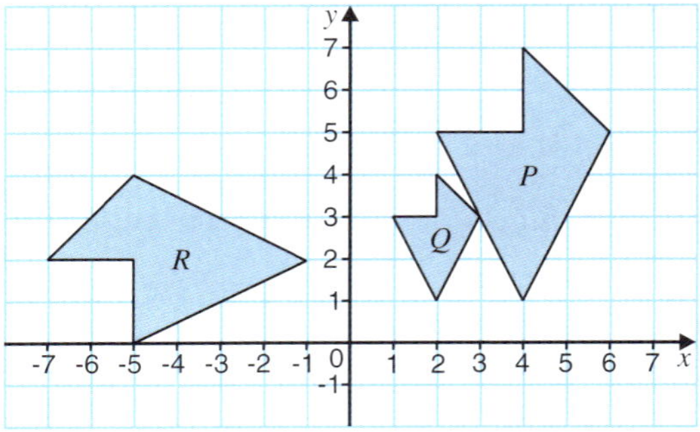

(a) Describe fully the single transformation which takes P onto Q.

(b) Describe fully the single transformation which takes P onto R.

21

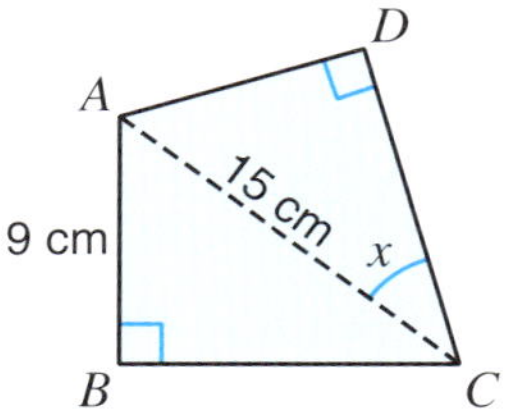

The diagram shows a quadrilateral $ABCD$.
$AB = 9$ cm and $AC = 15$ cm.

(a) Calculate the length of BC.

(b) Given that $\cos x = 0.7$, calculate the length of CD.

AQA

22
(a) List the values of n, where n is an integer, such that $3 \leqslant 3n < 18$.
(b) Solve the simultaneous equations $2x + y = 9$ and $x - 2y = 7$.
(c) Factorise the expression $n^2 - n$.
(d) Simplify $3a^2b \times 2a^3b$.

AQA

23
(a) Factorise completely. $3x^2 - 6x$
(b) Expand and simplify. $(3x + 2)(x - 4)$
(c) Make t the subject of the formula. $W = \frac{5t + 3}{4}$

AQA

24 You are given the formula $a = bc^2$.
(a) Calculate the value of a when $b = 100$ and $c = -\frac{3}{5}$.
(b) Rearrange the formula to give c in terms of a and b.

25
(a) The diagram shows the line $4y = x + 5$.
(i) What are the coordinates of the point marked P?
(ii) What is the gradient of the line?

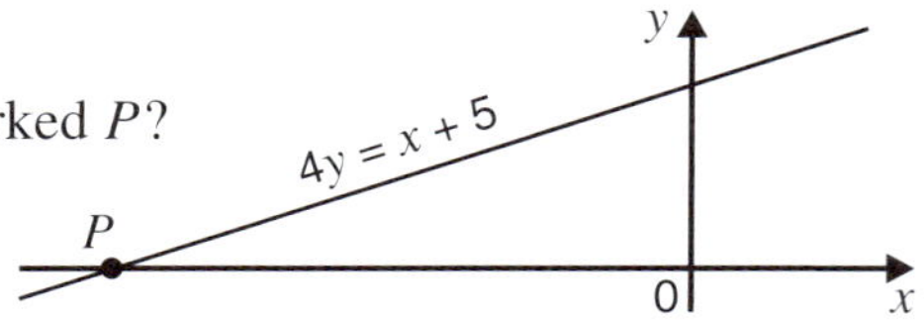

(b)

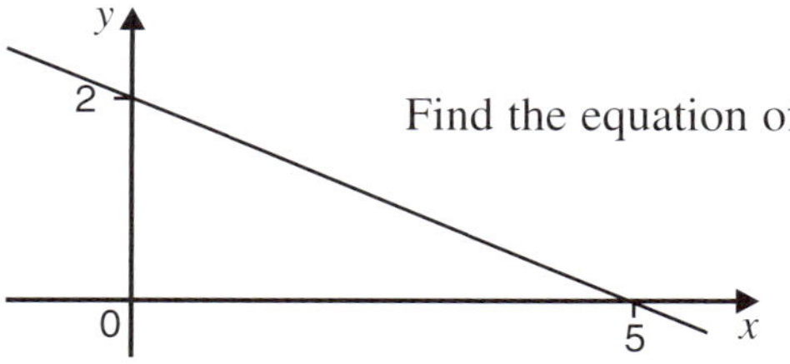

Find the equation of the straight line shown in this diagram.

26 These formulae represent quantities connected with containers, where a, b and c are dimensions.

$2(ab + bc + cd)$ $\quad abc \quad$ $\sqrt{a^2 + b^2}$ $\quad 4(a + b + c)$

Which of these formulae represent lengths? Explain how you know.

27 The sum of two numbers is 8. The product of these numbers is 15.
If one of the numbers is x, show that $x^2 - 8x + 15 = 0$.

AQA

28
(a) Simplify (i) $2a^3 \times 3a^2$, (ii) $4a^6 \div 2a^3$.
(b) Solve the quadratic equation $x^2 + 3x - 10 = 0$.
(c) Solve the inequality $3 < 2x + 1 < 5$.

AQA

Module 5 Exam Practice Calculator Paper

You may use a calculator for this exercise.

1 The first four numbers in a sequence are: 15, 11, 7, 3, …
(a) What are the next two numbers in the sequence?
(b) Explain how you found your answers.

2 (a) Simplify $5m - m + 5$.
(b) Solve (i) $3x = 1$, (ii) $4y + 3 = 19$.
(c) Find the value of $m^3 - 3m$ when $m = -2$.

3 (a) The diagram shows a regular pentagon.
How many lines of symmetry does a regular pentagon have?

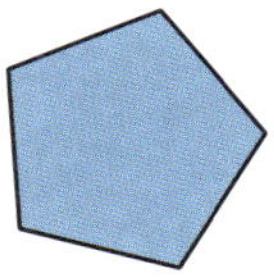

(b)

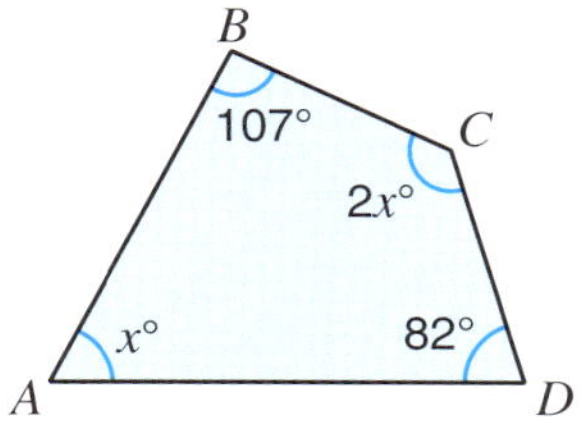

ABCD is a quadrilateral.
Work out the value of x.

AQA

4 An input-output diagram is shown.

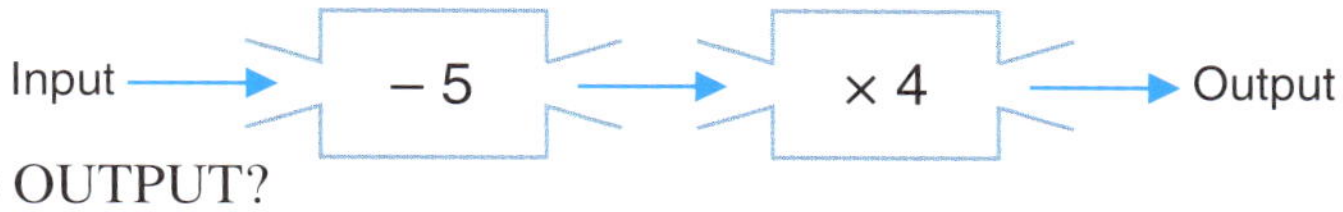

(a) When the INPUT is 8, what is the OUTPUT?
(b) When the OUTPUT is 36, what is the INPUT?

AQA

5 A jigsaw puzzle is a rectangle measuring 17.6 cm by 8.5 cm.
35% of the area of the puzzle is blue.
Calculate the area of the puzzle which is blue.

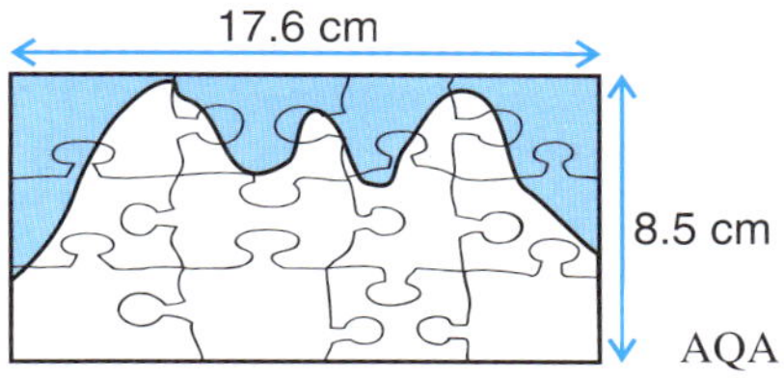

AQA

6

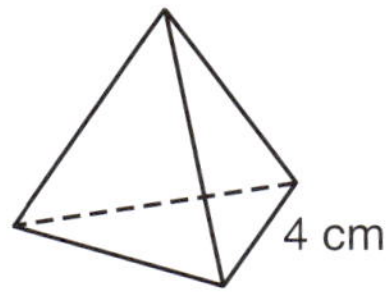

The diagram shows a regular tetrahedron.
Each edge is 4 cm long.
Draw an accurate net of the tetrahedron.

7 A toilet roll has 240 single sheets per roll.
Each sheet is 139 millimetres long and 110 millimetres wide.

Calculate the total area of paper on the roll.
Give your answer in square metres.

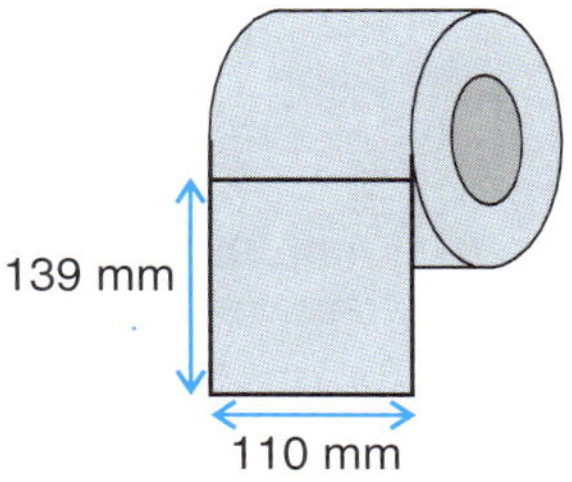

AQA

8 A hang glider flies 2.8 km on a bearing of 070° from *P* to *Q* and then 2 km on a bearing of 200° from *Q* to *R*.
(a) Make a scale drawing to show the flight of the hang glider from *P* to *Q* to *R*.
Use a scale of 1 cm to 200 m.
(b) From *R* the hang glider flies directly back to *P*.
Use your drawing to find the distance and bearing of *P* from *R*.

9 The graph shows the journey of a cyclist from Halton to Kendal.
The distance from Halton to Kendal is 30 miles.

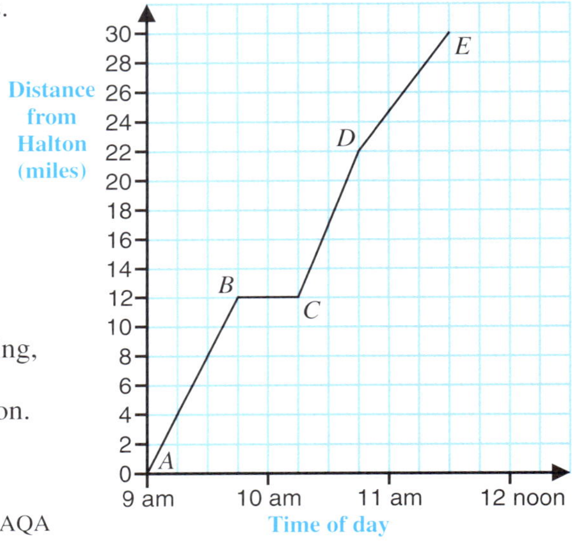

(a) For how long did the cyclist stop during the journey?

(b) What was the average speed for the part of the journey from A to B?

(c) On which section of the journey was the cyclist travelling at his fastest speed? Explain clearly how you got your answer.

(d) The cyclist stayed in Kendal for 2 hours. He then returned to Halton, without stopping, at an average speed of 12 miles per hour. Calculate the time he arrived back in Halton.

AQA

10 Calculate the area of a circle which has a radius of 9 m.

11 A regular polygon has 9 sides. Work out the sum of its interior angles.

12 Solve these equations. (a) $5y - 3 = 1 - 2y$ (b) $\frac{x + 5}{7} = 3$ (c) $3(x - 3) = 6$

13 A recipe for plum jam states:

2 kg of plums and 2 kg of sugar are needed to make 3.6 kg of jam.

(a) Kevin makes 4.5 kg of jam.
How many kilograms of plums did he need?

(b) Kevin puts the jam into 1 lb jars.
How many jars are needed for 4.5 kg of jam?

AQA

14 A solid plastic cuboid has dimensions 3 cm by 5 cm by 9 cm.
The density of the plastic is 0.95 grams per cm^3.
What is the weight of the plastic cuboid?

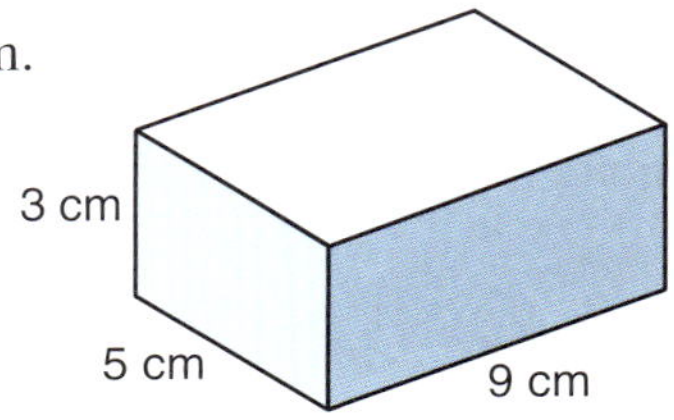

AQA

15 (a) Draw and label the lines $y = x + 1$ and $x + y = 3$ for values of x from -1 to 3.

(b) The region R is satisfied by all of these inequalities:

$$x > 0 \qquad y > x + 1 \qquad x + y < 3$$

Label the region R on your diagram.

16 Use a trial and improvement method to find a solution to the equation $x^3 + x = 57$.
Show all your working and give your answer correct to one decimal place.

17 The diagram shows a semi-circle with diameter AB.
C is a point on the circumference.
$AC = 6$ cm and $CB = 8$ cm.
Calculate the area of the shaded triangle as a percentage of the area of the semi-circle.

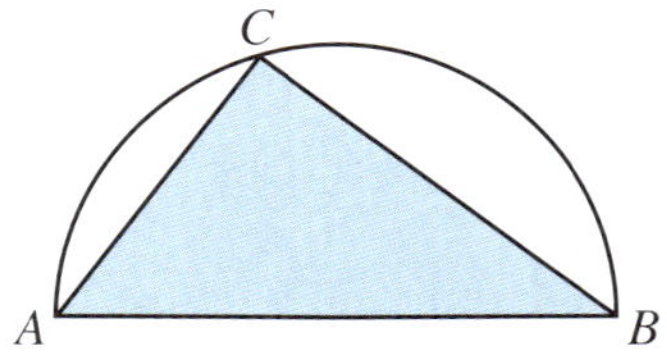

18 The volume of a cylinder is 75 400 cm^3. The height of the cylinder is 60 cm.
Calculate the radius of the cylinder.

19 Simplify (a) $36y^6 \div 9y^3$, (b) $4m^2 \times 3m^3$.

20 The diagram shows a zig-zag path which joins the upper and lower gardens at a holiday resort.

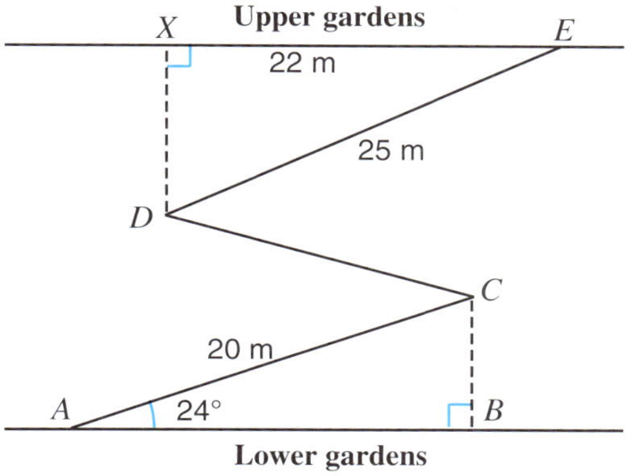

The path DE is 25 m long and $XE = 22$ m.

(a) Calculate XD.

The path AC is 20 m long and slopes at 24° to the horizontal.

(b) Calculate BC.

AQA

21 You are given the equation $y = ax + 4$.

(a) Rearrange the equation to give x in terms of y.

(b) The line $y = ax + 4$ passes through the points $P(0, 4)$ and $Q(2, 0)$. Find the value of a.

22 P, Q, R and S are points on the circumference of a circle with centre O.

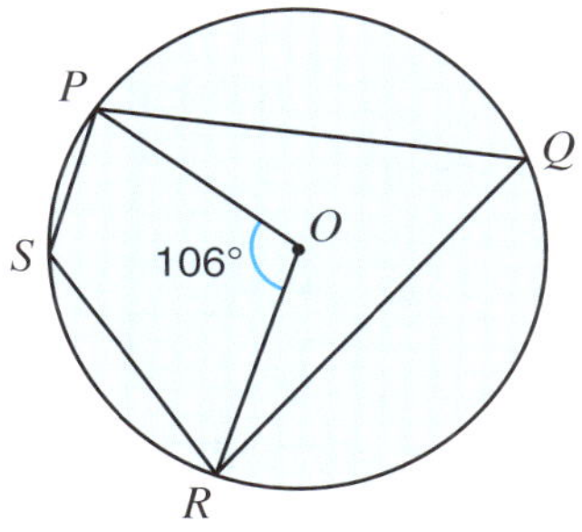

(a) Find the size of angle PQR. Give a reason for your answer.

(b) Find the size of angle PSR. Give a reason for your answer.

23

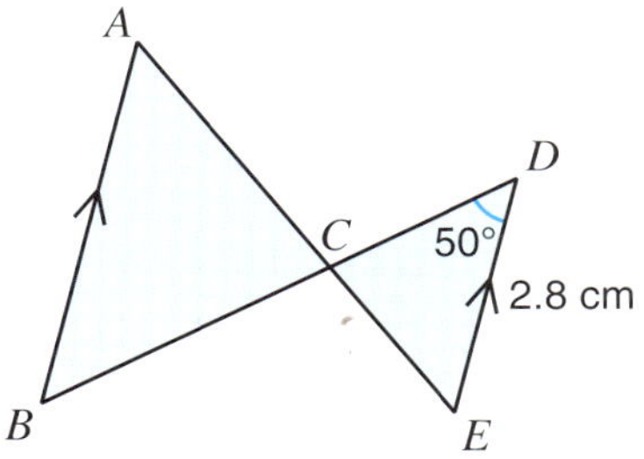

In the diagram AB is parallel to DE and ACE and BCD are straight lines.

(a) Explain why triangles ABC and EDC are similar.

The ratio of $BC : CD$ is $3 : 2$.
Angle $CDE = 50°$ and $DE = 2.8$ cm.

(b) (i) What is the size of angle ABC?
(ii) Calculate the length of AB.

24 (a) Write down the values of n, where n is an integer, which satisfies the inequality $-1 < x + 2 \leqslant 3$.

(b) Solve the inequality $2x + 3 < 4$.

25 (a) Solve the simultaneous equations
$$5x - 4y = -11,$$
$$3x + 2y = 0.$$

(b) Factorise fully (i) $3xy^2 + 6xy$, (ii) $ma - nb - mb + na$.

(c) Multiply out and simplify $(2x - 3)(x + 2)$.

(d) Solve the equation $x^2 - 7x + 12 = 0$.

26 The diagram shows part of a roof structure.

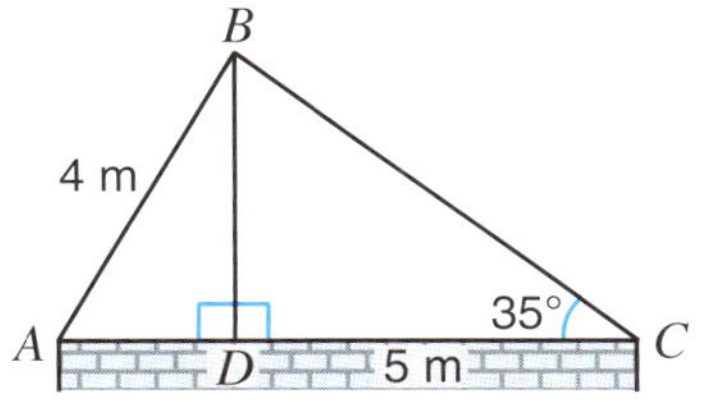

$AB = 4$ m, $DC = 5$ m and angle $BCD = 35°$.
BD is perpendicular to AC. Calculate angle BAD.

27 (a) You are given the formula $p = \frac{n^2}{4}$.
Rearrange the formula to give n in terms of p.

(b) Simplify $\frac{3x - 6}{x^2 - 5x + 6}$.

Index